D0958234

Also by Timothy Good

UNEARTHLY DISCLOSURE

Conflicting Interests in the Control of Extraterrestrial Intelligence

Timothy Good

With a Foreword by Admiral of the Fleet
The Lord Hill-Norton GCB
Chief of the Defence Staff (1971–3)
Chairman of the NATO Military Committee (1974–7)

arrow books

Published by Arrow Books in 2001

12

Copyright © Timothy Good 2000

First published in Great Britain in 2000 by
Century
Random House, 20 Vauxhall Bridge Road,
London SW1v 2SA

www.randomhouse.co.uk

Addresses for companies within The Random House Group Limited
can be found at: www.randomhouse.co.uk/offices.htm

The Random House Group Limited Reg. No. 954009

A CIP catalogue record for this book
is available from the British Library

ISBN 9780099406020

The Random House Group Limited supports The Forest Stewardship
Council® (FSC®), the leading international forest-certification organisation.
Our books carrying the FSC label are printed on FSC®-certified paper.
FSC is the only forest-certification scheme supported by the leading
environmental organisations, including Greenpeace. Our
paper procurement policy can be found at
www.randomhouse.co.uk/environment

MIX
Paper from
responsible sources
FSC® C016897

Printed and bound in Great Britain by Clays Ltd, St Ives PLC

To Bruce Renton (1925–1998)

Contents

Contents

Acknowledgements

I would like to record my thanks in particular to the following individuals and organizations who have contributed directly or indirectly to the production of *Unearthly Disclosure*:

William S. Adams of Random House (UK) legal department; José Miguel Agosto; Walter Andrus and the Mutual UFO Network; John Auchettl and Phenomena Research Australia; Jesús Alberto Balbi and *Cuarta Dimensión*; Frank Bourke and the *National Star*, Lafayette, Indiana; the Brazilian Air Force; Andrea L. Buchanan and the *Daily Optic*, Las Vegas, New Mexico; Jonathan Caplan QC; the French Committee for In-Depth Studies (COMETA); Soraya Collazo and family; Dwight Connelly and the *MUFON UFO Journal*; Billy Cox and *Florida Today*; Dr James Deardorff and the *Quarterly Journal of the Royal Astronomical Society*; the Defense Intelligence Agency; Lucius Farish and the *UFO Newsclipping Service*; Salvador Freixedo and Magdalena Del Amo-Freixedo; Dorina Garcia Lugo and family; GeoSystems Global Corporation; José Orlando Golís; Patricia B. Grant; Jean-Gabriel Greslé; Dr Peter Hattwig; Sebastián Robiou Lamarche; Nikolai Lebedev and *Komsolomets Kirgizia*; Michael Lindemann and CNI News; Erwin Lohre; Gianfranco Lollino; M. Alvarez López; the *Los Angeles Times*; François Louange; Frank Macintyre and the *Times*; Molly Moore and the *Washington Post*; the National Aeronautics & Space Administration; Maria Ortíz; Pan American World Airways/ DynCorp.; Roberto Pinotti; Polaroid UK Ltd.; Nick Pope; G.P. Putnam's Sons, publishers of *America's Ancient Civilizations* by A. Hyatt Verrill and Ruth Verrill; Ronald Reagan, Hon. KBE; Nicholas Redfern; Milly Eufemia Rivas; Amaury Rivera; Felix Rivera; Nestor Rivera; Les Roberts; Ubirajara Rodrigues; Dr Edoardo Russo and the Italian Centre for Ufology Studies; Davis Sheremata and the *British Columbia*

Report, Vancouver; Dick Sherman and *Raytheon News*; Dr R. Leo Sprinkle; Sir Mark Thomson Bt.; the United States Air Force Air Combat Command; the United States Air Force Office of Special Investigations; the United States Coast Guard; the United States National Transportation Safety Board; Dorothee Walter; Michael Wysmierski and *The Brazilian UFO Report*; Fabio Zerpa.

I am especially indebted to: Admiral of the Fleet The Lord Hill-Norton, for his courageous Foreword and steadfast support over the past 20 years, often in the face of derision from certain elements of the press; Dr José Alonso, for his interview with Graham Sheppard and me at the Arecibo Observatory, Puerto Rico; Dr John Altshuler, for helpful comments regarding animal mutilations and alleged alien implants; Maurizio Baiata, for help with the Filiberto Caponi case; Margaret Barling, for Spanish and Italian translations and additional assistance; Jeannie Belleau, for excellent research on my behalf and for unforgettable transportation in New Mexico; Joseph Bohunko, manager of the US Air Force Tethered Aerostat Radar Site at Lajas, Puerto Rico, for his interview with Graham Sheppard and me; Robert Bigelow and Dr Colm Kelleher of the National Institute of Discovery Science (NIDS), for generous use of a NIDS report on the investigation of a cow mutilation in Utah; Graham Birdsall, editor of *UFO Magazine*, for extracts from several articles; Mark Ian Birdsall, editor of *The Unopened Files*, for his interview with Kelly Cahill and for his donation of an Aldus PageMaker programme for my computer; Vivienne Birdsall, Mark's late wife, who installed the programme and spent much time patiently helping me to understand it, even as she bravely fought cancer; Mark Booth, my editor at Century, for his unswerving loyalty and wise counsel regarding the many problems that beset us with *Unearthly Disclosure* (not least the title!); Hannah Black, Mark's assistant, and Anna Cherrett, for their patience in coping with my perfectionism; Gildas Bourdais, for excerpts from his article in the *MUFON UFO Journal* on the COMETA report, *Les OVNI et la Défense: A quoi doit-on se préparer?*; Kelly Cahill, for her interview with Mark Ian

Birdsall and for extracts from her book, *Encounter*, published by HarperCollins; Filiberto Caponi, for his wonderful pictures and story, and for his unstinting co-operation and faith in me; Enrique Castillo Rincón, for so generously allowing me to make a three-chapter synopsis of his book, *UFOs: A Great New Dawn for Humanity* (Blue Dolphin Publishing), and for providing me with a synopsis from his second book, prior to publication thereof; the Civil Defence of Canóvanas, Puerto Rico, especially Ismael Aguayo and Edwin Vazquez, for assistance with investigations, including on-site interpretation; Agent Juan Collazo Vazquez of the Canóvanas Police Department, for the interview with Graham Sheppard and me; Gordon Creighton, editor of *Flying Saucer Review*, for extracts from a number of articles published in this indispensable journal; Chad Deetken, for the article on his research in Puerto Rico, and for additional information; Robert Fairfax, for much of the article he wrote in the *MUFON UFO Journal* (together with Peter Davenport, Kathleen Anderson and Ruben Uriarte) on the abduction of an elk in Washington State; Massimo Fratini, for help with Filiberto Caponi's case, including transportation in Italy; Professor Roger Green, for his exhaustive analysis of the Caponi photographs; Andrew Lownie, my agent, for his constant support and sensible advice; Jorge Martín, editor of *Evidencia OVNI*, for numerous extracts from his magazine and from his book, *La Conspiración Chupacabras*, and for assistance with my investigations in Puerto Rico; Dr Edgar J. Mitchell, for checking and approving quotations attributed to him, and for his photograph; Ted Oliphant III, for lengthy excerpts from his article on cattle mutilations; Vitório Pacaccini, co-author of *Incidente em Varginha*, for much assistance with my chapter on the Varginha case; Alessandro Piccioni, for the invaluable assistance he rendered in translating Filiberto Caponi's letters and other related material; Bob Pratt and Cynthia Luce, for generous extracts from their articles in the *MUFON UFO Journal* on Lieutenant-Colonel Hollanda's official investigations and the Varginha case in Brazil; Yasmin Renton, who together with her father Bruce (to whom this book is dedicated) translated Filiberto Caponi's manuscript so impeccably; Antonio Ribera, for his articles on the Julio Fernández abduction case, published in *Flying Saucer Review*, and for additional information; Hon. José R. Soto Rivera, Mayor of Canóvanas, Puerto Rico, who together with his assistant, Jorge Pérez, provided much help with investigations; Dr Pedro Rosselló, Governor of Puerto Rico, for responding frankly to my questions and for reviewing some of the Puerto Rican cases described herein; Graham Sheppard, my principal associate, for the report on his mysterious displacement while flying in Puerto Rico, and for a great deal of help and humour during our research – on the ground and in the air - in the 'Island of Enchantment'; Simon & Schuster, for extracts from *The Day After Roswell*, by Col. Philip J. Corso with Andrew J. Birnes; Jackie Stableforth, for material from *The Brazilian Roswell*, a television documentary which she produced on the Varginha incidents (directed by Bruce Burgess), and for additional help; Hal Starr, who provided me with information regarding an alleged alien base in the Marshall Islands; Bernard Thouanel and Presse-Communication, for material from *Les OVNI et la Défense*; Sarah Harrison, my publicist at Random House (UK), for a first-rate job organizing the promotion of *Unearthly Disclosure*; Rubens Junqueira Villela, for his article, 'UFOs in Antarctica', and for a great deal of additional information relating to his communications with extraterrestrials in Brazil; Ilsa Yardley, for her copy-editing of the manuscript.

Finally, I am indebted to my sources – 'John' in particular – and to others who have also contributed or helped but are not named.

Foreword

Admiral of the Fleet
The Lord Hill-Norton GCB
Chief of the Defence Staff 1971–3
Chairman of the NATO Military Committee 1974–7

I have known Tim Good for about 20 years and have been in close touch with him for all that long time, during which I have written a Foreword for two of his books and a Commentary on a couple of others. It is a pleasure for me to have been asked to do it again, for I have the highest regard for his absolute integrity, his determination and skill as a researcher, and his wide and detailed knowledge of the whole fascinating UFO experience. Were this not so, I confess at once that I should have serious difficulty in accepting several passages in this riveting book and the astounding revelations he now shares with the public. Foremost among these, perhaps, are his reports on widespread alien bases, including some undersea and their craft (USOs), and the possibility that the occupants have been collaborating with the Americans in the transfer of technology.

In this new work the author starts from the premise that there can no longer be any serious doubt that extraterrestrials have been visiting our planet for many years. He deals here with their activities, rather than with speculation about the craft in which they travel. We learn in his Introduction that the French Institute of Higher Studies for National Defence reported last year to their President and Prime Minister that 'the physical reality of UFOs under the control of intelligent beings is now *almost certain*' and, as I have said publicly elsewhere, I share that view. Indeed, it seems to me that the position of even a few years ago is now reversed and that anyone who does not believe it should be required to prove why they do not, rather than the other way round.

Good cites the 'giggle factor' in his Introduction to describe the reaction of people, who should know better, to disclosures about UFOs and their occupants, and their origin, behaviour and purpose. Such expressions are unfortunately commonplace and most usually appear in the writings of lazy second-rate journalists. Many share their views or, perhaps more accurately, say that they do. This reaction can only be driven by fear or ignorance and, as far as scientists are concerned, what they fear most is an attack on their own discipline; they fear their ignorance being exposed to public derision and they actually fear their inability to cope with what Good and all serious ufologists assert is the reality. As for the 'journos', they have found that it is easier to write a knocking piece about what I have called the 'little green men ha-ha-ha' syndrome than it would be to do some quite difficult but elementary work on analysing books such as this one.

Anyone who reads these words will very soon realize that they must disregard this foolish and superficial view of UFOs, and their occupants, called for convenience 'aliens'. Tim Good refers in his Introduction to the sensible, proper and highly satisfactory way in which this whole important subject is treated in China. How much better it would be for all of us if our scientific community and the media would give it the same treatment.

Discerning readers will find here a wealth of material upon which they can make up their own minds. I would suggest that before doing so they should try to imagine what their grandparents, perhaps even their parents, would have made in the 1920s, even in the 1950s, of the idea that men would shortly be walking on the Moon, that space probes would arrive at the precise time forecast years before on Jupiter or Saturn or Mars, and send back precise and detailed information, that instant communication by voice or image from one spot on the globe to any other would be just routine, that human hearts can be successfully transplanted, babies conceived in a test tube and that all this would be common-place in 2000. They would have found such happenings as bizarre, fanciful and incredible as some of the matters which have been reported all over the world to Good by reliable and corroborated witnesses, such as Rubens Villela, a distinguished scientist who has worked for the CIA as well as the US and Brazilian navies.

I have laboured this point because I believe it is important, particularly to new readers of the genre, to start with the notion that this is not a work of fiction; it is a carefully considered report by a distinguished and experienced researcher. Let me go over to the attack – UFO protagonists now have no need to be defensive, if they ever had. So if after reading Chapters 8–13 you still do not believe that there was a creature of Pretare, try answering the following questions: Why on earth should Caponi make up such an unlikely tale? How, if he made it up, did a young unsophisticated artisan from a remote Italian village manage to convince such an experienced, hard-headed researcher as Good? Why was a hostile Carabinieri unable to break his story or to discredit his photographs? Why did the US Embassy in Rome try to steal the photographs? If, after reading Chapters 2, 16 and 17, you still do not believe that there is something very odd going on in Puerto Rico, then you have brought scepticism to an art form. Why does almost the entire population believe in the existence of the so-called *chupacabras*? Why does the US military deny access to part of the island which is reported to contain an alien base and is sometimes guarded by armed sentries? These and many more strange stories from the island have been checked out with the author by Graham Sheppard, a recently retired British Airways captain, who relates in Chapter 2 a remarkable experience he had there himself, not far from an area where two other pilots simply disappeared some years before. He and his aircraft flying there in good weather inexplicably suffered what he describes as 'an enormous lateral displacement', which took him miles off his course and nearly into a forbidden zone? Is it likely that a man whose very career depends on his airmanship and total integrity would make up such a yarn?

All these, and many other astonishing and well-documented experiences, await you in this remarkable book. It will appeal, I have no doubt, to the new explorer in this strange territory as well as to the regular UFO buff. Readers of either persuasion cannot fail to be impressed – as I was – that many incidents reported by the author are corroborated by more than one independent witness, frequently a member of the police, or the military, whose integrity there can be no reason to doubt. Good has given me in confidence the names of many of his sources who do not at present wish to be identified, and I can vouch for their record of probity and good standing, frequently in government service. This alone makes *Unearthly Disclosure* worthy of serious attention and allows me to recommend it with confidence. It is a first-class read and an important contribution to the UFO lexicon.

HILL-NORTON

Admiral of the Fleet The Lord Hill-Norton was educated at the Royal Naval Colleges Dartmouth and Greenwich. During the Second World War he served in Arctic convoys, the North-West Approaches and on the Admiralty Naval Staff. From 1953 to 1955 he served as Naval Attaché in Argentina, Uruguay and Paraguay. He commanded HMS *Decoy* (1956–7) and HMS *Ark Royal* (1959–61). In 1968 he was promoted Admiral and in 1969 became Commander-in-Chief of all British Forces in the Far East. In 1970 he was appointed First Sea Lord, the professional head of the Royal Navy, and, from 1971, shortly after his promotion to the rank of Admiral of the Fleet, he became Chief of the Defence Staff of the United Kingdom and, as such, the British government's principal defence adviser. From April 1974 to 1977 he was Chairman of the NATO Military Committee, the highest military office in the Alliance.

Lord Hill-Norton is author of *No Soft Options: The Politico-Military Realities of NATO* (1978) and *Sea Power* (1982), which he also presented personally in a popular television series.

Introduction

Asked how they would react to undeniable proof that aliens are visiting Earth, 32 per cent of 1971 influential men and women in the United States said they were 'fully prepared to handle it'. When asked how they thought others would react to the same news, however, 25 per cent said that 'most people would totally freak out and panic', according to a nationwide survey conducted by the Roper Organization for the National Institute of Discovery Science in 1999. Eighty per cent said they thought that the US Government would classify or suppress evidence of extraterrestrial life.[1]

It is difficult to assess precisely how people would react to an official announcement confirming an alien presence on Earth, although if reactions to unofficial announcements hinting at such a presence are anything to go by, few people seem to be bothered. When President Reagan asked, 'Is not an alien force already among us?', during an important speech to the United Nations General Assembly in 1987, after stating his conviction that 'our differences worldwide would vanish if we were facing an alien threat',[2] hardly anyone paid attention (least of all at the UN). In 1999 a 90-page report, *Les OVNI et la Défense: A quoi doit-on se préparer?*[3] ('UFOs and Defence: What must we be prepared for?'), written mostly by former auditors at the French Institute of Higher Studies for National Defence (IHEDN), concluded that the physical reality of UFOs, under the control of intelligent beings, was 'almost certain'. Submitted to President Jacques Chirac and Prime Minister Lionel Jospin prior to its public release, the report was ignored by the international media, except in France, where it was rubbished by the few newspapers which mentioned it at all.

1

Gildas Bourdais, a leading French researcher and author, explains that the French report is the result of an independent study by the 'Committee for In-Depth Studies' (COMETA), whose members include General Denis Letty (President), General Bruno Le Moine, General Pierre Bescond, General Alain Orszag, Admiral Marc Merlo and Denis Blancher, chief National Police superintendent at the Ministry of the Interior. There is a preface by Air Force General Bernard Norlain, a former director of IHEDN as well as former commander of the French Tactical Air Force and military counsellor to the prime minister, and an introduction by Dr André Lebeau, former president of the National Centre for Space Studies (CNES), the French equivalent of NASA. Outside contributors included Jean-Jacques Vélasco, head of SEPRA (*Service d'Expertise des Phénomènes de Rentrée Atmosphérique*), the French government's official UFO study group.[4]

COMETA states that the extraterrestrial hypothesis for the origin of unexplained UFOs is 'by far the best scientific hypothesis . . . if [UFOs] were terrestrial craft, they could only be of American construction and, despite every secret precaution, that fact would have been uncovered'.[5]

'What situations must we be prepared for?' is a key question posed by COMETA. The report addresses situations such as extraterrestrial moves for official contact; discovery of an alien base; invasion (deemed improbable) and localized or wide-scale attack; and manipulation or disinformation aimed at destabilizing other states. The report also explores political and religious ramifications associated with alien visitation.[6]

Surprisingly, given France's traditional independent stance on matters of national security, particularly where the United States is concerned, COMETA recommends that European states and the European Union seek diplomatic initiatives with the US regarding this 'capital question', within the framework of political and strategic alliances. However, the report notes, 'faced with a persistent attitude of secrecy, how can we conceive of harmonious political and military relations between allies which . . . should rest on mutual trust if, in particular, access to technological information of incalculable importance is denied?'[7]

COMETA comments further on American policy in this regard:

> It is true that the attitude of this country has been extremely strange since the June 1947 wave of sightings, followed by the Roswell affair. If the Americans managed, on that occasion or on others, to recover at least some pieces of debris or complete wreckage of extraterrestrial vehicles, in more or less good condition, or even humanoid corpses, then some kind of contact would indeed have been established.

'Why and how could a secret of such magnitude be kept, in spite of everything, up to the present day?' COMETA asks, emphasizing the unique level of secrecy shrouding the subject since 1947. 'The simplest answer would be that the United States wants to protect, at all costs, military technological superiority derived from the study of UFOs, and, perhaps, a privileged contact.'[8]

The COMETA report is not without its critics, especially among members of the UFO research community, who tend to overlook the fact that reports of this nature are directed at the general public as well as specialists. Most, however, concede its significance. 'In spite of some minor mistakes and inappropriate hints,' writes the author Jean Sider, 'this report is nevertheless making quasi-official the UFO phenomenon. It is the first time in France, even in Europe, and maybe in the world, that these unusual manifestations are admitted publicly under the cover of a body close to the Ministry of Defence (IHEDN) as being possibly created by an unknown intelligence, maybe extraterrestrial.'[9]

'It was neither an accident nor a coincidence that [the committee members] possessed good scientific training or practice in several technical disciplines,' writes Jean-Gabriel Greslé, a retired military and airline pilot who has also written several books on UFOs.

> The aim of the committee members, every one of them a specialist of good standing, was to convince their colleagues that a problem, too long neglected, was worthy of their attention . . . None of the gentlemen who agreed to make their identity public, and a few

others who did not, are given to flights of fancy. The muted sense of urgency that pervades the whole report suggests that the committee members knew a few things that the population at large did not . . .[10]

An American report by an international panel of scientists (including two COMETA members), directed by Dr Peter Sturrock, issued a year before the one by COMETA, concludes that scientists could learn much about unexplained physical evidence for UFOs if the 'giggle factor' could be overcome.[11] In contrast, thus far, to the COMETA study, the Sturrock report, *Physical Evidence Related to UFO Reports*,[12] received wide, sensible media coverage.

The 'giggle factor' is not a problem in China. In my book *Beyond Top Secret*, I devoted a chapter to encounters with UFOs reported by military and civilian pilots, and other credible witnesses in that country, and showed how seriously the subject is treated in the academic community. In 1992 the China UFO Research Organization, which is a member of the China Association for Science and Technology, had 3600 formal members as well as 40,000 research associates.[13] 'The level of interest and acceptance is rising rapidly,' said Sun Shili, a retired Foreign Ministry official who heads the Beijing UFO Research Society, in January 2000. 'Because of the frequent sightings recently in Beijing, Shanghai and other cities that have had many witnesses, even the media, which are very serious and careful, have been paying attention.'

Most of China's UFO researchers are scientists and engineers, and many UFO groups require a college degree and published research for membership. The Beijing UFO Research Society includes many Communist Party cadres or managers, and Air Force officials regularly attend important meetings. 'If our conditions for membership weren't so strict we'd have millions of members by now,' explains Sun. Ironically, a country renowned for its repression of liberalism now leads the world in liberal academic discussion relating to this controversial and multi-faceted subject. 'In the US, scholars investigating this are under pressure and have been derided,' Sun points out. 'But in China, the academic

```
INQUIRE=DOC17D
ITEM NO=00502993
ENVELOPE
CDSN = LGX487   MCN = 92107/10876   TOR = 921070814
RTTUZYUW RUEKJCS6879 1070816-UUUU--RUEALGX.
ZNR UUUUU
HEADER
R 160816Z APR 92
FM JOINT STAFF WASHINGTON DC
INFO RUEALGX/SAFE
R 160758Z APR 92
FM FBIS OKINAWA JA
TO AIG 4581
RUCIAEA/FASTC/TAI WRIGHT PATTERSON AFB OH
ACCT FBOW-EWDK
BT
CONTROLS
UNCLAS 1L

SERIAL:  OW1604075892

BODY
COUNTRY: PRC
SUBJ:     UFO RESEARCH ORGANIZATION TO HOLD CONFERENCE IN BEIJING

SOURCE:  BEIJING XINHUA IN ENGLISH 0717 GMT 16 APR 92
TEXT:


   ((TEXT))  BEIJING, APRIL 16 (XINHUA) -- THE CHINA UFO RESEARCH
ORGANIZATION (CURO) WILL HOLD A NATIONAL CONFERENCE NEXT MONTH IN
BEIJING.
   WANG CHANGTING, ACTING CHAIRMAN OF THE CURO, SAID THAT SEARCHING
FOR CREATURES THAT MIGHT BE LIVING IN OTHER SOLAR SYSTEMS IS ONE OF
THE THEMES OF THE "1992 INTERNATIONAL SPACE YEAR".
   MORE THAN 100 CHINESE AND OVERSEAS RESEARCHERS WILL BE PRESENT,
MAKING THE ACTIVITY THE LARGEST OF ITS KIND EVER HELD IN CHINA.
   UNIDENTIFIED FLYING OBJECTS, ALSO KNOWN AS FLYING SAUCERS, BECAME
A HOT TOPIC IN CHINA IN THE LATE 1970S.  THERE HAVE BEEN OVER 5,000
SIGHTINGS OF UNEXPLAINED AERIAL PHENOMENA IN CHINA.
   THE FIRST REPORT OF UFOS CAME FROM AMERICA, AND THERE HAVE BEEN
400,000 REPORTS OF SIGHTINGS WORLDWIDE.
   IN 1978 THE UNITED NATIONS CALLED ON THE GOVERNMENTS OF ALL
COUNTRIES BE ON FULL ALERT FOR SIGHTINGS AND ESTABLISH UFO
INVESTIGATION BODIES.
   CHINA SET UP ITS OWN UFO INVESTIGATION BODY, CURO, IN 1978, AND
IT IS NOW A MEMBER OF THE CHINA ASSOCIATION FOR SCIENCE AND
TECHNOLOGY, LARGELY SUPPORTED BY THE GOVERNMENT.
ADMIN
(ENDALL) 160711        504.00        0759Z APR
BT
```

Approved for Release
Date   SEP   1997

UNCLASSIFIED

Figure 1. A 1992 US intelligence electrical message alluding to the UFO
situation in China. (The first reports of UFOs did not come from America,
and '400,000 reports of sightings worldwide' is an underestimation.)
(*Defense Intelligence Agency / Nicholas Redfern*)

discussion is quite free, so in this area American academics are quite jealous of us.'[14]

In February 1971 Dr Edgar D. Mitchell, pilot of the Apollo 14 lunar module, became the sixth man to walk on the Moon. He has discussed the UFO subject with a number of people in the military and intelligence community who have convinced him that the US Government has covered up the truth about UFOs for over 50 years. He wants Congress to grant his sources immunity to reveal 'the real story' of events, such as that involving the crash of a flying disc near Roswell, New Mexico, in July 1947. 'Many of these folks were under high-security clearances; they took oaths and they feel they cannot talk without some form of immunity,' said Mitchell in 1998. 'It takes a brave person to come out on something like this.'[15]

'I am convinced there is a small body of valid [UFO] information, and that there is a body of information ten times as big that is total disinformation put out . . . to confuse the whole issue,' Dr Mitchell told a reporter, Billy Cox, in 1996.

> The dangerous part is, they're still operating under a black budget, which has been estimated at over $30 billion a year. And nobody knows what goes into black budgets. The prime requisite is security first and everything else second. Imagine an organization that has a black budget, an unquestioned source of funds, reports to no one, and has this exotic technology that they can keep to themselves and play with. The information is now held primarily by a body of semi- or quasi-private organizations that have kinda spun off from the military intelligence organizations of the past. Just like we build a rocket through a private contractor, there have been private groups involved with this issue for a number of years because they have the expertise.

Dr Mitchell stresses that he has no first-hand knowledge of the existence of recovered alien artefacts and the subject of UFOs never arose during his Apollo-era training. 'NASA at that time was so sure there were no such things . . . I would say, however, that if there was knowledge of ET contact existing within the government, and we were sent into space blind and dumb to such information, I think it is a case of criminal culpability . . .'[16]

I share Dr Mitchell's conviction that information about the alien situation is held primarily in the US by organizations that have 'spun off from the military intelligence organizations of the past', operating under a black budget. In this book I reveal information supplied by my own sources which, as suspected by COMETA, tends to confirm that certain American military and scientific personnel have indeed established 'privileged contact' with extraterrestrials, and that a number of scientists from other countries have been recruited in an 'unearthly alliance'. As Lord Hill-Norton confirms, I have provided him in confidence with the names and backgrounds of a number of my sources for these remarkable disclosures.

All manner of strange creatures associated with the alien phenomenon are featured in *Unearthly Disclosure*. I have also included stories involving contact with quasi-human beings. Although seemingly ludicrous in many respects and often involving confabulation, deception or delusion on the part of the witnesses and disinformation by the aliens, it is my contention that important elements of truth are contained in the stories I have selected.

Whatever the aliens' agenda, continuing reports of abductions, animal mutilations, as well as stories of submarine and subterranean bases, described herein, reinforce my belief that our planet is being used as a centre of clandestine operations by several alien species. We are told by astronomers and exobiologists that Earth may be unique in this particular part of the galactic neighbourhood. If this is the case, it should come as no surprise that other intelligent beings regard our planet as a target of opportunity. 'Your world is marvellous,' Julio Fernández was told by his alien abductors (Chapter 7). 'Its biological richness is unbelievable. There are very few worlds like it. It is a well-nigh inexhaustible mine of many of the things that we need, and that we do not have . . .'

Unearthly Disclosure is dedicated to the late Bruce Renton, who alerted me to the remarkable story of Filiberto Caponi and his photographs showing an apparently alien creature in Italy. Together with his daughter, Yasmin, Bruce translated Caponi's manuscript, which I edited for this book (Chapters

8–13). Bruce earned a first in Russian and Italian at St Edmund's Hall, Oxford, and went on to learn many other languages. He served in the British Army and with the Secret Intelligence Service (MI6) during the Second World War, before becoming a correspondent for *The Times*, in Italy. Afterwards he wrote for the *New Statesman* and the *Spectator*, among others, and became a venerated member of the Foreign Press Association in Rome. His colourful career included a period as manager of public relations for British Airways in Italy and as a representative for official tourism in Asia, Hong Kong, Macau and Thailand. I shall never forget his kindness and support.

NOTES

1 Press Release, National Institute of Discovery Science, Las Vegas, 7 June 1999.
2 Verbatim text, 42nd General Assembly of the United Nations, 21 September 1987.
3 COMETA, *Les OVNI et la Défense: A quoi doit-on se préparer?*, GS Presse-Communication, 79-83 rue Baudin, 92309 Levallois-Perret Cedex, France, July 1999.
4 Bourdais, Gildas, 'Quasi-official French document looks at defense issues related to UFOs', *MUFON UFO Journal*, no. 377, September 1999, pp. 10–13. Copyright 1999 by the Mutual UFO Network, 103 Oldtowne Road, Seguin, Texas 78155.
5 COMETA, op. cit., p. 55.
6 Bourdais, op. cit.
7 COMETA, p. 58.
8 Ibid., p. 57.
9 Sider, Jean, 'A second view of the COMETA report', *MUFON UFO Journal*, no. 377, September 1999, p. 13.
10 Greslé, Jean-Gabriel, *The COMETA Report*, December 1999.
11 Sawyer, Kathy, 'Panel Urges Study of UFO Reports', *Washington Post*, 29 June 1998.
12 'Physical Evidence Related to UFO Reports: The Proceedings of a Workshop Held at the Pocantico Conference Center, Tarrytown, New York, 29 September–4 October 1997', *Journal of Scientific Exploration*, vol. 12, no. 2, 1998, pp. 179–229.
13 Good, Timothy, *Beyond Top Secret: The Worldwide UFO Security Threat*, Sidgwick & Jackson, London, 1996, pp. 209–22.

14 Rosenthal, Elisabeth, 'In UFOs, Beijing Finds an Otherworldly Interest It Can Live With', New York Times Service, *International Herald Tribune*, London and Paris, 12 January 2000.
15 Rhodes, Tom, 'Aliens exist – just ask the man on the moon', *Sunday Times*, London, 11 October 1998.
16 Cox, Billy, 'Apollo 14 astronaut searches for the truth', *Florida Today*, 12 January 1996, as published in *MUFON UFO Journal*, no. 342, October 1996, p. 20. Copyright 1996 by the Mutual UFO Network. Dr Mitchell has confirmed to me the accuracy of his statements as quoted in this report.

Chapter 1

A Source of Unknown Energy

It was shortly before dawn on 28 July 1962, when the captain of a 46-foot chartered fishing boat spotted lights, low in the water, apparently stationary, about six miles south-east of Avalon, Santa Catalina Island, 30 miles off the coast of Long Beach, California. Changing course towards the tip of San Clemente Island, bringing the lights to dead ahead, the captain used his binoculars for a better look. A squat, lighted structure in which several men were working could be seen. Another member of the fishing-boat crew joined the captain and both continued to watch.

'It appeared to be the stern of a submarine,' stated the captain in his report to Marvin Miles, aerospace editor of the *Los Angeles Times*. 'We could see five men, two in all-white garb, two in dark trousers and white shirts, and one in a sky-blue jump-suit. We passed abeam at about a quarter-mile and I was certain it was a submarine low in the water, steel gray, no markings, decks almost awash, with only its tail and an odd aftstructure showing.'

When the submarine started towards their boat, the skipper turned hard to keep clear as it swept past them at a surprising speed and, still on the surface, headed for open sea. Although there was a 'good-sized swell', no noise could be heard and the 'submarine' left no wake. The men decided to report the incident to the US Navy. Detailed statements were taken, and the men were shown silhouettes of various foreign submarines. Questioned by the *Los Angeles Times*, the Navy responded that there was 'nothing to it'.[1] The submarine was assumed by the *Times* to be possibly of Soviet origin, yet the absence of engine noise and wake, combined with the relatively high surface speed, remains unexplained.

Unidentified submergible objects (USOs) have been reported for centuries. What leads me to suspect that the Santa Catalina 'submarine' might not have been of Soviet origin is that four days later another, similar craft was sighted, this time in the Mediterranean Sea, as recounted in my previous book, *Alien Base*. On 1 August 1962 three fishermen observed a large, metallic, submarine-shaped object, with around a dozen 'frogmen' coming out of the sea and climbing aboard it. The fishermen believed they were watching a submarine on manoeuvres, that is, until it rose silently about 20 metres out of the water, hung stationary for a few minutes, then shot off horizontally in the air at tremendous speed.[2]

These and many similar USO reports suggest that alien beings not only are as capable of travelling in our oceans and lakes as they are in our atmosphere, but that they have established permanent submarine bases on our planet.

COSTA RICA

On the morning of 4 September 1971 four members of the National Geographic Institute of Costa Rica were flying in a twin-engined aircraft 10,000 feet above Lake Cote, near Arenal, Arajuela (10°35N, 84°55W), to take a series of cartographic photographs. A special automatic large-format camera, fitted underneath the plane, took pictures at 20-second intervals. On returning to the institute's laboratory in San José, the team was astonished to discover that one of the frames (no. 300) showed what looked like a metallic disc, which appeared as though it had just left, or was on the point of entering, the lake. It had not been seen from the aircraft.

Had it been at ground level the object (see Plate 2) would have been about 50 metres in diameter. It does not appear on photos 299 and 301. After analysing the original negative, Jacques Vallée, the well-known author and researcher, eliminated tricks of light as an explanation. Further studies by Dr Vallée, Dr Richard Haines, François Louange and C. Perrin de Brichambaut revealed that the object appears to be self-luminescent and that it made a sudden manoeuvre at the instant the photo was taken.[3,4]

According to the Costa Rican investigators, Carlos and Ricardo Vilchez, there have been numerous reports of unknown submergible craft entering and leaving Lake Cote, which is extremely deep. One morning at about 09.00 (no date given), two men heard a metallic noise coming from the lake and an object, shaped like a submarine with three 'domes' on its top, emerged, hung level with the water for a few seconds, then suddenly shot off towards the mountains to the north. Local fishermen, out on the lake in the small hours, are reported to have seen various objects, giving off coloured lights, submerged below them. Sometimes the movement of these objects caused the men to lose their balance. The Vilchez brothers claim that these underwater activities led to a reduction in the fish population, to the concern of those whose livelihood depended on it.[5]

USA

Also associated with a reduction in the local fish population is a unique encounter with a USO reported in Pascagoula, Mississippi, on the night of 6 November 1973. Here follow extracts from the official Coast Guard report:

1. 2130S TWO LOCAL FISHERMEN REPORTED IN PERSON TO THIS UNIT THAT THEY WERE FISHING IN APPROX. POSITION 88–36W, 30–20N WHEN THEY LOCATED A STRANGE ILLUMINATING OBJECT WHICH WAS APPROX. [IN] 4–6 FT OF WATER AND MOVING AT APPROX. 4–6 KTS . . . FISHERMEN TRIED TO DETERMINE WHAT OBJECT WAS BUT COULD NOT. THEY TRIED TO HIT IT WITH PADDLES AND OBJECT WOULD GO OUT AND MOVE TO ANOTHER POSITION . . . FISHERMEN APPEARED SOBER AND EXTREMELY CONCERNED ABOUT THE OBJECT.
2. 2140S THIS UNIT DISPATCHED CG 163519 WITH BM NATIONS AND BM3 CREWS ABOARD TO INVESTIGATE. STATION PERSONNEL DID IN FACT LOCATE OBJECT, WHICH HAD AN AMBER BEAM APPROX. 4–6 FT IN DIAMETER AND ATTACHED TO SOME BRIGHT METAL OBJECT MOVING AT 4–6 KTS. OBJECT DID IN FACT CEASE ILLUMINATING, CHANGED TO A DIFFERENT COURSE AND RE-ILLUMINATE ITSELF

```
CG DE PS"

P 061815Z NOV 73
FM COGARD STA PASCAGOULA
TO COMCOGARD GRU MOBILE
BT
UNCLAS
UNIDENTIFIED SUBMERGED ILLUMINATED OBJECT SIGHTING
A. MY 070615Z NOV 73
1. THE FOLLOWING STATEMENT HAS BEEN RELEASED TO NEWS MEDIA
THIS DATE CONCERNING SUBJECT SIGHTING: QUOTE AT 0930 PM
LOCAL TIME 6 NOV 73 TWO LOCAL FISHERMAN RPTD IN PERSON TO
CG STA PASCAGOULA THAT THEY WERE FISHING IN A POSITION
BETWEEN THE WEST BANK OF PASCAGOULA SHIP CHANNEL AND ROUND
ISLAND, WHEN THEY NOTICED AN ILLUMINATING OBJECT BENEATH THE
WATER , THE FISHER MEN STATED THEY ATTEMPTED TO DETERMINE
WHAT THE OBJECT WAS BUT COULD NOT. THE FISHERMEN APPEARED
EXTREMELY CONCERNED. CG STA PASCAGOULA DISPATCHED ITS
SMALL BOAT WITH TWO STATION MEMBERS ON BOARD TO INVESTIGATE
THE OBJECT WAS RELOCATED BY UNIT MEMBERS AND APPEARED TO BE
4-6FT IN DIAMETER AND SHOWING   AN AMBER COLOR. THE GLOW
EVENTUALLY BECAME EXTINGUISHED AND COULD NOT BE RELOCATED.
A DAYLIGHT INVESTIGATION ON THE MORNING OF 7 NOV PROVED
NEGATIVE UNQUOTE.
2. THE FOLLOWING PERSONS WERE ON SCENE AND SAW THE REPORTED
GLOW:
        RAYMOND RYAN, AGE 42,1403 LARSON ST, PAS.
        EARL RYAN, AGE 16
        EDWARD RICE, AGE 48
        FREDDY RICE, AGE 35
        VELMA RICE, AGE 37
        EDDIE RICE, AGE 15
3. FURTHER INQUIRIES FROM MEDIA RELATING TO SUBJ WILL BE
DIRECTED TO YOUR OFFICE.
BT

TOD 06/QI
TOD 08/1849Z NOV PDL K
DE CG R NJ AR
```

Enclosure (4) to WILBANKS/DORMAN
Trip Report of 12 NOV 73

Figure 2. Two pages from a US Coast Guard report relating to sightings of an unidentified submergible object (USO) witnessed by fishermen and coast guards in Pascagoula, Mississippi, November 1973. (*US Coast Guard*)

14

EI O9 DE PS

P 070615Z NOV 73
FM COGARD STA PASCAGOULA
TO COM COGARD GRU MOBILE
INFO COGDEIGHT
BT
UNCLAS
UNIDENTIFIED SUBMERGED ILLUMINATING OBJECT
1. 2130S TWO LOCAL FISHERMEN REPORTED IN PERSON TO THIS UNIT
THAT THEY WERE FISHING IN APPROX. POSITION 86-36W, 30-20N WHEN
THEY LOCATED A STRANGE ILLUMINATING OBJECT WHICH WAS APPROX.
4-6 FT OF WATER AND MOVING AT APPROX. 4-6 KTS. SUBJ FISHERMEN
TRIED TO DETERMINE WHAT OBJECT WAS BUT COULD NOT. THEY TRIED TO
HIT IT WITH PADDLES AND OBJECT WOULD GO OUT AND MOVE TO ANOTHER
POSITION. SUBJ FISHERMEN APPEARED SOBER AND EXTREMLY CONCERNED
ABOUT THE OBJECT.
2. 2140S THIS UNIT DISPATCHED CG 163519 WITH BM2 NATIONS AND
BM3 CREWS ABOARD TO INVESTIGATE. STATION PERSONNEL DID IN FACT
LOCATE OBJECT, WHICH HAD AN AMBER BEAM APPROX. 4-6 FT IN
DIAMETER AND ATTACHED TO SOME BRIGHT METAL OBJECT MOVING AT 4-6
KTS. OBJECT DID IN FACT CEASE ILLUMINATING, CHANGED TO A DIFFERENT
COURSE AND RE-ILLUMINATE ITSELF. SUBJ OBJECT TRAVELED SEVERAL
COURES WHILE ILLUMINATED. STATION PERSONNEL COULD NOT IDENTIFY
OBJECT AND HAS NEVER SEEN ANY THING LIKE IT. 2230S CG 163519
MOORED STATION AND STATED FISHERMEN WILL RETURN TO STATION AT
A LATER TIME. THIS UNIT WILL OBTAIN THEIR NAMES AND ADDRESSES.
BT

TOD 07/0656Z NOV CC K
DE EI R WL AR
DE OQ R KD AR

Enclosure (3) to WILBANKS/DORMAN
Trip Report of 12 Nov 73

... OBJECT TRAVELED SEVERAL COURSES WHILE ILLUMINATED. STATION PERSONNEL COULD NOT IDENTIFY OBJECT AND [HAVE] NEVER SEEN ANYTHING LIKE IT ...

When the coast guards themselves had located the USO, they too attempted to deal with it by striking it with an oar. 'The object again dimmed and/or moved (at 4–6 knots),' the Coast Guard report states, 'and after 10–15 minutes extinguished and could not be relocated.'

Object travelled in SW direction, toward deeper water, and appeared to remain in or near a 'gully' on the seafloor ... Current during period of sightings was 'negligible'; object moved in various directions, though primarily to SW in relatively straight course, and at speeds up to 4–6 knots. Object did not consistently move when disturbed or passed over in boats.

Light from object was directed toward surface; it appeared to come from a coherent source approximately 3" in diameter, with a surface intersection circular or elliptical in shape and approximately 10' × 12' in size. Color was generally described as yellowish-amber, or with a light red tint. Intensity varied from 'almost too bright to look right at' to zero, depending on amount of disturbance (brightest when first approached). When seen from the side, it was described as looking like a parachute underwater.

Object felt metallic when struck, but could not be consistently struck. Portion of oar underwater was not visible from surface when in light beam from object. Object 'turned off' when struck with beam from flashlight; when light [was] removed, object reilluminated to previous intensity in about 1 minute ... Phenomena observed were not consistent with any known fish or other marine life, nor with flashlight, lantern, navaid, or other known light source.[6]

'When I hit it with my oar, it felt like metal and when the Coast Guardsman took my oar and hit it, he said it felt like metal,' declared Raymond Ryan, one of the fishermen. 'It looked like a mini-submarine I once saw on TV.'[7]

The Coast Guard report concludes: 'At least nine persons witnessed an undetermined light source between the hours of 1930 and 2200 on the night of 6 November 1973, at two locations separated by approximately ½ mile . . . The presence of the object was associated with a significant variation in the fish catch in the area.'[8] Interestingly, the USO was reported near the mouth of the Pascagoula river, where less than a month earlier the incredible abduction of two credible fishermen, Charles Hickson and Calvin Parker, took place.[9]

PUERTO RICO

Much of my research in the 1990s has focused on the United States Commonwealth of Puerto Rico, where so many sightings of unidentified flying and submergible objects, as well as encounters with a variety of unearthly beings, have been reported that I have come to believe in the existence there of an alien base.

José Orlando Golís, who works for the Puerto Rican government, lives in Río Grande, close to El Yunque, the 28,000-acre Caribbean National Forest in the north-eastern part of the island, a focal point for anomalous activity. In 1998 he was introduced to me by Jorge Martín, Puerto Rico's leading investigator. 'Many people have seen UFOs flying over the water close to the surface,' Orlando told me. 'Once, at one a.m., we saw one with many coloured lights flying next to the sea just over the surface. At first we thought it was a boat. It seemed to be dark underneath and had lights – mostly red and blue – at another, upper level. Then it angled and moved upwards. It made a humming sound, and seemed to head in the direction of El Yunque.'[10]

Felix Rivera, a diver with an underwater salvage and maintenance company based in Ceiba, near the US Navy's Roosevelt Roads Naval Air Station, which adjoins El Yunque on the east coast, confirmed to me that USOs have frequently been observed, often by qualified witnesses. 'Navy SEALs have seen USOs here,' he revealed. 'Some have told me that these things will often come up close to boats, then shoot off. They move too fast underwater to be ours.'[11]

Another focal point of activity in Puerto Rico is the south-west coast. In an area known as Cayo Margarita, about 15 miles out in the Atlantic, many local fishermen as well as commercial and private pilots have seen USOs entering or

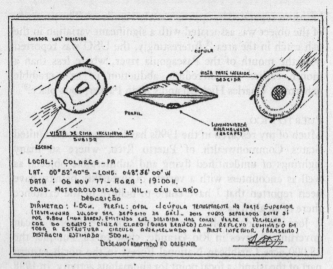

```
LOCAL: COLARES - PA
LAT. 00°52'40"S - LONG. 048°38'00"W
DATA : 06 NOV 77 - HORA : 19:00H.
COND. METEOROLOGICAS : NIL, CÉU CLARO
                    DESCRIÇÃO
DIÂMETRO: 1.50m.  PERFIL: OVAL C/CÚPULA TRANSPARENTE NA PARTE SUPERIOR
(TESTEMUNHA JULGOU SER DEPÓSITO DE GÁS) - DOIS TUBOS SEPARADOS ENTRE SÍ
POR 0.80m (mais BAIXA), EMITINDO DAS CORES VERDE E VERMELHA.
COR DO CORPO : CINZA CLARO (QUASE BRANCO) COM REFLEXO LUMINOSO EM
TODA A ESTRUTURA. CIRCULO AVERMELHADO NA PARTE INFERIOR. (BRASEIRO)
DISTÂNCIA ESTIMADA   500m.
            DESENHO (ADAPTADO) AO ORIGINAL.
```

1977- 06.11 - 19:00P - RELATO 47A - CL.8 - F20 - Corpo ligeira-
mente iluminado, de cor Cinza(celeste)clara,de formato circular
com uma cupula ovalada na parte superior, com dois tubos na parte frontal, na parte inferior um circulo avermelhado (braseiro),
seu diâmetro foi estimado em 1.50m, não fazia ruido e a luminosidade se refletia em toda a sua estrutura.Nos tubos frontais /
foi observada a emissão de feixes de luz de cores : verde e ver
melha.Baixa altura (?), distância 500m.
Nota- Causou interferência no televissor que o relator trabalha-
va.

Figure 3. Two pages from a Brazilian Air Force report describing UFO and
USO sightings by witnesses in north-east Brazil in 1977–8. Led by
Lieutenant-Colonel Uyrange Hollanda, the Air Force Intelligence team
interviewed nearly 300 people. (*Forca Aérea Brasileira*)

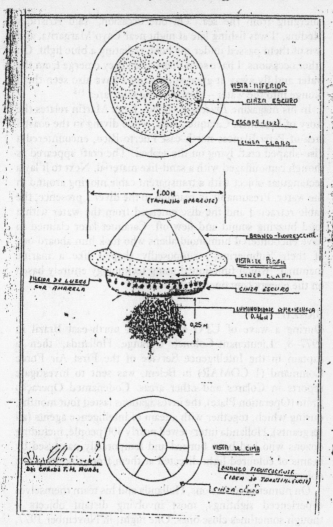

VISTA: INFERIOR

CINZA ESCURO

ESCAPE (LUZ)

CINZA CLARA

1.00 M
(TAMANHO APARENTE)

BRANCO-FLUORESCENTE.

VISTA: PERFIL

FILEIRA DE LUZES
COR AMARELA

CINZA CLARA

CINZA ESCURO

LUMINOSIDADE AMARELA
(0.46µ)

0,25 M

VISTA DE CIMA

DEN. CONDÉ T. M. RUADI

BRANCO FLUORESCENTE
(IDEA DE TRANSPARENCIA)

CINZA CLARA

emerging from the sea. 'On one occasion,' said Arístides Medina, 'I was fishing late at night near Cayo Margarita, and two of them passed under my boat, radiating a blue light. On other occasions, I have seen them when they emerge from the water and fly away at great speed, and I have also seen them plunge into the water – always in the same area.'[12]

In his magazine *Evidencia OVNI*, Jorge Martín relates the story of Inocencia Cataquet, who, while diving in the coastal area of Peña Blancas north-east Puerto Rico, encountered a disc-shaped craft lying on the seabed. The craft appeared as though camouflaged with a sand-like material. Next to it lay a rectangular object with a transparent cable moving around in the water. Presumably in reaction to the diver's presence, the cable retracted and the disc emerged from the water with a loud buzzing sound and flew off. Cataquet later claimed to have encountered humanoid aliens who took him aboard one of their 'submarines', supposedly shaped like a marine mammal, 'which functioned using technology entirely based on the energy contained in the water'.[13]

BRAZIL

During a wave of UFO sightings in north-east Brazil in 1977–8, Lieutenant-Colonel Uyrange Hollanda, then a captain in the Intelligence Service of the First Air Force Command (1 COMAR) in Belém, was sent to investigate reports in Colares and other areas. Codenamed Operação Prato (Operation Plate), the investigations lasted four months, during which, together with a team of intelligence agents (all sergeants), Hollanda interviewed nearly 300 people, including dozens who had been burned and temporarily paralysed by beams of coloured light directed at them from the unknown objects.

On numerous occasions, Hollanda and his team themselves experienced sightings, most involving distant objects – though sometimes close ones. One night, in November 1977, near the village of Baía do Sol, north of Belém, a structured craft hovered about 100 metres above the men. The incident occurred just after 19.00. 'I was terrified,' Hollanda told investigators Bob Pratt and Cynthia Luce, during an interview in 1997. 'We never saw anything approaching. Suddenly a big disc-shaped object 30 meters in diameter . . . was hovering exactly above us!'

> It made a noise like an air conditioner, and in the midst of that we could hear a sound like a bicycle sprocket when you pedal backwards. It was emitting a yellow glow that would grow and dim, every two or three seconds . . . about five times. As we watched we could see small yellow and orange lights in the middle of it. And after the fifth time, the lights turned light blue, dimmed – and then it disappeared with incredible speed toward the sea.

Hollanda interviewed fishermen from Colares who had seen USOs going in and out of the water and who, like the fishermen in Puerto Rico, reported seeing blue lights moving around underwater. 'Several weeks later I saw a light near a fishing boat,' said Hollanda. 'The light was blue. It circled the boat once or twice about 300 meters away and then it dived into the water . . . I saw it. It really happened.' The fishermen told Hollanda that the object 'made no sound, like a blade going into water'. Another crew of fishermen reported seeing a blue light underwater, which circled their boat, then emerged from the water.

Hollanda's team took several hundred photos of UFOs. At first, the photos showed little detail but, with the use of special filters and ultraviolet and infrared film, eight different-shaped objects were discerned:

> The first was a disc with windows. The second was rectangular, like a barrel on its side. The third was trapezoid, or like a pyramid with its top cut off. The fourth was like [the fuselage of] a Boeing (jetliner). The fifth was triangular or like an arrowhead. They flew very high in the sky [and] were also seen leaving the water. The sixth was domed. The seventh was pointed on the top and bottom and was black on top and white on the bottom. The eighth was like a ball with three sticks coming out the back, with lights on the sticks.

On one occasion a ninth shape, a 'huge mother ship', was seen by Hollanda and his men, near Baía do Sol.

It was maybe 100 meters long with windows in it . . . And little ones (flying saucers) would come out of it and later go back in, three, four, five, six sometimes. We photographed this several nights.[14]

One of the experts we used said the cylinder looked like a 200-litre oil drum. We concluded the object was reacting to our pictures. They seemed to know what we were doing, possibly looking for us. When we least expected it, there they were – right above us. And something else – shortly after we began seeing these things, our eyesight started to deteriorate, slowly at first. We ended up, most of us, having to wear glasses.[15]

Encounters with humanoid occupants were also investigated by the Brazilian Air Force intelligence specialists. Although most reports described beings of about one and a half metres in height, in two cases the beings were taller. A pilot known to Hollanda, driving near Colares one night, saw a disc land behind trees. 'He was alone on the road, it was completely dark, and he became frightened,' said Hollanda. 'Then he saw a man walking toward him. The stranger was tall and had blond hair. He walked close to the car, looked at the driver, and looked into his eyes. The driver started to cry and the tall man shook his head, glanced at the license plate, turned, and walked back into the forest. Then the disc took off.'

Regarding the numerous cases involving witnesses paralysed and burned by the flying objects – called *chupa-chupas* by the locals, who believed they sucked blood from their victims – Hollanda said he was convinced that blood samples were somehow being withdrawn via a beam of red light. 'First came a green light that would hit the person and paralyze them, then the green light would turn off and a red ray of light would hit, burning them,' he explained. 'They were not attacking people. They were collecting material.' Although at least two people died in Colares after being burned by the rays, those particular cases did not come to Hollanda's attention during his investigations.[16] 'Hollanda told Cynthia and me in 1997 that people in *all* of the 30 villages in the flap area were burned by rays of lights from UFOs, not just in Colares as previously had been believed,' Bob Pratt pointed out to me.[17]

'We had reports of mostly women being struck by some kind of ray from these lights in the sky, usually leaving marks of two punctures in the middle of a dark red blotch on their breasts,' Hollanda explained to investigators A. J. Gevaerd and M. A. Petit.

> Sometimes men had similar marks on their arms and legs. The ratio was about four women to one man affected.
>
> Once we interviewed one woman who had been sitting at home, singing her baby to sleep when suddenly the temperature went up sharply. She looked up at the roof and it turned red. Then it became transparent and the woman could see stars through the roof. It was as though it had turned to glass. She saw a bright green light in the sky, felt drowsy and then suddenly a red ray hit her on her left breast. Like the others who told us their stories, the woman seemed genuine and I felt she was telling the truth.
>
> We kept the authorities informed at every step. The government sent medical experts to examine the people we had spoken to and they monitored them and the places involved, but that's all. They couldn't do anything else.[18]

All reports on these investigations were sent to the Brazilian Air Force headquarters in Brasilia. Operação Prato was classified. 'You were forbidden to speak about this when you were in the Air Force, as an officer,' said Bob Pratt to Hollanda. 'What were the specific orders about not speaking?'

'Well, I had obligations, military obligations,' replied Hollanda. 'I was in a classified mission. Not secret missions – [but] classified. And the Brazilian government and the Air Force were not interested in publicizing the subject because three questions often were made to the government and Air Force: Who are they? Where do they come from? What do they want? And the Air Force did not have any answer to the three questions.'

'They didn't know?'

'I believe only the Americans are advanced. Russians, I don't know. But the Brazilian Air Force cannot answer.'

'But did your commander ever specifically say: "You cannot speak about these things . . . in public?"'

'Yes.'[19]

On 2 October 1997, less than two months after giving the

above interview, Lieutenant-Colonel Uyrange Hollanda was found hanged in his home. Although some believe he died in suspicious circumstances, Bob Pratt assures me that all the evidence points to suicide.[20] Hollanda was 57 years old. For many years, he had obeyed orders not to reveal publicly what he had learned as a result of Operação Prato. But by 1996 he no longer felt under that obligation. 'Thus, he began to speak out,' report Bob and Cynthia, 'giving interviews to magazine and television reporters, revealing with his first-hand testimony what governments around the world deny . . .'[21]

THE ARCTIC

Numerous sightings of USOs have been reported by personnel of the former Soviet Navy and other seamen. Paul Stonehill, a Ukrainian-born US citizen, author of *The Soviet UFO Files*, has learned that veteran officers of nuclear-powered submarines at Soviet naval bases and installations in the northern Arctic Ocean revealed, during formal lectures, that incidents had occurred when submarine sonar operators tracked unidentified submarines that appeared to be pursuing them. 'The pursuers changed their speeds at will – speeds that were much, much faster than the capabilities of any submarines in our world at that date,' reports Stonehill.[22]

In December 1977, in the vicinity of Novy Georgiy Island in the Arctic Ocean, the crew of the Soviet fishing trawler *Vasiliy Kiselev* reported a USO take-off from the water. Rising vertically from out of the sea came a doughnut-shaped object, the diameter of which they guessed at between 1000 and 1600 feet, claims Stonehill. 'It hovered at an altitude of three miles. The trawler's radar was immediately rendered inoperative. The object hovered over the area for three hours, and then disappeared instantly.'[23]

ANTARCTICA BASE

Antarctica, the most remote continent on Earth, is unpopulated except for a few hundred international scientists and support staffs engaged in a variety of experiments. Rubens Junqueira Villela is a Brazilian meteorologist and explorer, the veteran of 12 expeditions to Antarctica: two with the US Navy, nine with the Brazilian Antarctic Programme (the most recent in early 2000) and another on the sailing ship *Rapa Nui*. 'As far as UFOs are concerned,' writes Villela, 'Antarctica is no exception to anywhere else in the world. UFO sightings have been reported and even abduction attempts have allegedly been made. In some respects, however, events in this barren land are somewhat different.'

> Many of the incidents are reported by highly qualified people, who work in observatories and scientific facilities equipped with some of the most advanced scientific resources available for detecting geophysical phenomena . . . Furthermore, I have had access to UFO reports from other nations' Antarctic programmes, which are unknown to the public. These reports suggest the phenomenon is very real.

Villela himself had a sighting during his first trip to Antarctica. 'I was aboard the US Navy icebreaker *Glacier*, which had set sail from New Zealand at the end of January in 1961. Our principal objective was to explore an unknown territory on Antarctica, and the Eights Coast (south of the Bellingshausen Sea).' On 16 March, while collecting samples on the seabed, between the peninsula and the South Shetland Islands, *Glacier* was struck by a fierce storm, forcing it to retreat to Admiralty Bay in the King George Islands.

> I noticed we were inside Martel Inlet . . . Around me, from mountains which towered 600 metres, the ice was melting and crashing noisily into the sea. Nearby, US Navy sailors were busy assembling spotlights on the boat, for it was necessary to keep a vigilant eye on the ice blocks which could change the anchorage of our vessel.
>
> It was at this point that the most astonishing experience of the entire expedition occurred. A strange light suddenly crossed the sky, and everyone started to shout. The excitement was widespread and growing. Trying to describe the light which appeared over Admiralty Bay wasn't easy, for many of us were lost for words. I wrote in my diary: '. . . the colours, the configuration and contours of the object . . . with geometric forms, did not seem to be from this world, and I did not know what could possibly reproduce it'.

The object was multi-coloured and had a luminous body – oval-shaped. It left a long tube-like orange/red trail. Suddenly, it split into two equal pieces, as if it had exploded. Each part shone even more intensively, with white, blue and red colours projecting 'V'-shaped rays behind it. Quite quickly they moved away, and could be seen around 200 metres above the ground. Before the object had divided, I would estimate its size to that of a fist at arm's length. Throughout the sighting no noise was heard by any of the witnesses. The light moved horizontally and slowly, around 80 k.p.h., from northeast to southwest. It had possibly originated from behind the mountains on the other side of the island.

The sighting was registered officially by the US Navy as 'a meteor or some other natural luminous phenomenon', the 'explosion' used to substantiate the meteor theory. Villela was not convinced. How, he wondered, could a meteor be confused with an object carrying what seemed like 'antennae', 'completely symmetrical and followed by a tail, without any sign of atmospheric turbulence'?

As a meteorologist, the evidence didn't support such a theory, even allowing for the fact that many strange optical and luminous phenomena, including mirages, auroras, etc., can be seen on Antarctica. Similarly, I had already accumulated practical experience in the observation of artificial satellites in Brazil, and participated at a secret conference relating to UFOs in 1958.[24]

Villela has enjoyed a varied career. In 1952, while attending the University of Maryland as an engineering student, he was invited to work for the US government's Foreign Broadcast Information Service (FBIS). 'It was the best job I ever had,' he told me. 'At the time, FBIS had been transferred to CIA. The monitoring station was located in an "antenna farm" at Indian Head, by the Potomac river, south of Washington, DC.' Before joining CIA, Villela independently specialized in Soviet air communications, 'trying to break their secret codes for identifying locations'. At CIA he monitored signals from Guatemala during the CIA-backed anti-communist revolution which overthrew Colonel Jacobo Arbenz Guzman, drawing praise from Allen W. Dulles, then CIA Director.

Feeling that his life's dream lay in Antarctica and disillusioned by the suffering that the revolution brought to Guatemala, Villela turned down a promising career in the CIA and, in 1955, transferred to Florida State University to complete his Bachelor of Science degree in meteorology.[25] Currently, he is a professor with the Department of Atmospheric Sciences of the Astronomical and Geophysical Institute at the University of São Paulo.

While attending a training course at NASA's Goddard Space Flight Center, Greenbelt, Maryland, between October 1962 and June 1963, Villela was asked by a scientific colleague to submit a report on his Antarctica sighting to the National Investigations Committee on Aerial Phenomena (NICAP), then headed by the late Major Donald E. Keyhoe. In 1968, in Paris, Villela participated in a 'closed-doors' meeting with other scientists to discuss the UFO subject, the 'Invisible College' so called by the French researcher Aimé Michel.

Villela had further UFO sightings, mostly in Brazil. For a number of years he belonged to the now defunct Associação de Pesquisas Exologicas (APEX), a research team which included two distinguished pioneers, Dr Max Berezowski and Professor Flávio Pereira, then President of the Brazilian Institute of Aeronautics and Space Sciences.[26] On several research trips craft appeared before the team. The first sighting was 'arranged' via Eromar Gomes, who claimed to be in communication with the craft's occupants, Villela explained to me. Gomes, an individual with 'special neurophysiological features' allegedly adapted by the aliens, was placed under hypnosis by Dr Berezowski. 'The subject is not under terrestrial hypnosis,' the entities communicated, 'he is under a cataleptic state induced by us.'

'A field experiment was proposed,' said Villela. 'We were to meet somebody who was also an ET contactee in Limeira, a city about 100 miles north of São Paulo, on the night of 18 November 1978.' Two objects were seen, the second of which impressed Villela. 'When I first saw this second craft,' he told me, 'I really got a jolt: a beautiful coloured prismatic object turning around its own axis . . . the ETs seemed to read your mind, answering questions even before you finished asking.'

Another impressive event, also witnessed by others, occurred in Itanhandu, a small city in the southern part of Minas Gerais state, on the night of 21 April 1996, as Villela disclosed to me.

We had seen small moving lights ('sondes') and two small craft flying together. The ETs said they would give a demonstration of their weapons, by shooting down a 'rival's' observation device, hovering in the sky. The object blew up silently, growing from a star-like point to a larger, tear-drop shape . . . The ETs said it had been disintegrated before it hit the ground so as not to disturb the neighbourhood, and it emitted only a high frequency sound.[27]

This reads like something out of *Star Wars*. Villela, though, is a cautious scientist and, as a meteorologist (and pilot, incidentally), he is unlikely to have confused what he saw with anything conventional. He tells me that he has witnessed other, similar 'acts of aggression'. If true, a conflict of interests, on the part of those here from elsewhere, is implied.

The occupants apparently told me about their presence in Antarctica, and, to obtain my trust, they supplied information about NASA's space programme and created atmospheric effects in the sky . . . even though it was a bright clear night. I have to say I accepted the contacts as something quite normal, [like] some kind of radio communication.

In one of the 'conversations' made through our contactee acting as a link, they told us that they do indeed have a base in Antarctica, 'in a gulf occupied by many nations'. They are apparently 'self-adapting beings, who could survive in any part of the world', be it in the desert, our oceans, or the frozen regions of Antarctica. In a further amazing communication, they informed me that they required our water as a 'source of energy' in a form still unknown to us. This was apparently drawn from Artesian wells in the Antarctic . . .[28]

In response to my questions, it is interesting to recall that 'my' ETs said that it might be a good idea to establish open contact with earthlings under controlled conditions in Antarctica. But precautions would be needed on both sides. For instance, no [aircraft] weighing under 20,000 kilos should fly over the alien base as it might be attracted by their force field . . .[29]

'After my first UFO sighting in Antarctica, followed by

28

some incredible experiences, my perception of life has changed,' declares Rubens Villela. 'Today, I accept the UFO phenomenon as factual. The existence of life in the universe is not a belief many of my colleagues share. But as we approach the new millennium, astronomers and journalists will probably feel very frustrated; the astronomers for ignoring the existence of other life forms, the journalists for having missed the greatest news story of the century . . .'[30]

NOTES

1 *Los Angeles Times*, 25 October 1962, cited in Lorenzen, Jim and Coral, *UFOs Over the Americas*, Signet Books, New York, 1968, pp. 51–2.

2 Good, Timothy, *Alien Base: Earth's Encounters with Extraterrestrials*, Century, London, 1998, pp. 229–30.

3 *Les OVNI et la Défense*, COMETA, GS. Presse-Communication, July 1999, p. 43.

4 *Contacto OVNI*, Mexico, no. 55, February 1998, pp. 2–5, translated by Margaret Barling.

5 Ibid., pp. 6–7.

6 US Government Memorandum, Naval Ship Research and Development Laboratory, Panama City, Florida, 12 November 1973.

7 'Pascagoula Fisherman Says USO Not Fish', *Mobile Press*, Alabama, 9 November 1973.

8 US Government Memorandum, 12 November 1973.

9 For a comprehensive account, see Blum, Ralph and Judy, *Beyond Earth: Man's Contact with UFOs*, Corgi, 1974.

10 Interview, Río Grande, Puerto Rico, 11 April 1998.

11 Interview, Ceiba, Puerto Rico, 12 January 1999.

12 Martín, Jorge, 'US Jets Abducted by UFOs in Puerto Rico', *The UFO Report 1991*, ed. Timothy Good, Sidgwick & Jackson, London, 1990, p. 201.

13 Martín, Jorge, 'Blond Aliens on El Yunque', *Evidencia OVNI*, no.16, 1998, p. 6, translated by Margaret Barling.

14 Pratt, Bob and Luce, Cynthia, 'Former Brazilian intelligence officer relates experiences', *MUFON UFO Journal*, no. 372, April 1999, pp. 3–8. Copyright 1999 by the Mutual UFO Network.

15 'Operation Prato', *UFO Magazine*, May–June 1998, pp. 27–8.
16 Pratt and Luce, op. cit.
17 Letter to the author, 25 September 1999.
18 'Operation Prato', op. cit.
19 Extract from interview with Hollanda by Pratt and Luce, supplied to the author.
20 Letter to the author, 21 December 1999.
21 Pratt and Luce, op. cit.
22 Stonehill, Paul, 'UFOs in the Soviet Waters', *Flying Saucer Review*, vol. 44, no. 1, 1999, pp. 13–15, 19.
23 Stonehill, Paul, *The Soviet UFO Files: Paranormal Encounters Behind the Iron Curtain*, Quadrillion Publishing Ltd, Godalming, Surrey, and Quadrillion Publishing Inc., New York, 1998, p. 73.
24 Villela, Rubens Junqueira, 'UFOs in Antarctica', *UFO Magazine* (UK), November–December 1998, pp.10–13. Translated by Ricky Seraphico from 'Discos Voadores na Antarctica', *Revista UFO Brasil*, May 1998. Villela has corrected some translation errors in this article and added a few details.
25 Letter to the author, 5 November 1999.
26 Villela, op. cit.
27 Letter to the author, 14 October 1999.
28 Villela, op. cit.
29 Letter to the author, 5 November 1999.
30 Villela, op. cit.

Chapter 2

Displacements

For many years Graham Sheppard, an airline pilot, has been my principal research associate. Before we met, in 1990, he had written to me describing his radar-confirmed sightings of UFOs observed from the flight deck of Vanguard airliners in 1967. As pointed out in my book *Beyond Top Secret*, it is due in no small part to Graham that the Civil Aviation Authority (CAA) now takes pilot sighting reports more seriously than once it did, particularly those involving 'near misses': in 1995 he briefed the CAA's Joint Airmiss Working Group, advising that 'the commercial sensibilities of the airlines should now be set aside along with the media's inability to give serious treatment to the subject. Otherwise this discrete and notifiable hazard to aircraft safety will continue to be concealed and gratuitously omitted from the briefing syllabus.'[1]

In August 1966 Graham graduated as a qualified commercial pilot at the then British European Airways (BEA)/ British Overseas Airways Corporation College of Air Training at Hamble, Southampton, to fly as First Officer on the Vickers Vanguard airliner. (Coincidentally, Graham had been First Officer on a Vanguard chartered by the London Symphony Orchestra, with whom I played for 14 years, on our return to London from Budapest, following a series of concerts in Europe in September 1970.) 'In the aviation world,' Graham explains, 'Hamble was renowned for the rigour and quality of the training, not least in the now endangered art of dead reckoning navigation, a skill that was taught by veteran original aviators. The fundamentals of this art are aid-free and call on discipline, common sense and awareness, embedded as instinctual by those determined flying instructors at the start of my career.'

Graham flew with BEA as co-pilot on the Vickers Vanguard Merchantman (the cargo variant of the Vanguard), the BAC 1-11 jet airliner, then took a two-year sabbatical in Africa in the mid-1970s, first with the Zambia Flying Doctor Service (ZFDS) out of Ndola, then with Air Malawi flying the Islander on domestic routes and the BAC 1-11 475 as co-pilot on the international network. 'Bush-flying with the ZFDS refreshed and refined those old dead reckoning skills to a high degree, based entirely on the quality training imparted at Hamble,' he explained to me. 'In 1979 the now merged British Airways [BA] moved me to the left seat as Captain of the Vickers Viscount, followed over the remainder of my time with BA by command of Boeing 737, Boeing 747 Jumbo, Boeing 757 and 767, ending in December 1994 on the Airbus A320. "Retirement" has included a year's contract flying the Boeing 767 for Alitalia, and a year on Boeing 747 Classic for Cathay Pacific Cargo.'

Graham and I have conducted a great deal of research in Puerto Rico, where alien-related phenomena are widespread, and it is to Puerto Rico that we now turn our attention for the most bewildering experience in Graham's entire flying career. Although nothing unusual was seen during the experience, we both have no doubt that what occurred is indeed related to the alien phenomenon.

UNSCHEDULED DISPLACEMENT

In March 1993 Graham was employed by British Airways, current in all the normal flying licence requirements. Just prior to visiting Puerto Rico he had flown a B767 to Paris and back to London, a routine duty. 'Up to and including the trip to the Caribbean my health was excellent,' he emphasizes.

On 1 March 1993 I completed the routine pre-rental checkride with one of the resident flying instructors at Caribe Aviation, San Juan Isla Grande Airport, Puerto Rico [Plate 5]. The weather was fine and sunny, a light northerly breeze enabling a rapid 50-minute completion of the required stalls, steep turns, circuits and landings.

The following day, 2 March, at 0905 local time, I taxied out in a Cessna 172, registration N92256, to depart on a cross-island route that was to be coastal tracking west to the town of Arecibo, thence south to the famous radio telescope of the same name, 10 to 15 minutes over the site photographing the telescope and environs, then direct track to Mayagüez airport on the west coast to land for a break.

The flight went exactly as planned, the weather improving rapidly from overnight rain, a northerly breeze at 2000 feet easily assimilated in initial tracking and certainly borne in mind for the track from the telescope to Mayagüez. Once over the site, the cloud was a little lower than expected, but the light and altitude were good enough for well lit perspectives of the telescope, using a Panasonic NVS-7 video camera.

Having completed the filming within the planned time, I set course for Mayagüez airport, climbing to an altitude of 2200 feet on the pressure altimeter. This apparently random height was a compromise between the terrain and the cloud base, i.e., any higher, say to 2500 feet, would have seen me in and out of cloud, losing sight of the ground and, possibly, other aircraft. As I was still using the video camera from time to time, this altitude of 2200 feet, crucially important as it happened, is clearly recorded on the film of the trip.

In general terms, the airport of Mayagüez is 25 miles west of the telescope. Strictly, the true bearing of Mayagüez from Arecibo is 250 degrees. This is measured using a standard protractor on a Lambert Conformal Conic Projection, the true orientation being provided by a superimposed grid. By simply applying the 360-degree protractor to the track line, the direction of the track relative to true North can be seen. As any compass orientates to the magnetic lines of force around the planet, the true direction has to be converted to a magnetic direction, given that the primary direction indicator on the aeroplane is the E2 compass.

The arithmetic difference between true direction and magnetic direction at any point on the earth's surface is known as 'variation', and this figure, plus for westerly variation, minus for easterly variation, is applied to the chart-measured true direction. In this case, in early 1993, the magnetic variation is shown on the chart as 11 degrees West. This figure is added to the true track to give 261 degrees, i.e., the heading required in still air to make good the track from Arecibo to Mayagüez. By flying a heading on the compass of a little north of that westerly track to allow for the north wind, i.e., 270 degrees, one should arrive very close to destination; in fact, by steering a little more into the wind, the airport should appear on the left-hand side of the aeroplane. This is known as gross error technique, that is, by making a large and deliberate correction for wind drift, then any major line feature such as a coast or railway line that is across-track can be followed unambiguously to the destination point. There's nothing worse than to arrive over such a feature and be uncertain whether to turn left or right!

The distance of 25 miles divided by the estimated ground speed of 90 knots (nautical mph) or 1.5 miles per minute, gives a time of 17 minutes. It seemed reasonable to expect that steering roughly west for a quarter of an hour would see me easily in sight of Mayagüez airport. But the reality was totally unexpected.

Lateral Displacement

I set course, as planned, from Arecibo telescope towards Mayagüez, settling down at a film-recorded altitude of 2200 feet, steering 270 degrees on the gyro compass, also clearly shown on the video film. I was certain that, given the perceived wind strength and direction at that altitude, my heading of 270 would bring me to the coast a few miles to the north of Mayagüez airport, thus facilitating entry to a left-hand circuit for landing on the east-facing runway.

Some five minutes or more after leaving the telescope, happily cruising and filming, a feeling of unease and growing confusion came over me, particularly in relation to my position, temporarily uncertain to say the least. However, I knew without doubt that by maintaining my heading of 270, the track would easily resolve itself in the 25 miles to the coast. I was also aware that the north wind was less than earlier and that this gave me a greater 'gross error' margin for the predicted position of the airport to my left. Over such a short distance, my estimated time of arrival would be little affected.

Minutes went by with no positive idea of my position, but I was confident that the major coastline feature, at right angles to my track, would soon appear. Once there, a left turn would quickly bring me into the Mayagüez circuit area. Even so, the underlying unease persisted.

I recall the shock of seeing the coastline, not at right angles to my track, but parallel. In other words, the coast that I was now flying *along* was totally wrong and unexpected. The E-W North coast of the island was out of the question since the wind was from the north and I had been steering west, and there was sea on my left side. Could it then be a headland on the west coast, and I was tracking the south part of that headland? Within seconds it became alarmingly clear that I was flying along the *south* coast, was past Guánica and could clearly see the south-west tip of the island at Cabo Rojo in the near distance. Worst was the realisation that I was about to infringe Restricted Area R-7105, the US Air Force Tethered Aerostat (balloon) Radar Site at Parguera. The navigation error here is enormous and, as will be seen, should be impossible.

In stark terms, there was an unscheduled lateral displacement which was so bizarre that I was able to rationalize it with the comment in my flying log book: 'Arecibo telescope – nav error/mishap!!!'

Several years went by before Tim Good and I revisited and reflew the same track, at the same altitudes and in the very same aeroplane, N92256. What we found was, and remains, a disturbing and unsettling probability.

First Re-run

On 24 October 1998 Tim and I departed Isla Grande Airport, Puerto Rico, at 1125 local time, to fly exactly as the flight planned on that day in March 1993. In fine weather, with similar northerly wind, our achieved schedule was as follows:

Taxi	1125
Take Off	1133
Arecibo Town	1157
Arr. Telescope	1203
Dep. Telescope	1210
Land Mayagüez	1228
Engine off	1230

The time from Arecibo telescope to landing at Mayagüez is 18 minutes, which means that time to abeam the airfield in the circuit would have been 15–16 minutes. On this particular day, fine and clear, we could see the west coast of the island five minutes after departing the telescope, and the airport at Mayagüez shortly after – a matter of minutes. This is a very short 25-mile leg, and even in the cloudy conditions of 2 March 1993, should have presented absolutely no difficulty. On this revisit, the ease and rapidity of the sector reinforced the absurdity of my previous experience.

This re-run of my ill-fated flight served only to underline the probability that something abnormal had occurred; that this was not prolonged inattention, a deliberate and dangerous exposure to the cloud-shrouded Cordillera Central, or imagination. There was one important and unresolved question to be addressed before I could declare, with 100 per cent certainty, that I was not directly responsible for the navigation error. Would it have been possible for me, maintaining an altitude of 2200 feet, to fly due south from my planned track (Arecibo telescope to Mayagüez) to the Guánica area without hitting high ground? To answer this, we had to wait another three months before Tim and I again hired Cessna 172, N92256, to fly the alternative possibility.

Second Re-run

On Thursday, 21 January 1999, we departed Isla Grande Airport at 1040 local time. Again, we flew the same track, Arecibo town, south to the telescope, climbing to 2000 feet as we progressed inland. This time, instead of pausing overhead the telescope we carried on tracking southwest towards the obvious barrier of the Cordillera Central. The US Sectional Chart, Puerto Rico–Virgin Islands, shows spot heights along this feature of up to 3900 feet, with the 3000-foot contour an indisputable factor in the track segment that I would have had to have flown through, given my start and finish points. There is no doubt that to maintain cloud and terrain clearance on the day in question, I would have been obliged to turn back away from the Cordillera. Somehow, I had arrived over the south coast having traversed the hills without hitting anything!

So, on this January day, as we passed Adjuntas airfield, 2340 feet, it became obvious that to cross the Cordillera at any point, we would have to climb to at least 3000 feet. In the event, we made 3400 feet to skim over a col near the town of Castaner, peaks on either side, and were immediately on the southern slopes to the plain between Ponce and Guánica. Landing later at Mayagüez, removal of any lingering suspicion that I may have deliberately or unwittingly flown that dangerous track only served to deepen my unease over the incident.

The Radar Factor

Civilian radar takes an interest in aircraft flying in controlled airspace in a well-defined boundary surrounding San Juan and Isla Grande airports. In that environment, you have to be identifiable and in two-way communication. Once outside that boundary of controlled airspace (vertical delineation) you can opt for Radar Advisory Information. I generally opt for it so I know what other aircraft are around. Within that controlled airspace (vertical delineation) it is mandatory to use a transponder (Secondary Surveillance Radar) which gives the radar controller altitude and position information, and in some cases, speed. Once outside the controlled airspace – in this case about five miles to the west of the airport – one enters a Radar Advisory Environment. At low level, further to the west, as in the Arecibo area, it's probable that the radar controller would lose returns therefore would take no further interest. I have no way of knowing to what extent *military* radars, which may have unknown capabilities, might take an interest. In theory, someone, somewhere, could have been aware of my displacement, but the chances of me ever knowing it are zero.

The Meteorological Record

There is one final aspect which has been examined in some detail, and that is the meteorological record for that day, 2 March 1993. There was just a chance that an unseasonal freak wind had been blowing at 2000 feet that would explain the 60-degree track error. Notwithstanding the complete absence of turbulence associated with high winds, I needed to find evidence of a minimum of 70 knots cross-track component, i.e. a storm-force northerly wind, given that my deviation started at the point of departing Arecibo telescope. From points further west along my planned track to Mayagüez, the north component would have to have been such as to blow me sideways at 90 knots with no forward progress at all. To answer this question, I obtained from the excellent National Climatic Data Center, Asheville, North Carolina, the following:

'Radiosonde balloon data. 02 March 1993. Time 8am local. Height 726 meters, 2380 feet. Wind 005 degrees (Northerly) at 10 knots.'

This shows just what I found in practice, that the cruise level wind was light from the North. The surface actual weather for San Juan at 0850 local time, 15 minutes before my take off, was: Wind North 5 knots; Cloud scattered at 2000 feet; Visibility 8 miles; Temp. 76 Fahrenheit – a nice day for flying. The surface actual weather for Mayagüez at 1050 local time, as I landed there was: Wind N. East 10 knots; Cloud broken at 3000 feet; Visibility 10 miles; Temp. 81 Fahrenheit. How was it possible to become disorientated in such weather?

Summary

To summarise the main points:
  1. An inexplicable lateral displacement affected a routine, simple navigation exercise.
  2. The weather/wind conditions could not have been a factor.
  3. Terrain considerations make the apparent achieved track unlikely if not impossible.
  4. Video film confirms flight parameters, altitude and heading,

cloud base, start position at Arecibo telescope and end position on the south coast.

5. Promulgated magnetic anomaly warnings 'up to 9 degrees at *ground* level' could not account for the track error.

6. Aircraft instruments appeared normal at all times, updating of gyro compass with E2 magnetic compass routine practice, and was only needed on the ground.

Such unplanned displacements are relatively common in automobiles, and have certainly been reported in the past by aviators, so the experience is not unique – only weird and unwelcome. To have revisited the happening in such detail, to confront the possibility of manipulation by agencies unknown for what can only be whimsical intent, serves only to sharpen my vigilance and increase the attention I pay to the stories of others.

In 14,000 hours of flying worldwide, I have never experienced such a bizarre and unnerving incident as this one. I do remember, though, a colleague recounting how, when flying a light aircraft across the Mona Passage from the Dominican Republic to Puerto Rico, he noted an uncontrollable compass spin on the E2 standby instrument. There seemed no rhyme nor reason, and that is how my experience will have to remain – a total mystery.[2]

None of the pilots to whom I sent copies of Graham Sheppard's report was able to rationalize the unscheduled displacement. Having flown with Graham in the right-hand seat of the same Cessna 172 on those two re-runs in Puerto Rico, in 1998 and 1999, I too can offer no explanation. Sir Mark Thomson, a former Royal Navy jet pilot who currently flies a Beechcraft Baron twin-engined aircraft and who knows Graham, is as baffled as he is impressed. 'It is undeniably one of the most important pieces of evidence I've ever seen,' he told me. 'A lifelong airline pilot flying the simplest aircraft in good weather, and in Puerto Rico, where the evidence for so long has been so strong and getting stronger. There is no explanation, in *our* laws of physics, for his aircraft movement. It unquestionably happened. It proves to me their mastery of space, time *and* distance. But why did "they" move him . . .?'[3]

PACIFIC OCEAN

In the spring of 1966 a Boeing C-97 Stratofreighter of the US Air National Guard, flying from Kwajalein Island to Guam, in the Pacific Ocean, unaccountably found itself miles off course. The navigator was Lieutenant Colonel Frank P. Hopkins, at the time Air Force Advisor to the 106th Air Transport Group, New York Air Guard. 'Kwajalein weather gave me a pleasant forecast, no significant weather, winds at our level approximately 040/10–12 knots,' Hopkins's report begins.

Terminal weather at Guam was standard, and we all looked forward to a pleasant night flight of approximately 6 to 6+30 hours . . . We climbed out to about 12,000', levelled off, and settled down . . .

Second hour out, since the weather was so good, I decided to use a Celestial Fix for a position [and] shot what developed on the chart as a perfect three-star fix [leaving] no doubt as to where the aircraft had been at that point in time . . .

Third hour out . . . I shot a second celestial fix. Weather was excellent: high, broken overcast, no turbulence, wonderful results. Another pinpoint fix. Only problem was [that] this last fix was about 340 nautical miles down intended course. A C-97 at that altitude works at a true air speed of about 220 knots. With the pertinent information stuck on a computer I came up with a wind of approximately 110 knots from 070. I rechecked and re-rechecked. There was no error. It is . . . a very serious thing in the business when ground speed changes for inexplicable reasons by a full third.

Fourth hour out . . . I was using good Loran [long-range navigation] and shooting celestial. Ground speed was down to about 230 from the previous fix. Some slight left drift. No problems. Except for the fact that, in ostensibly good weather, a plugging old '97 had, in fact, covered 340 nautical miles in one hour of time for no apparent reason.

At Guam Hopkins learned that he was not alone in reporting such a displacement. The head of the weather section informed him that he was aware of such inexplicable phenomena: it always occurred at night, perhaps eight to ten times a year and lasted not more than two hours.[4] Graham Sheppard's displacement, however, occurred in broad daylight, at relatively low altitude and over clearly visible ground, versus Hopkins's night-time event, at 12,000 feet, over open water.

DISAPPEARANCES

Puerto Rico lies within a corner of the legendary 'Bermuda Triangle' where, for many years, bizarre incidents have been reported, such as the famed disappearance of six Grumman Avenger torpedo-bombers off the coast of Florida in December 1946. In Puerto Rico itself I interviewed two groups of witnesses who, on two separate occasions in 1988, watched as US Navy Grumman F-14 jets apparently were 'captured' or otherwise 'absorbed' in mid-flight by the large, unknown aerial craft they were pursuing.[5] It seems reasonable, therefore, to link these kinds of phenomena with aerial displacement.

Jorge Martín learned from a high-ranking officer connected to the US Navy that American authorities were alarmed because, periodically, aircraft of both the US, the Puerto Rico Air National Guard, as well as some private aircraft had disappeared in an area to the north-west of Puerto Rico known as the San Juan Trench (which drops to 9200 metres in the Milwaukee Depth, the deepest part of the Atlantic Ocean). The Navy and Air Force found that, on a regular basis, a huge, disc-shaped craft would come out of the sea in the Trench, sometimes 'hanging stationary in the air on a great column of water before vanishing or before submerging again'. Pilots reportedly were ordered to approach the object and on several occasions, when they got too close, their aircraft appeared to 'explode silently, to vanish into thin air'.[6]

Graham Sheppard cites the case of a colleague who noted 'an uncontrollable compass spin' while flying a light aircraft across the Mona Passage from the Dominican Republic to Puerto Rico. More serious cases have occurred in the area, such as the following.

On 28 June 1980 José Luis Maldonado Torres, a 31-year-old pilot, was flying an Ercoupe 415-D, together with José A. Pagán Santos, a 22-year-old student pilot, on the return leg to San Juan from Santo Domingo in the Dominican Republic. Shortly after 20.00 local time, Maldonado began transmitting 'Mayday' distress calls on the 121.5 MHz International Distress Frequency, which is continuously monitored. For some reason, these calls were not picked up by the approach control facility at San Juan International Airport, but a Spanish airliner (Iberia), en route from the Dominican Republic to Madrid, served as a link with San Juan, via the Federal Aviation Administration's (FAA) mast on El Yunque. Here follow extracts from the 65-page US National Transportation Safety Board (NTSB) accident report, obtained by Graham Sheppard. The Ercoupe (erroneously named Air-Coupe, a later version of the same aircraft) is identified by its registration number N3808H, and the Iberia Airlines plane by its flight number, IB976. Greenwich Mean Time (GMT) is used in the transcript:

0003:00 GMT N3808H Mayday Mayday Air-Coupe ocho cero eight zero zero Hotel we can see a strange object in our course we are lost Mayday Mayday

0003:25 GMT N3808H Mayday Mayday we are lost we found a strange object in our course

0003:35 GMT IB976 Station calling Mayday Mayday Iberia nine seven six Iberia nine seven six go ahead

0003:45 GMT N3808H Ah we are going from Santo Domingo to ah San Juan International but we found (Ah a weird object in our course that made us change course about three different times we got it right now in front of us at one o'clock our heading is) zero seven zero degrees . . . our altitude one thousand six hundred at zero seven [zero] degrees . . . our VORs [VHF Omnidirectional Range] got lost off frequency

0004:15 GMT IB976 Station calling one two one five Mayday Mayday Iberia nine seven six go ahead

0004:20 GMT N3808H Mayday Mayday this is Air-Coupe three eight zero eight Hotel in flight from Santo Domingo to San Juan Puerto Rico we have a very weird object in front of us that make us lose course . . . our present heading is one thirty degrees at one thousand five hundred feet sir

0004:55 GMT N3808H We lost signal off of Aguadilla VOR

0005:00 GMT IB976 Ah station calling Mayday station calling Mayday San Juan request to Ah SQUAWK one one zero zero one one zero zero

0005:10 GMT N3808H We do not have transponder sir we do not have transponder

0005:25 GMT IB976 Station transmitting Mayday San Juan request you transmit one one zero zero

0005:35 GMT N3808H We do not have transponder sir we do not have transponder

0005:40 GMT IB976 OK which is your call sign and estimate position

0005:45 GMT N3808H Right now we supposed to be at about thirty five miles from the coast of Puerto Rico but we have something weird in front of us that make us lose course all the time I change our course a second [unintelligible] our present heading right now is three hundred we are right again in the same stuff sir

0006:30 GMT IB976 Station transmitting Mayday station transmitting Mayday Iberia nine seven six San Juan requests you to call one three four three or one three five seven say again frequency one three four three or one three five seven do you copy

0007:10 GMT IB976 Station transmitting Mayday call San Juan one three four point three or one three five point seven . . .

No response was heard from the Ercoupe. Extracts follow from the NTSB's Narrative Statement of Pertinent Facts, Conditions, and Circumstances. Times are local.

At 2007, the San Juan International Flight Service Station [IFSS] advised the San Juan Combined Center Radar Approach Control (CERAP) watch desk that he was not getting anything on his Direction Finder (DF) on Frequency 121.5 Mhz.

At 2012 the Atlantic Fleet Weapons Range (AFWR) [based at Roosevelt Roads Naval Air Station] advised San Juan CERAP that they had N3808H on radar for a while and heard his Mayday but could not make out what he was trying to say. San Juan CERAP asked AFWR the flight's position when they last observed him on radar. AFWR responded that the flight was observed at about 35 miles west of Puerto Rico.

At 2015 AFWR advised the San Juan CERAP that they had a target bearing 266 degrees and about 110 miles from their location. The target was moving east.

At 2017 CERAP advised the San Juan IFSS that AFWR thought they had the aircraft on radar but nothing definite. The target was never identified. A search for the aircraft and occupants was launched by private aircraft and the U.S. Coast Guard at about 2144 or about 1½ hours after radio communications with the flight were lost.

> The search . . . continued until [30 June 1980] in the afternoon at which time a message was sent to all ships and aircraft in the suspect area to look out for the survivors. All attempts to locate the aircraft and occupants have been to no avail. The aircraft is presumed ditched at sea and both occupants deceased.

It is unfortunate that some sections of the recorded transmissions are either unintelligible or apparently missing.

'An Emergency Locator Transmitter [ELT], which can be activated manually, or possibly automatically on immersion – if afloat – was fitted to the Ercoupe,' Graham Sheppard explains. 'Had it been activated, it would have provided direction finding [DF] on the 121.5 MHz International Distress Frequency.'

The NTSB's *Narrative Statement* continues:

> Based on the only information available, it is estimated that the pilot possessed about 200 hours total flying experience of which 117 were flown as pilot-in-command and 15 hours were flown at night . . . it is estimated that the student pilot possessed about 16 hours total flying experience all of which was flown dual . . . the aircraft received an annual inspection on [16 May 1980] and the tach recorder indicated 640.3 hours at the time . . .
>
> The actual weather conditions at the place and time of the accident can not be determined since an accurate geographical location of crash site is unknown . . .
>
> It is noted that the pilot stated in his distress call that there was a weird object in the flight's path which made him change course about three times. The pilot did not describe the object except for saying at one time, 'We are in the same stuff again.'
>
> It is also significant to note that at 2003 the pilot stated his heading was 300 degrees magnetic, at 2004 he stated his course was 130 degrees magnetic and at 2006 the pilot said his course was 300 degrees magnetic.[7]

Graham points out that at 20.16 local time, 11 minutes after the stricken Ercoupe's last communication, Roosevelt Roads Naval Air Station (AFWR) made an intriguing comment to San Juan Approach Control, which is not further referenced in the official report: 'It looks like we may see a few of them out there but not too [unintelligible].' Presumably, several radar contacts – including the Ercoupe – were detected in the

TRANSCRIPTION OF THE C3 POSITION
RECORDING OF FREQUENCY 121.5 LOCATED AT THE
LAS MESAS RCAG SITE

2358:00 GMT

2359:00 GMT

0000:00 GMT

0001:00 GMT

0002:00 GMT

0003:00 GMT   N3808H   Mayday Mayday Air-Coupe ocho cero ocho zero
zero Hotel we can see a strange object in our
course we are lost Mayday Mayday

0003:25 GMT   N3808H   Mayday Mayday we are lost we found a strange
object in our course

0003:35 GMT   IB976   Station calling Mayday Mayday Iberia nine seven
six Iberia nine seven six go ahead

0003:45 GMT   N3808H   Ah we are going from Santo Domingo to ah San Juan
International but we found (Ah a weird object in
our course that made us change course about three
different times we got it right now in front of us
at one o'clock our heading is) zero seven zero
degrees... our altitude one thousand six hundred
at zero seven degrees... our VORs got lost off
frequency.

0004:15 GMT   IB976   Station calling one two one five Mayday Mayday
Iberia nine seven six go ahead

0004:20 GMT   N3808H   Mayday Mayday this is Air-Coupe three eight zero
eight Hotel in flight from Santo Domingo to
San Juan Puerto Rico. we have a very weird ah object
in front of us that make us lose course... our
present heading is one thirty degrees at one
thousand five hundred feet sir

0027   QUALITY CONTROL CHECK

Figure 4. Two pages from the 65-page accident report by the US National
Transportation Safety Board relating to the disappearance of José Luis
Maldonado Torres and José A. Pagán Santos in their aircraft off the west
coast of Puerto Rico, June 1980. (*National Transportation Safety Board*)

44

0004:55 GMT	N3808H	We lost signal off of Aguadilla VOR
0005:00 GMT	IB976	Ah station calling Mayday station calling Mayday San Juan request to Ah SQUAWK one one zero zero one one zero zero
0005:10 GMT	N3808H	We do not have transponder sir we do not have transponder
0005:25 GMT	IB976	Station transmitting Mayday San Juan request you transmit one one zero zero
0005:35 GMT	N3808H	We do not have transponder sir we do not have transponder
0005:40 GMT	IB976	OK which is your call sign and estimate position
0005:45 GMT	N3808H	Right now we supposed to be at about thirty five miles from the coast of Puerto Rico but we have something weird in front of us that make us lose course all the time I change our course a second (unintelligible) our present heading right now is three hundred we are right again in the same stuff sir
0006:30 GMT	IB976	Station transmitting Mayday station transmitting Mayday Iberia nine seven six San Juan requests you to call one three four three or one three five seven say again frequency one three four three or one three five seven do you copy
0007:10 GMT	IB976	Station transmitting Mayday call San Juan one three four three or one three five seven call San Juan Center one three four point three or one three five seven point seven
0008:00 GMT		

QUALITY CONTROL CHECK

0028

45

same area. Might the 'strange object' have been one of them?

Graham's calculations show that, at the time of the last communication, the Ercoupe was some 30 nautical miles off the coast of Puerto Rico and several miles to the east of Mona Island. Three interesting points arise here. First, a colleague of Graham's noted 'an uncontrollable compass spin' while flying a light aircraft across the Mona Passage; second, one of Jorge Martín's US Navy sources disclosed that a huge subterranean alien base existed in Puerto Rico, extending under the sea as far as Mona Island (Chapter 17); and third, the Brazilian scientist Rubens Villela was informed by his alien contacts that aircraft weighing less than 20,000 kilos (48,501 lb/24.25 tonnes) might be jeopardized by a 'force field' emanating from their base in Antarctica (Chapter 1).

Jorge Martín has played me a copy of some of the recorded transmissions from the Ercoupe, leaked to him by a Federal Aviation Administration source, and there is no doubting the tone of urgency in the pilot's voice. Puerto Rican authorities suggested that the 'accident' had been due either to an inexperienced pilot or to the age of the plane. Neither explanation is valid. José Pagán Jimenez, the student co-pilot's father who owned the plane and flew it himself, was assistant chief of the aerial division of the police. True, the Ercoupe was registered in 1947 but, according to Pagán Sr, it was in perfect condition. He told Martín that he had only recently replaced the old engine with a new one. Significantly, nowhere in the transcript is a fault reported.[8]

Like Frederick Valentich, the young pilot who disappeared together with his light aircraft while flying over the Bass Strait, Australia, in October 1978, after reporting the close proximity of a UFO,[9] Pagán Jr was a firm believer in the reality of the UFO phenomenon. It is not known if the young Puerto Ricans were actually abducted. 'But what we do know,' said Pagán's father, 'is that [a UFO] was in some way or other involved in what happened . . .'[10]

NOTES

1 Good, Timothy, *Beyond Top Secret*, pp. 36–8, 102–3.

2 Report prepared for the author, April 1999.

3 Letter to the author, 1 July 1998.

4 Sanderson, Ivan T., *Invisible Residents*, The World Publishing Company, New York and Cleveland, 1970, pp. 152–3.

5 Good, Timothy, *Alien Liaison: The Ultimate Secret*, Century, London, pp. 5–7.

6 Martín, Jorge, 'The Alien Presence in Our Seas', *Flying Saucer Review*, vol. 44, no. 1, 1999, pp. 9–10, translated by Gordon Creighton from *Evidencia OVNI*, no. 13, 1997.

7 National Transportation Safety Board Accident File No. MIA-80-D-A079.

8 Martín, Jorge, 'A Valentich type of UFO case off Puerto Rico', *Flying Saucer Review*, vol. 43, no. 4, Winter 1998, pp. 6–8, translated by Gordon Creighton from *Evidencia OVNI*, no. 3, 1994.

9 Good, *Beyond Top Secret*. See also Haines, Richard F., *Melbourne Episode: Case Study of a Missing Pilot*, LDA Press, Los Altos, California, 1987.

10 Martín, 'A Valentich type of UFO case off Puerto Rico', op. cit.

Chapter 3

Soul Vampires

On the night of 8–9 March 1993 Erwin Lohre, an artist and former military pilot, was sleeping at his family home in Braunschweig, north-central Germany. At around 00.30, he suddenly awoke with a stabbing pain in the area of his spine. 'I at once took a painkilling tablet and lay down again,' he recounted to Dr Peter Hattwig, a UFO investigator. 'Meanwhile, my wife had also awakened, simultaneously.'

> Suddenly, we heard a clear humming sound coming from the sky. After three or four seconds this noise, which seemed 'metallic', as though produced by a centrifugal force, grew louder, and then, through the bedroom window, we saw a bright round shining object stationary at a height of some 10 metres or so above the birch trees to the east. There was a full Moon at the time. But despite that, our bedroom and terrace outside was lit by something even more powerful than the moonlight – a bluish-white colour like neon lighting. At the same time we both felt a strange metallic sort of taste on our tongues.
>
> Up till then I had scarcely given a moment's thought to UFOs, but it was now immediately quite clear to me that I was looking at an unknown flying object, and I said to my wife: 'Look! See what it is! They are going to land here!' Being a former fighter pilot myself, I wanted of course to see what was going on. But when I tried to stand up, I found that I couldn't move, and with my wife it was just the same. Also our two kittens, which sleep on the foot of the bed, were both sitting there, bolt upright, and looking as though turned to stone. Meanwhile, our bedroom window was being bathed, on and off, in a bright yellow beam of light apparently coming down from above.
>
> I didn't get frightened because I was so completely spellbound. Indeed, if anything, my feeling was rather one of annoyance

because I was immobilized and unable to get to the window. But my wife . . . afterwards had a thorough fit of the shakes. The eerie apparition lasted altogether about 40 seconds or so, and then the vivid light ended abruptly. Then, some 30 or 40 seconds later, we saw the UFO fly over our bedroom window in a westerly direction and vanish. Simultaneously the paralysis ended for both of us. My wife was too upset to be able to sleep any more, and so was I.

Then, about half an hour later, we heard the same sound again, coming from the other direction. Our bedroom has windows on the two sides, and so we got a full view of the UFO for the first time. From a distance of about 300 metres we watched it flying straight towards us. Again we heard the same sounds as before, and for about six seconds or so we could see its shape absolutely clearly. [It] shimmered with all the colours of the rainbow . . . the cupola was a bright, shining silver. The underside had three coloured apertures and a central light . . . Then, just as the disc – which I estimated to be about 10 metres wide – was nearly right over us, something quite unbelievable happened. It simply dissolved into thin air – between one-tenth of a second and another – and it was gone, without any transition!

Lohre reported the encounter to a local newspaper. 'After the newspaper had published the report,' he said, '25 people contacted me, including one whole bowling team which had been travelling home at the time. Unfortunately none of them was prepared to go public as eyewitnesses.' (In Germany, I should point out, there is considerable reluctance on the part of its generally conservative citizenry to report such incidents. For this reason, I am sure, relatively few reports reach the media.)

Dr Hattwig asked Herr Lohre if he had the impression that the craft was 'seeking' him personally. 'Absolutely!' replied Lohre. 'For it was hovering there right beside my bedroom window, as though they knew exactly where I was. It is true that my wife and I were both paralysed, but unlike me she felt no pain in the spine.'

AFTERMATH

The day after the incident, a number of peculiar developments occurred. 'At 4 p.m.,' recounted Lohre, 'my wife and daughter and I – who were all in different rooms at

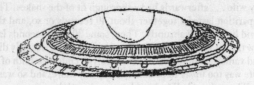

Figure 5. A sketch by Erwin Lohre, a former military pilot who, together with his wife, was temporarily paralysed as this craft hovered outside their house in Braunschweig, Germany, in March 1993. (*Erwin Lohre/FSR Publications Ltd*)

the time – saw a light like a photo–flash in front of our TV sets, accompanied by a crackling sound.'

> Then, an hour later, phenomenal discharges came from the TV sets downstairs. Furthermore, we found that our computer had packed up. We never found any reason for that, and it has never happened again. Then, at about 10 p.m., suddenly a tremendous banging started up inside our wardrobe, as though somebody was shut in there. But despite all our efforts and searching, we could find absolutely no reason for the noise. And every time we opened the wardrobe, the din stopped.

These events continued for two months after the incident. It is interesting to compare the 'tremendous banging' noise with the violent sounds and vibrations reported in the home of Enrique Castillo Rincón, following his initial encounter in Costa Rica in 1963 (Chapter 4).

'After the encounter I had constant pain in the spine,' Lohre told Hattwig, 'and a week later, using a mirror, I discovered on my spine, at the level of the buttocks, two red marks, about two centimetres apart.'

> I went to see a doctor, who then found two black spots below the skin. He applied an ointment, and he referred me for a CAT scan, but before I was able to go there two little black lens-shaped things came out of my back. I put them away very carefully, to show them

to the doctor, but by the second day following they had simply evaporated.[1]

Several aspects of this case impress me. As a former pilot, Erwin Lohre is unlikely to have mistaken the craft he and his wife saw for any kind of conventional aircraft. Also, he had never heard about alien abductions or alien implants, reacting in disbelief when questioned on this by Dr Hattwig.

In recent years several operations to remove alleged alien implants have been performed on a number of abductees, some with rather dubious results. At the time of writing, proper, peer-reviewed scientific analysis has yet to be conducted in this field, despite the interesting claims of Dr Roger Leir, who is the first to have written a book on this aspect of the abduction phenomenon.[2] Dr John Altshuler, a haematologist and pathologist who was the first to examine an animal reportedly mutilated by aliens on a ranch in Alamosa, Colorado, in 1967,[3] was also first, I believe, to remove implants from abductees. He told me that years ago he had performed surgical procedures on two patients. 'One object was cylinder-shaped, about five millimetres long. I had very thin sections made and conducted a variety of different tests, but I was unable to elucidate what it actually was. In the other case, I could find no evidence other than that it had been a fibre.' Dr Altshuler is sceptical about some of the purported medical findings thus far published, and urges caution in this potentially promising field of study.[4]

ENCOUNTER AT EUMEMMERRING CREEK

Mark Ian Birdsall, one of Britain's leading UFO researchers, takes a highly sceptical view of the whole concept of alien abductions. In 1996, however, he interviewed a woman whose compelling account gave him pause for thought. Kelly Cahill, an attractive and intelligent Australian, was 25 years old at the time of the incident. The following is taken partly from her book, *Encounter*, but mostly from the interview she gave to Mark, which includes further developments.

On 7 August 1993, at dusk, Kelly and her husband, Andrew, were driving to visit friends near the Dandenongs, east of Melbourne. As they headed up into the mountains from Cranbourne, driving along the Belgrave–Hallam road on the outskirts of Belgrave South, Kelly fleetingly glimpsed something unusual. 'I was just sort of gazing out of the window and I saw this circle of round, orange lights, back in a paddock,' she told Mark. Andrew, who was driving, saw nothing. The incident was forgotten until Andrew brought it up in conversation with their friends later that evening.

Between 23.30 and 23.45, following a game of bingo with their friends, the couple set off for the return journey to their home in Gippsland, a trip normally taking one and a half hours. Around midnight, as they drove along the unlighted Belgrave–Hallam road, in Eumemmerring Creek, Narre Warren North, near the location of the earlier sighting, similar orange lights appeared. As Kelly reported:

> At first, from a distance, it looked like a blimp, hovering above the road at about 400 metres in front of us, but as we got closer to it, you could see it wasn't a blimp. And there were these silhouettes standing there, like people, in the orange lights. I said to my husband, 'It looks like there's people in there!' There were people looking at us – that's the way I saw it. And the minute I said that, it shot off to the left and just disappeared, like in two seconds flat, into the distance, to the east of Melbourne.

A few kilometres later Kelly and Andrew encountered a blinding white light in the middle of the road. Kelly held her hand up to her eyes so she could see through the windscreen. 'Do you see that?' she asked Andrew. He replied in the affirmative. 'What are you going to do?' she continued.

'I'm going to keep on driving,' he responded.

'Because of what we'd seen back there,' said Kelly, 'I was saying to him that we were going to see a real UFO. And, you know, my heart was pumping and the adrenalin was pumping through my body.' The couple continued driving, but suddenly everything seemed to change. 'I don't know how to explain it,' said Kelly. 'It was really strange. The car had slowed down. We were doing about 40 kph but had been doing 110–120 kph. And I'm sitting there totally relaxed, and really, really disorientated. And I said to my husband, "I've had a blackout. What happened to the light? Did we see a UFO?" He said, "I think so. We must have turned a corner or something." I felt like I had experienced a blackout.'[5]

On the way home, the couple began to argue about what happened. A distinct smell, similar to that of vomit, permeated the air inside the car, although no traces could be found. In addition, Kelly complained of a dull pain in her stomach, extending to her shoulders.[6] Arriving home, they were shocked to discover that the time was 02.30. 'We had left our friends [Yvonne and her family] no later than 11.45 p.m.,' explained Kelly. 'We had done this journey on many occasions, and it always takes around 90 minutes. I was shocked when I noticed the clock. I had no interest in UFOs at that time, and certainly had no knowledge of "missing time" and so on. I didn't know what had happened. I sat there thinking that I may have had an epileptic fit or something.'[7]

PHYSICAL ABNORMALITIES

Shortly after arriving home, Kelly discovered that she was losing blood, which was puzzling because her most recent menses had ended a few days earlier. She also noticed a red, triangular-shaped mark below her navel. 'At first it was a red triangle, a perfect centimetre each side,' she reported. 'I didn't realize until later how important it was, though just in the back of my mind I had a suspicion that it was connected to the incident. Four to five months later, the red mark had gone, but this perfect triangular scar was there: it was only the outline of a scar, like it had actually been cut.'[8] Such triangular marks have been reported in a number of abduction cases.

Initially, Kelly did not seek medical help for the excessive bleeding, having experienced a similar gynaecological problem when she was younger. 'I had pre-cancerous cells without knowing it, and had to have laser treatment,' she explained. But when the bleeding persisted for over three weeks, she decided to go to hospital.[9] She also suffered from severe headaches, which she had never had before. She remained in hospital for a few days while various tests were carried out. A uterine infection was diagnosed, but since such infections are normally caused by a self-terminated pregnancy or from recent surgery – neither of which applied – this seemed peculiar. A course of antibiotics cleared up the condition in a few days.[10]

BEDROOM INTRUSIONS

On 6 September 1993 Kelly had the first of four night-time bedroom intrusions by an unknown entity. Via telepathy, the entity told her not to be afraid of what was about to happen. She then felt a physical sensation on her chest, as if a suction device were draining energy from her. As she lay there paralysed, the 'suction' process suddenly grew more powerful, and a tall, black figure in a full-length hooded cloak, with vaguely defined features and dull-red glowing eyes, could now be seen. The entity continued staring at Kelly, by now imbued with a sense of malevolence: she felt convinced that it was literally trying to take the life out of her. Eventually the entity vanished. Kelly insists she was fully conscious at the time and that the entity appeared quite solid.[11]

Nocturnal intrusions of this nature, commonly experienced by abductees, have been reported for centuries and are often attributed to an incubus or succubus – male or female demons, respectively – who attempt either to have sexual intercourse with, or to steal the souls of, victims. Whatever their origin and purpose, these entities are encountered throughout the world and have much in common with the abduction scenario.

In 1991–3, numerous witnesses in Czechoslovakia reported bedroom intrusions by various beings, invariably in the latter half of the night, preceded by a beam of light entering from outside the house. In these cases the entities typically were described as roughly human-shaped, semi-diaphanous, with an indiscernible face, dressed in either a 'white cowl', a 'diving suit', a 'space suit' or a suit 'like the protective clothes of workers in nuclear power stations'. In all cases the witnesses remained paralysed until the entities suddenly vanished. Dr J. S. from Zlín, in Moravia, had an encounter at the end of November 1992:

> I woke up about half an hour after midnight with a feeling that somebody was staring at me. There was an indistinct, tall figure in

the bedroom doorway . . . I was incapable of saying anything aloud. I got frightened because of this figure . . . I'm sure I was fully conscious. It took some minutes for me to pluck up my courage and to put [on] the light on my bedside table. The figure vanished. I got out of bed and and went out of the room. Going through the door I had an unpleasant feeling, and my back was stinging.[12]

There are parallels here with Kelly Cahill's case, also with that of Erwin Lohre, e.g., the sharp pain in his spine. Regarding 'sleep paralysis', I have experienced this myself on numerous occasions, although seldom in recent years. Typically, I wake up in the small hours, fully conscious, my body becoming progressively paralysed, my solar plexus and/or the bed apparently vibrating, and aware of a sense of malevolence. Only through a supreme effort of will am I able to 'dislodge' whatever it is. I have neither seen nor heard anything unusual on these occasions, however. Abduction proponents maintain that this is the initial stage of a typical alien abduction. They may well be right, but I have no intention of finding out! In any case, my feeling is that these particular 'presences' are not necessarily of extraterrestrial origin.

The generally accepted medical view of sleep paralysis is that it is a defence mechanism inhibiting our body movements during sleep, preventing us from physically acting out our dreams. 'In the borderline state between being awake and asleep,' explains Nick Pope in *The Uninvited*, 'the process of sleep paralysis can still be present for a moment, and can lead to situations where people wake up momentarily unable to move.'[13] This is certainly true in many cases, but not all, as Pope and other abduction researchers concede. In my own case, on some occasions the onset of paralysis has occurred when I am awake, as my girlfriend can verify: in fact, she too has experienced the phenomenon, which on one occasion, in Germany in 1989, was accompanied by blue light and strange sounds, the source of which could not be determined.

A Japanese survey reveals that 40 per cent of people claim to have experienced sleep paralysis. According to Dr Susan Blackmore, a psychologist at the University of the West of

England, who has studied around a hundred such cases, many descriptions by people who think they have been abducted by aliens match what often occurs during sleep paralysis, including strange whining, humming or machine-like sounds, vibrations and the sensation of an unseen, perhaps frightening, presence. Dr Blackmore argues that 'alien abduction' is a modern version of 'sleep paralysis myths' that date back centuries.[14]

Is it that simple? In discussing parallels between sleep paralysis in its various forms and the typical alien abduction scenario, author Ralph Noyes noted that:

> Allowing fully for a general sloppiness of approach on the part of many ufologists, coupled with a strong wish by some of them to cram the data into preconceived notions and to use such dubious techniques as hypnotic regression . . . there are far too many differences between the two experiences to enable us to assimilate the one to the other [though] these differences must not blind us to some very striking similarities.[15]

POLTERGEIST-TYPE PHENOMENA

Another similarity noted between alien abductions and psychic phenomena is the proliferation in some cases of poltergeist ('noisy ghost') activity following an encounter. Like Erwin Lohre, Kelly Cahill and her family were plagued by all sorts of bizarre happenings. Within days of the encounters their television set would switch itself on in the middle of the night, but when Kelly went downstairs to investigate it would switch itself off. A day or so later the video machine started playing up, on one occasion spontaneously ejecting a tape. Other electrical appliances went berserk, necessitating the replacement of several expensive items such as the refrigerator; light bulbs burned out within days of being replaced; the car starter-motor turned over by itself on several occasions, and Kelly began receiving electric shocks from objects that normally do not conduct electricity.[16]

Many jump to the conclusion that not only are UFO phenomena inextricably linked to psychic phenomena, but they are part and parcel of a *single* phenomenon. I reject this hypothesis. It is possible, for example, that contact with alien intelligences stimulates poltergeist and other psychic activity and causes witnesses to become psychically 'open', for reasons that we do not understand. It is also possible that some aliens may be thousands of years ahead of us in terms of mental development; therefore, what we regard as paranormal abilities may be second nature to them. They may be equally adept at functioning in other dimensions and manipulating spacetime. Thus, if mischievous, part of their repertoire might include inducing, or provoking, outbreaks of 'poltergeist' activity.

FLASHBACKS

On 16 September 1993 Kelly and Andrew were attending a barbecue with friends when the conversation turned to UFOs. Surprisingly, from being forgetful or sceptical about their experience the previous month, Andrew now began to talk freely, reminding Kelly of the object hovering in the middle of the road, which she had forgotten. For a while she did not believe him. Then, on the afternoon of 1 October 1993, she experienced a series of vivid flashbacks. Driving with Andrew along the Belgrave–Hallam road, where the incidents had occurred, en route to see the same friends, she suddenly felt very strange.

> I just got this sinking feeling through me, like sickened with horror for no reason, as if someone had just told me my child had been killed. And all of a sudden it's like this whole memory – it was a conscious memory, it was so real that I just wanted to sit there and scream that this can't be happening, this can't be real. And yet it was real memory: it's not like remembering a dream or remembering something or imagining. It was something that had happened and I had forgotten about it, and it was this sensation of horror, this dread . . . And that's when all the 'flashes' started, like pulling the car over, bending down to pick up my handbag, put it on my shoulder, walking across the road – and seeing these beings, seeing this craft. And I didn't even tell my husband: I was just sitting in the car freaking.

'During our interview,' reported Mark Birdsall, 'Kelly continually referred to the flashbacks as "triggers". One memory freed another, and she was basically reliving the entire event. Five or six more "triggers" occurred after they arrived at their friends' house.' By the end of the evening, she had recalled a great deal more about the frightening encounter.[17]

THE ENCOUNTER RECALLED

'We turned this bend, from where the light was, and there was this dirty big UFO sitting in the field,' Kelly related to Mark. 'No one could miss it, it was 50 metres in diameter.' Andrew stopped the car and pulled over to the side of the road. Another car was parked over 100 metres behind them. (Later, it transpired that a third car had also been present at the scene.)

I had got outside of the car, crossed the road, and picked up my handbag. As I went to look behind me, here was another car. I walked around the front of the car to meet my husband on the other side, started walking across the road, looked down the road again – and other people were walking across the road, too. They never saw us – they thought they were the only ones. I jumped the gully. There was about 10 metres of grass before the [electrified] fence . . . I stood there for about 30 seconds watching this dirty big craft [with] round circles of orange light; they were fluorescent, really hazy around the outside, but big enough for a man to stand up full-length in each one of these circles. And underneath was this blue stuff that came down to the ground in a conical shape, like a half-crescent of fluorescent light.

Then this one, tall, black being appeared in front of the craft – I don't know where it came from. It was really tall, like about seven feet, I guess. You couldn't see any features, it was like a silhouette. Its head was quite large. The first thing I thought was that I could talk to it, like I could say hello in my head. And I did. I heard the words, 'Let's kill them'. That's all I heard. I went into panic. The next thing, there were seven or eight of these other things right behind the first one, all identical. Then I felt this energy going through me. I don't know how to describe it – it was like waves of energy. I was extremely religious at the time, and I began screaming that they had no souls. Then all these eyes lit up red – 16 to 18 eyes, huge, big round things. This all happened in a few seconds. Then they moved across the field – the whole lot of them

– gliding, but so fast, and split up into two groups: some went towards the other people, and the other group came towards us. I felt this blow to my stomach, went flying through the air and landed on my back in the grass. I was winded, I couldn't breathe, and I was nauseous.

I managed to pull myself into a sitting position, because I thought I was going to die if I didn't, and I sat there. Then I called out to my husband, because I was totally blind: when I sat up, I couldn't see a thing, and for the rest of the encounter all I had was what I heard. I had ringing in my ears. Then I heard my husband say, 'Let go of me!' And he was a few metres away from me. I think part of what knocked me out was perhaps because I'd been hit in the stomach somehow – I don't know with what – then I'd literally been lifted off the ground and landed flat on my back – luckily it was on grass.

Then I heard this male voice saying, 'We don't mean you any harm' and my husband saying, 'Well, why did you hurt Kelly then?' I remember sitting on the ground, raving hysterically about demons and evil, because it really fitted into my Church beliefs. I began to be sick and put my head between my legs. Then I passed out. I came to – I don't know how long I was out – lifted up my head, then heard this male voice, using stupid cliché lines, like, 'We are a peaceful people'. It wasn't like he was talking to me, and I thought maybe it was to the other group. I was still totally blinded. And I started screaming, 'They tried to trick you, they want to steal your souls!' like a raving, hysterical maniac. Then this male voice said, 'Will someone *do* something about her', and I felt this hand on my shoulder. At that point, terror turned to this sort of incredible anger, and that's when I started screaming out, 'In the name of God, get out of here!' and so on. And then – I'm back in the car.

'I knew all these were real memories,' Kelly insists. 'I was in total shock. There was no way in the world that they could have been anything else but real. I knew that I'd been through that physically, though I did have the thought that the only other explanation was that I could have something wrong with my brain – that I might have a brain tumour.

'All I did was think about the incident constantly. I told my husband about it, but he cracked up laughing.'[18]

THE INVESTIGATIONS BEGIN

A few days later, Kelly decided to contact someone in authority. 'I wanted to tell the government, I wanted to tell the whole world. I didn't know then that there was such a thing as a UFO researcher. I was dead serious and I was going to do something about it.' After speaking to a couple of universities and the Department of Civil Aviation, she was put in touch with a local UFO group in Melbourne, then Bill Chalker, the well-known researcher from New South Wales. Chalker referred Kelly to John Auchettl, who heads Phenomena Research Australia (PRA), based in Mulgrave, Victoria. A few days later Kelly phoned Auchettl. She was astonished to learn that other people had had encounters with UFOs. 'John made me feel really secure. He told me not to touch any books or read anything about the subject, and that I was to keep a journal of my recollections.'

Auchettl and his team began a series of painstaking investigations, one of which was to place an advertisement in a number of local newspapers, asking merely for UFO witnesses to contact him. To further prevent contaminating the evidence, he kept Kelly in the dark about most of the results of his investigations.

John got heaps of calls from people who had seen objects in the sky, and then, in November 1993, he got this call from two ladies, whose mother had seen the advertisement, and they said they had had this really strange experience out on Belgrave-Hallam road – he hadn't mentioned the road in the ad – and [I learned much later] they described a craft very similar to what I had, and these tall black beings, and getting out of their car, and that there was another car behind them. At that point in the road where I had seen the light and had a blackout, these other people [Glenda, Jane and her husband Bill] had reached that point 10 minutes earlier. They all suddenly felt violently sick, lost control of their car and spun out, hitting a pole. The car wasn't really damaged, though there was some damage to the pole (which was checked later). They waited at the side of the road until they felt well enough to move. This was around midnight.

Two vehicles overtook them as they were about to pull onto the road. A speeding car went past and then another one came by. We assume the first one was us, and the second one was the other

people, because when we all rounded the turn, we parked right up
the top of the hill, and the third car was parked at least 100 metres
behind us. Then they all looked and saw exactly the same thing –
this dirty big UFO thing in the middle of the field . . . then they
saw the third car pull back.

'What else did they describe to John?' asked Mark.

'They pulled over, and there was this other car parked – a
single white male in a stationary vehicle,' Kelly continued.
'Something happened to him, too, apparently, because he got
the same marks on his body. While all this was going on, Jane
said she saw a "red, fluorescent dragon" pass her. The
researchers didn't know what that was until this year – a
month ago [October 1996]. Jane said to her husband, "Did
you see the red dragon?" and he said, "What red dragon?" –
and they passed out. Then they got out of their car and
crossed the road.'

Bill remembers nothing, except seeing the big craft and all the
black beings. We got out the car before them, then they got out –
I'm looking back across the road at them just leaving their car.
They got to the side of the road in enough time to see all the
beings; they didn't see them appear, they were already there by
that time. Then the two women reported a loud humming sound,
and blacking out. The next conscious recollection Linda had was
being back in the car again, wondering what the hell had happened
to the can of Coke she was holding.

John arranged for the women to have hypnotic regression: he
didn't feel it was advisable in my case. In Victoria, regression by
amateurs is illegal – you have to have a professional, government-
registered psychiatrist to do it. Under regression, the women
found themselves strapped down to tables on their back. I don't
remember anything like that. They were able to see the ceiling,
they were able to see the tips of their toes, but they couldn't move.
And they saw these other beings – Glenda's drawn one – then this
tall one, the same tall, black being that I saw . . . They underwent
medical examination, especially a vaginal examination – instru-
mental probing of some sort. Jane is a nurse: she got most of her
medical data, including photographs, and her own doctors to
examine her, and having records done, because of this.

The women both claimed that, even though they weren't
together, they were in the same situation, telepathically, with each

other, and both knew what was going on with the other the entire time. Glenda had the most incredible ligature mark on one of her ankles, like she'd been strapped down to something so tightly that it brought all the blood to the surface. Both had the triangle mark below their navel: Jane got a photograph of it and had it all documented. It was very similar to my mark. Both women also had three marks on the inside of their thighs, on one side. Bill remembered nothing, but under hypnotic regression he did have some memory of knowing that activity was going on around him, but he couldn't see, he was totally blind: it was like he'd lost a lot of his normal senses. After the incident, he lost a whole lot of hair on the back of his head.

'These were all professional people,' Kelly explained to Mark. 'The reason they didn't go public is that Bill is terrified of losing his job as a bank manager.'[19]

THE RED DRAGON
In September 1996 Kelly gave an interview for *Who*, a popular Australian weekly magazine. Following publication, the editor received an interesting letter, dated 1 October 1996:

Dear Mr Moore,

. . . I read with interest an article [about the Kelly Cahill] encounter on the night of 8th August 1993. Then, on Tuesday 10th September, I also listened to a radio programme about the same case, and my husband noticed, and I agree, that there is a possibility that he was involved in this encounter . . . we know that on the radio, Kelly and the others reported seeing another vehicle located at the bottom of the hill . . .

Could you ask any of the witnesses, Kelly, Jane or Glenda, *without revealing the below information* [a section for Moore's eyes only appeared at the bottom of the page] I have now presented to you, to see if any of them remember what I am about to tell you.

On the right hand, rear side of my husband's vehicle, he had a mounted spare wheel with a very unique protective cover over it. This design was produced by me and it is not commercially available. On the cover is a red reflective material, shaped like a dragon . . . This image is most striking, and my husband and I feel one would find it very difficult to miss . . . Do they recall seeing the dragon? To also support his case, I have enclosed a new set of colour photographs from his original photographs of skin marks found on his body after what I believe was a UFO encounter. The originals will have to remain with us, however, you have our permission to show others and print them if you wish. My husband's occupation, Victorian Government Law Department, prevents him at present revealing to you his or my true identity. My husband and I wish to remain anonymous until we feel more comfortable with future decisions.

You may find this revelation a little strange and somewhat late. I acknowledge this obvious problem. At first he did not want to believe that he could have witnessed such an event. It has been three years of disbelief and denial. He did make an attempt to [explain] his interrupted drive home by contacting the RAAF [Royal Australian Air Force] in late November, 1993. They put him in contact with a Melbourne [UFO] group, [which proved] unhelpful. I then telephoned the RAAF, who were most helpful, and they put me in contact with a [well-known researcher] in Sydney [who] never returned our call. After these most unhelpful contacts, my husband decided the situation was too unusual to explain to anyone and it would be far more beneficial to let this matter rest. It was not until last week after we read your positive and balanced article that we (at my insistence) decided we should write to you in support of the others and their case, and to look into his situation again . . .[20]

It must be emphasized that Kelly had no knowledge of the 'red dragon' reported by Jane until she read the letter in October 1996, because Auchettl had deliberately, and wisely, refrained from telling her – or anyone else – about it. '*No one else was aware about the dragon*,' she said. 'When I got on the phone to John, he got so excited, and that's when he came out and told me the whole thing.'[21]

SCIENTIFIC FIELD DATA

For about a year, John Auchettl and members of Phenomena Research Australia conducted a thorough survey of the paddock where the craft is alleged to have set down on the night of 7–8 August 1993. 'They actually went out to this field 14 times,' Kelly related to Mark, 'but he told me nothing about what was going on. They had this field cordoned off into one-metre squares, doing chemical analysis, magnetometer readings, and so on.' Equipment from Monash University worth $200,000 was used in the analyses. Auchettl's team, which included independent analysts, discovered a number of anomalies, such as higher magnetometer readings at the same place where Kelly and the others reported seeing a cone of light coming from the craft. 'Also, all of the foliage in the entire area had gone through some sort of abrasion; there were tiny little holes all through everything,' she explained to Mark.

> The ground was compacted in that area as if under high pressure, and there were also – I don't know what you call it – like worm-holes through the soil. The soil had been rapidly dehydrated, though the area is [originally] a marsh. And inside that semi-circular area were three marks – three round circles. The other women had drawn this tripod under the craft, which I hadn't seen.[22]
>
> We all reported seeing the semicircular shell [of light] under the craft, but I hadn't noticed that there was also a triangular tripod support. The other people had seen that. I don't know how I could have missed the tripod, except for the fact that I probably wasn't wearing my glasses.
>
> John and his people found the soil changes and the magnetic anomalies, which corresponded to our descriptions of the craft's dimensions. But they also found some unusual chemical traces . . . essentially the whole area was laced with sulphur. They thought at first that the marks in the ground were burns, but it turned out they had been produced by a chemical called pyrene. Although this is often found in coal lodes, it shouldn't have been present in this particular location . . .
>
> John told me they found unusually high amounts of tannic acid in the semicircle. He said it was strange because the tannic acid should have dissolved over the months, due to the rain we'd had, but the acid was locked in by a coating of some sort of unidentifiable waxy substance.[23]
>
> The fact that you have three separate parties of people who saw the same thing, who had marks on their bodies, who all had over an hour of missing time, and that there's a whole heap of scientific evidence, proves that something physical occurred out there.[24]

THE BLACK HELICOPTER

There is yet more to this extraordinary story, including bizarre incidents that happened to Kelly two years earlier. For example, she describes in her book how, at around 19.00 one evening in October 1991, in Lalor, a suburb of Melbourne where she and Andrew were living at the time, a black helicopter hovered noisily no further than 10 to 15 metres away from her position on the second-storey veranda. She called out to her husband and her friend Sylvana, who were downstairs, but they seemed uninterested.

> It sat there for fifteen minutes at least – it seemed like a very long time to me. I kept going out on the verandah, getting blown around, looking at the figures and wondering what they were up to. But they just sat there. I couldn't see their faces, but I was sure they could see me. It had no lights on the outside, and it was totally bizarre. In the end I just had to ignore it, as Andrew had suggested, and eventually it did go away.[25]

At the time, Kelly knew nothing of the link between black helicopters and UFOs, i.e., that such helicopters have sometimes been reported by abductees and have often been at the scene of unexplained animal mutilations associated with UFO activity, particularly in the United States (to be discussed in Chapter 15).

LIFE-FORCE

Although an extraordinary focus on human reproduction is evident in many abduction cases – perhaps for purposes of alien hybridization – Kelly Cahill shares my feeling that some alien entities might be more interested in our 'souls', or 'life-force', than in our bodies. 'This possibility sheds some light on the motivation of these beings, or at least the ones that I had to deal with,' she writes, in a fascinating, and I believe important, hypothesis propounded in her book.

> Ironically, the beings seemed to be dealing with and manipulating things that we are still debating the existence of. That may be why we can't understand the abduction phenomenon. The body/life-force relationship appears to be important to them, but this is something that we find intellectually vague . . . they could

primarily be after the life-force in us, and only secondarily interested in our biology and culture. Because of our biology, they have to deal with us on that level as well, but there's something about our spirits that keeps them coming back . . . [26]

NOTES

1 Hattwig, Dr Peter, 'A Noteworthy UFO Sighting over Germany', *Flying Saucer Review*, vol. 41, no. 4, Winter 1996, pp. 4–5, translated by Gordon Creighton.

2 Leir, Dr Roger K., *The Aliens and the Scalpel: Scientific Proof of ET Implants in Humans*, Granite Publishing LLC, via the Twiggs Company, PO Box 2875, Rapid City, South Dakota 57709, 1988.

3 Good, Timothy, *Alien Liaison*, pp. 21–3.

4 Interview, Denver, Colorado, 7 March 1997.

5 Interview by Mark Ian Birdsall with Kelly Cahill, Leeds, 18 November 1996.

6 Cahill, Kelly, *Encounter*, HarperCollins, Sydney, 1996, pp. 54–5.

7 Birdsall, op. cit.

8 Ibid.

9 Ibid.

10 Cahill, op. cit., pp. 72–3.

11 Ibid., pp. 76–80.

12 Babícek, Stanislav, 'Silver Beings of the Night', *The INFO Journal*, Winter 1996, p. 31.

13 Pope, Nick, *The Uninvited: An Exposé of the Alien Abduction Phenomenon*, Simon & Schuster, London, 1997, p. 253.

14 Von Radowitz, John, 'Sleep state may explain alien tales', *The Scotsman*, 11 September 1996.

15 Noyes, Ralph, 'Abduction: The Terror That Comes . . . ', *The UFO Report 1991*, ed. Timothy Good, p. 92.

16 Cahill, op. cit., pp. 95–7.

17 Birdsall, op. cit.

18 Ibid.

19 Ibid.

20 Webster, Di, 'Alien Nation', *Who*, 16 September 1996 (as dictated by Kelly Cahill to Mark Birdsall).

21 Birdsall, op. cit.

22 Ibid.
23 Cahill, op. cit., pp. 213–15.
24 Birdsall, op. cit.
25 Cahill, op. cit., pp. 186–8.
26 Ibid., pp. 160–1.

Chapter 4

Operation Andromeda

Before returning to the stronger evidence for alien encounters, this and the following three chapters are devoted to certain outlandish claims. While these present problems in terms of credibility, in my opinion there is a core of information contained therein which deserves consideration.

In *Alien Base*, I recount numerous stories of the so-called contactees, some dating back to the early 1900s, describing aliens similar in appearance to human beings. To many researchers these stories are of little or no relevance, due in part to the frequently banal and evangelical messages imparted by the 'space brothers', or because these aliens do not conform to preconceived notions of alien appearance, behaviour, or origin. Nowadays, abductions by small bug-eyed beings – the so-called 'Greys' – have become fashionable. In many cases these stories are far more outlandish than those reported by the contactees yet, paradoxically, they are taken far more seriously, particularly in the United States. Academics such as Dr John E. Mack, Professor of Psychiatry at Harvard Medical School, and Dr David M. Jacobs, Associate Professor of History at Temple University, Philadelphia, have both published books endorsing many of the abduction claims.[1,2,3,4]

A major problem in assessing the evidence for alien contact is that many abductees tend to confabulate – to fabricate imaginary experiences as compensation for loss of memory – owing either to 'missing time', to a 'screen memory' imposed upon them by the aliens, or to make their story (and themselves) more interesting. Compounding the problem, there are others claiming abduction by, or contact with, extraterrestrials whose stories are simply the product of deception or delusion.

Here follows the incredible story of Enrique Castillo Rincón, whose claimed contacts with extraterrestrials – none of which involved abduction – covered a long period. As one of Castillo's friends remarks: 'I don't believe what Enrique says at all, but he's a great friend and brother. Either he's concocted an amazing and very elaborate story, or what he says is true.'[5]

THE CURTAIN RISES

In June 1963 Castillo, then 30 years old, was employed by the maintenance department of the Costa Rican Institute of Electricity (ICE). During the visit of President John F. Kennedy to Costa Rica that month, when Castillo had been working on a communications network to connect Costa Rica with the rest of the world to cover the visit, the country was subjected to a number of earth tremors arising from the eruption of one of its largest volcanoes, Irazú.

Eruptions continued for weeks. The Civil Guard organized an observation post near the crater, 3342 metres above sea level, to monitor the lava flow and ICE established a telecommunications network to co-ordinate an evacuation of the capital, San José, should the need arise. At around 17.30 on the day they began work, Castillo and two colleagues, dressed in asbestos suits, set about taking photographs and measurements, and selecting the best site for the observation post. At 17.45 the engineer next to him drew his attention to an unusual orange aircraft in the sky, followed closely by another, similar aircraft. It was the beginning of a series of extraordinary encounters for Castillo, most of which are described in his fascinating book, *UFOs: A Great New Dawn for Humanity*.[6]

'Our first guess,' wrote Castillo, 'was that these could be some type of aircraft from President Kennedy's escort forces; however, we could not identify them . . .'

At 5.47 p.m. the two craft hovered together, stationary, at an altitude of some 300 meters above the crater. The object closest to us suddenly dropped a few meters in a straight line, stopped abruptly, and then started falling slowly, gently swaying from side to side, like a dead leaf falling from a tree. It finally 'parked' three meters above the surface of the volcano's crater, about 60 meters from us.

This 'vehicle' was lenticular in shape, about 45 meters in diameter and 12 meters high. A series of windows emitting blue light was visible around its diameter. It had a well-proportioned, greenish dome, seamlessly joined to the main body, which was smooth and the color of lead. When the two machines approached, they looked orange or reddish in color, but when they stopped, they lost that hue.

The second object moved towards the far side of the crater and, having crossed the column of ashes, performed similar manoeuvres before disappearing behind the volcano, in full view of the principal engineer, who was some distance away from Castillo and his colleague. Both craft seemed to induce a kind of whirlwind effect, as though 'produced by a propeller rotating at high speed', Castillo reported.

At that moment, far from feeling fear, with our will-power numbed, we felt at first as though we were pinned to the ground, and then as if we were standing on top of an ant hill, because we felt a strong itch all over our bodies, which blocked our . . . intentions to flee for cover.

We had been watching this imposing spectacle for only a few seconds, when a piercing, high-pitched, whistle-like noise assaulted our ears and made them ache almost unbearably. A door opened over the dome, and something like a periscope emerged through it. Above this, another object, shaped like a hammer, rotated rapidly while emitting a violet light, a different hue from the blue that filtered through the peripheral windows. The periscope rose about a meter and stopped . . . The hammer continued to rotate, and, in spite of our earache, we could perceive a low-frequency, quite rhythmic, musical tone.

Totally conscious of everything around us, with our senses more alert than ever, but at the same time perplexed and immobilized, we feared for the worst. [Then] the periscope retracted, the door closed, and after a fraction of a second, the craft lifted up a few meters, as if it were falling upwards; then it tilted slightly and shot off into infinity at a fantastic speed. The second ship followed silently, leaving behind a multi-colored trail, first white, then orange, then reddish, changing to strong blue, and finally fading into violet. The stupendous speed made the craft look oval rather than round. As suddenly as they had appeared a few minutes earlier, they were gone, and we saw them no more.

This event lasted seven minutes. Castillo noticed a sharp pain in his left shoulder, as did his nearby companion. 'In our work, we were acquainted with electrical fields,' said Castillo, 'and these could explain the uncomfortable itch and our loss of freedom of movement, presumably induced by the machine.' At first agreeing to remain silent about the incident, the witnesses changed their minds when, as they headed back to San José, they began to feel ill – 'a strange discomfort, marked by dizziness and vomiting'.

Fearing that we might have received a strong dose of radiation from the objects, we drove our jeeps quickly to the nearest health center, located in the city of Cartago, some 45 minutes from Irazú. Along the way, we were forced to stop several times, distressed by stomach cramps and the need to evacuate our bowels, always with negative results. These false alarms scared us, because our bodily functions seemed altered, and in our panic we feared that we might even die.

At the health centre in Cartago, Castillo and his colleagues persuaded the doctor to examine them, on the grounds of possible poisoning from the noxious volcano emanations. The doctor sent the men to the San Juan de Dios Hospital in San José for a more thorough check-up. 'Our eyes and tongues were examined, and we were given a white powder in a glass of water. They sent us home with the assurance that nothing was wrong with our health . . . I told the full story to Beatriz, my wife at the time, who did not believe a word of it.'[7]

DISQUIETING DEVELOPMENTS

One night, two months after the incident at Irazú, Castillo began experiencing disquieting symptoms. 'At 1 a.m.,' he wrote, 'a violent sound reverberated in my head. I woke up startled and indescribably frightened, trying to identify the origin of the noise. It was like a swarm of bees fighting inside my brain. Covering my ears did not help at all . . . I recalled suddenly that only once before had I heard such a noise: at Irazú, in front of the UFO!'

Castillo got out of bed and, grabbing an old broom handle, inspected the entire house. Nothing could be seen. Neither his wife nor his children were awakened by the noise and, when Castillo mentioned it to his wife the next morning, she accused him of being psychotic. The next night, before dawn, the noise returned: this time she heard and felt it, although the children remained asleep. 'A strong tremor woke both of us up,' said Castillo. 'Beatriz, visibly disturbed, tried to call my attention to a strange noise that was mercilessly jostling the house.'

> I walked to the bathroom, where everything shook. The window panes seemed ready to fall to the floor. The walls 'danced' to the same tune . . . Our ears ached desperately. Deathly afraid, I ran for the door, and when I opened it, all noises ceased, replaced by a sudden, eerie quiet . . . It was possible to compare the two latest frightening events: I discerned that the awful noise this time had been louder and more piercing than the first time. I stepped out into the yard and surveyed the beautiful, starry sky. There was nothing in sight . . .[8]

It is possible that the 'strong tremor' felt in the house may have been seismic in origin, especially in a country where such tremors are commonplace, yet it was not reported by others and it is hard to reconcile a tremor with the loud, piercing noise, as well as with the earaches experienced by Castillo and his wife.

THE FOLLOWER

Castillo formed a UFO study group in San José and continued to study everything he could about the subject. A practising member of the Church of Jesus Christ of the Latter Day Saints at the time, he once mentioned the Irazú incident to a Mormon minister, hoping for an explanation. 'Not only was there none,' said Castillo, 'but I received a severe warning from my superiors to keep silent.'[9]

In 1964 Castillo moved to Cali, Colombia and the following year he was appointed chief engineer in charge of outdoor installations for General Telephone International's public central phone system, in Bucaramanga, northern Colombia. Here he also founded a new branch of the Mormon church, as he had done in Cali. Then, in 1968, he accepted a job offer in Brazil and moved to Brasilia.

In the small hours of an October morning an unusual encounter happened while Castillo was driving at speed on the highway from São Paulo towards Brasilia. 'It was 4 a.m., and for a long stretch the road was completely empty,' he reports.

> At 100 k.p.h., my car was performing beautifully. It was a clear, cloudless night, with no wind. Suddenly, an unknown force shook the steering wheel with a strong vibration.
>
> Through the windshield, I saw a ball of fire that crossed the sky and lit up the tops of the jungle trees. I stopped at once, parking at the side of the road. At first, I thought it might be a plane in trouble, but it looked more like a luminous sphere. It pulsed, as if it were breathing! . . . I got into the car, exceedingly scared, and accelerated, intending to put distance between the object and myself [but] the object followed me for many kilometers, ahead or above the car, moving to the left or to the right. When close, the steering wheel shook and the radio lost the station to which it was tuned, and garbled unintelligibly. This circumstance was repeated several times . . .
>
> It moved parallel to the car, keeping pace, whether I increased or decreased the velocity. Several times, when it dove over the car, I thought it would crash, but in the end nothing happened. In the distance, a light became visible over the road. The object, sensing it, quickly got lost over the jungle. There was no witness . . .

The light turned out to be a toll gate. Unnerved by this experience, Castillo asked an officer and a soldier there for a glass of water, then related to them what had happened to him on the road. Such apparitions of 'spirits' were frequent in the area, the officer responded.[10]

Was Castillo being followed by something – or someone – from elsewhere?

THE REPRESENTATIVE

Castillo's six-month contract in Brazil having expired, he moved to Caracas, Venezuela, eventually settling in an apartment in San Bernardino. One Sunday in 1969, after attending his church, Castillo went alone to the Canaima cinema to see *Barbarella*, starring Jane Fonda. Standing near the queue was a young man, who approached Castillo in a friendly manner. At first Castillo took him to be a Mormon priest and greeted him thus: 'Hello, elder!'

'Sorry, but that is not my name,' replied the man. He introduced himself as Cyril Weiss, of Swiss nationality, representative of a wholesale distribution company based in Switzerland, on business in Caracas to open a market in Latin America. He asked Castillo if he could join him in the cinema and handed over a ten-bolivar note for the ticket. After the film, Castillo drove Weiss back to his hotel, and the two agreed to meet the following day. 'He asked me to drop him at a corner, from where he walked off with great strides,' said Castillo. 'He was pleasant and very well-behaved, although cautious.'

Next day, after work, the two met at Castillo's apartment. Weiss made himself comfortable in the living room. Noticing some tape recordings on a table, he picked up one and asked if he could listen to it. The recording was of Schubert's 'Trout' Quintet. 'Pleased, he relaxed,' said Castillo, 'giving the impression of being lost in his thoughts at the harmonies of this beautiful musical composition. Once in a while he came back to reality and asked details about my collection of classical music.' Weiss expressed astonishment that, in addition to classical music, Castillo enjoyed, for example, tangos by Carlos Gardel, the famous Argentine singer.

Weiss appeared startled when Castillo told him that his religion prohibited coffee, liquor and tobacco. Offered cheese and sausage sandwiches, Weiss politely refused, explaining that he was a vegetarian. Castillo had to laugh, because he too had been a vegetarian for some time (the sausage sandwiches having been bought for Weiss). Castillo then steered the subject to UFOs, asking Weiss for his opinion. 'The latest investigations of the US government,' replied the Swiss, 'have shown that they do not exist. As of today, the phenomenon has been sufficiently explained. I do not wish to discourage you, but I agree that they are pure hallucinations. Furthermore, I dare to say that they are a safety valve, a product of the cold war among the world powers.' Castillo remained silent, not wanting to offend his guest.

Deeply involved in evangelical work for the Mormon church at the time, Castillo invited Weiss to attend a couple of services, which he did. 'Cyril did not want to be baptized,' said Castillo, 'nevertheless, he always was very respectful of other people's beliefs.'

Weiss was altogether an interesting if unusual man.

> [He] had the characteristic physical traits of the Nordic race. His looks enticed women. His blond, well-kept hair shone under the sun. He protected his fair, white skin from the sun's rays, staying in the shade as much as possible. He was about 1.78–1.80 meters tall (or almost six feet), and looked 27 years old at the most. His countenance was proud, but he dressed informally and neatly. His face projected serenity, and his speech denoted peace of mind. He was always calm and never completely lost control of his emotions.

Weiss's control of his emotions became disconcertingly evident when Castillo was driving his new friend in Caracas. A car ahead of them ran over and killed a boy's dog, and failed to stop. Castillo got out of the car and approached the boy, numb with shock. 'With my hands full, attempting to console the boy, I felt behind me a cold stare, alien, insensible to pain. It was Weiss, who had walked slowly to the [scene]. His coldness impressed me strongly.'

Resuming their drive, Castillo fumed about the brutality of people. 'Enrique,' said Weiss, 'don't worry so much about the boy; after a few hours, his sadness in the face of the inevitable will end. We all possess a brain mechanism that overcomes everything; even children have it. Thanks to that mechanism, we finally accept the events that hurt us, no matter how cruel and unjust they might be . . . '

Castillo was astonished. 'He hadn't even shown pity. In this way, Cyril was baffling. He seemed indifferent to everything.'

Despite being attractive to women, Weiss appeared

uninterested in them, provoking comments among the church group that he must be homosexual. Castillo felt certain this was not the case, however. On one occasion the girls in the group tried to provoke Weiss. 'For the first and only time I saw him mad,' said Castillo, 'although a few moments later he was back in his usual nonchalant mood.'

Weiss seemed to live a solitary life. Castillo found it hard to find any social activities that his friend enjoyed. On one occasion the two visited a beach. 'Cyril did not swim,' said Castillo, 'because according to him, salt water, wind and sun would affect his skin.' Instead, Weiss read a book in the shade. The book was about UFOs, thus the subject came up again. This time Weiss seemed more open-minded, expressing his reconsidered view that intelligent life must exist elsewhere in the universe, but that we had not yet been visited.

At a football match Weiss walked out of the stadium when the two teams began to fight each other, prompting police intervention. Castillo tried to interest his friend in other sports, such as boxing and bullfighting, to no avail. 'Haven't you noticed the bloodshot eyes of all the spectators of [these] type of shows?' asked Weiss. 'Violence is contagious, and violent shows, without a doubt, are for individuals who are insufficiently evolved.'

As if to reassure Castillo, Weiss frequently showed identification papers, as well as an attaché case containing his company's samples of men's toiletries – lotions, talc, deodorants, soaps and shaving creams. Still, Castillo continued to puzzle over this unusual man. 'His Castillian was excellent, for a foreigner, and was devoid of any accent. He had a very academic way of talking, carefully worded, and lacking any regional expressions that could expose his origin . . . and expressed his ideas, always profound, with precise words.'

A favourite topic of conversation was religion. 'It is my belief,' said Weiss, 'that all religions are the product of a temporary need inherent to people.' He encouraged Castillo, nonetheless, to study other religions. Although impervious when asked about his personal or emotional life, the emotions of others fascinated him. He frequently asked Castillo to read aloud the letters he received from his mother.

Cyril enjoyed the contents of the letters, and he stressed the notions of love, and of adherence to the highest standards of respect for all human beings, that were in them.

His interest was centered in learning, in detail, about what united my mother and myself with such a tremendous bond of love, besides the mother and son relationship, and on some wholesome advice towards accepting things that cannot be changed by religion or advice; acceptance for things as they are.

One day Weiss told Castillo that his headquarters had summoned him to another country. 'Surprised, I didn't answer,' said Castillo. 'I was moved. For the first time, his eyes expressed some feeling . . . He left pleasant memories, and he was a good friend. But things didn't end there . . .'[11]

OPERATION ANDROMEDA

In October 1969 Enrique Castillo returned to Bogotá, Colombia, owing to the pending death of his mother, and soon found a new job as manager of Instelco, the telephone company. Until 1971 he regularly attended meetings of the Mormon church, but resigned in disgust and disillusion when a young negro boy he had taught for the priesthood was rejected for belonging to a 'sinner's race' (a condemnation since rescinded by the Mormon church).[12]

One Friday afternoon in 1973 Castillo received a telephone call from a Mexican woman named Karen, who explained that she needed to discuss matters of mutual interest. 'She started talking about UFOs, and a message that some "Martian" masters had supposedly sent me,' said Castillo. 'I took this to be a jest from one of my friends [but] we agreed to meet in a well-known ice-cream parlor on the north side of town.'[13]

The following afternoon, Karen arrived at the ice-cream parlour. Castillo introduced Alfonso Blanco, a friend who was interested in the subject. Immediately, Karen spoke of her 'Martian masters' who had given her Castillo's telephone number, and about some courses run by another Mexican lady called Marla, who also spread the teachings of her masters, as well as 'techniques for communication with extraterrestrials'. Castillo agreed to arrange conference facilities for a three-day period, while Karen related her experiences with the 'Martians' to a group of people. 'Without exception,' said Castillo, 'we were all baffled and stared at her in disbelief.'[14]

Despite scepticism about Karen and her teachings, Castillo attended further meetings at various locations, during which some of the members – including the medium Graciela Torres – purportedly received messages via 'automatic writing' and 'direct voice', now originating with aliens from 'Andromeda' (the Andromeda Galaxy, lying a mere 2.3 million light years from Earth).

One night, in October 1973, members of the group, including Castillo, stood on top of a hill in a suburb north of Bogotá, having been told by the 'masters' to prepare for a physical contact. 'We are here, brothers,' announced the Andromedans, through Torres. 'We have decided that five of you will come on board.' Time passed and nothing happened, until midnight, when another message came through. 'Brothers, Operation Andromeda has been cancelled. Please go home. Tomorrow at noon we will get in touch with each of you.'

'A wave of protest was felt all around,' said Castillo. 'I shared in this feeling, offended and disillusioned, about being fooled by the "extraterrestrials", wasting our time.' Nonetheless, Castillo decided to give the promised individual communication a chance the following day. He asked his wife to leave him in the house for a couple of hours and, towards noon, he prepared pencil and paper and sat on the bed, beginning the special relaxation and concentration exercises, as taught by Karen. Suddenly, at 12.25, he got a shock. 'Enrique, write!' came a voice. He looked outside the room, but no one was there. The voice repeated the instruction, so he sat down and put pencil to paper. 'Pages were filled at the speed that my hands permitted. A strong shivering affected my whole body, and a strange force took hold of me. I was so moved that I could no longer think.'

The messages related to the previous night's meeting (the 'poor behaviour' of the group causing cancellation of the contact plan) and said there would be no contact that night either (another attempt had been planned), but that 'other space brothers had already arrived'. A coming 'Third World War' was also referred to. Staggering into the bathroom, still trembling, Castillo noted his eyes, bloodshot from crying uncontrollably, and a strange purple line around his nose and nails. Soon, however, he returned to normal.

The next day Castillo learned that there had indeed been no communication. The group agreed that he had been selected in some way. At a meeting a few days later he had begun his relaxation technique with the others, all looking at Torres, when suddenly he felt 'that same buzzing sound' and a voice again commanded him to write. 'We are messengers from the Pleiades,' it said, 'the same who gave knowledge to the Inca and other races.' (The Pleiades is a cluster of between 300 and 500 stars, some 30 light years across and 400 light years distant.) Castillo then fell into trance for half an hour, oblivious to the message received through him. 'The message read that I was the one selected in Colombia by the extraterrestrials to make direct physical contact on a date that they would give soon.'

Dr Rafael Contreras, a physician who participated in the meetings, examined Castillo and pronounced that, apart from a slightly higher than normal heart rate, he was in good health, although for a while Castillo was troubled with throbbing headaches each time he fell into a trance. These would recede, the aliens promised him, after two or three more sessions. Once, he was told that they were taking certain 'measurements' of his brain. 'According to them, the vibration rate of my brain was 829 "valiums"[!]. I thought maybe that was a voltage, the natural frequency of my brain. However, they never clarified this point.' That is hardly surprising, for gobbledegook typically features in such communications. To his credit, Castillo remained sceptical about the nature and purpose of his contacts.

Some members left the group (called the Colombian Institute for the Investigation of Extraterrestrial Phenomena), convinced that the whole thing was fraudulent, the manifestations of witchcraft, spiritism, or insanity. By the end of October 1973 the 'Pleiadians' announced, through Castillo, the date when they would establish physical contact with him.[15]

TAKEN ON BOARD

The date of the contact was to be 3 November 1973, although only an undisclosed lake was given as the site of the encounter. In the event, Castillo experienced a number of dreams in which he saw two faces pointing to a lake surrounded by forests and hills. Later he was given precise co-ordinates and a plan. 'I was told to follow the instructions from the dreams, for finding a clearing. There should be a tree, and under its roots, hidden by a medium-sized stone, I should find a sphere, take it in my hand, and walk to the designated place.'

Castillo travelled two and a half hours by bus, then walked for another two hours until he satisfied himself that he had located the site, at the edge of a lake (some 80 kilometres north of Bogotá). It was now sundown. Among a group of trees he saw a medium-sized stone and ran towards it. There was the sphere, about the size of a golf ball, which he picked up. 'It looked like stainless steel but was light in weight, ice cold, and its surface was punctured by several small holes, as if it had been drilled by a very thin needle.' Castillo kept the sphere in his hand, looking at it constantly as he walked and paying attention to the sky and the forest. Then he headed away from the lake shore and into the trees, until it got dark.

Just before 20.00 the sphere began to feel unevenly warm, then tiny, dark-blue rays of light emitted from it. 'The light emission must have been triggered by something, because it was increasing [although] never hot enough to burn my hands.' At 20.10 there came a low, rumbling noise and the entire area was flooded as if by direct sunlight. 'I perceived two craft slowly moving above, some 200 meters above the trees . . .'

Water dripped from their slanting surfaces. They were huge, 40 or 45 meters in diameter, by 12 to 15 in height. Over them, I could discern great domes, casting a surprising luminosity. The temperature changed noticeably. When they passed overhead, I felt heat. I was terrified. . . . They had been waiting for me at the bottom of the lake ... All nocturnal noises stopped, and time stood still. The momentary, day-like illumination extinguished. The ships hovered about 100 meters from where I was. One of them silently moved behind the other. Now there was no more light, just a small halo surrounding the closest one [which] approached ... Moving slowly and swaying slightly from side to side ... it shot downwards two beams of light, strong orange in color [which] do not radiate like regular light does. [Later] I saw how the beams of light retracted until reaching the bottom of the craft, apparently 'absorbed', or reeled in.

Two silhouettes slid down the beams until they disappeared behind the trees ... A crackling of branches [and] dry leaves announced the arrival of the two beings. Ten meters from me, I noticed a luminosity. They wore dull, lead-gray uniforms, orange or tangerine-colored boots, and helmets with glasses that permitted seeing their eyes, as I noticed later ... Their belts supported five odd-looking buttons, three on their right side, and two on the left. Some of them were larger than the others, and two emitted light: one white, the other green ... They both approached me. I smiled nervously, not knowing what to do, [then] a voice was heard in my brain: 'Enrique, don't be afraid; we are incapable of hurting you!' My reaction was of fear, walking backwards three or four steps ... until my back hit against a tree

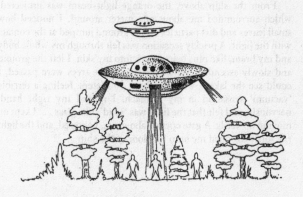

Figure 6. A drawing based on the description given by Enrique Castillo Rincón of being taken aboard an extraterrestrial spaceship, near an undisclosed lake north of Bogotá, Colombia, 3 November 1973. (*Jesús Alberto Balbi, Cuarta Dimensión, Argentina, 1975*)

. . . I heard the voice again: '. . . we are your friends . . . We are going to take you on board. Don't be afraid. If you don't want to come in, it is all right, but we need this meeting; it is vital.'

Castillo nodded, trying to control himself. The being on his right side came closer.

A flexible, corrugated piece around his neck connected the helmet to the rest of the uniform. At the height of the ears, some coiled cables protruded and went towards his back. Looking at his eyes, I heard the voice say: 'Come with us.' They turned around, and I could see a backpack where the coiled cables ended. At the tops of their helmets was something like an 'electronic eye'. They walked ahead, and I followed closely. The elegant but very masculine shape of their bodies emphasized their height: 1.78 to 1.80 meters tall. One of them placed himself at my side, and the other walked firmly ahead . . . We arrived at a clearing, free of vegetation.

Castillo was told that he would now be 'lifted' on board.

The ship approached, as if having received a signal. The closest [astronaut] moved closer to me, and, touching slightly my right arm and shoulder, said: 'Enrique, I am your friend, don't be afraid.' When he said this, I finally relaxed [and] felt a great peace of mind.

From the ship above, the orange light-beam was projected, which surrounded me about one meter around. I noticed how small leaves and dirt particles on the ground jumped at the contact with the light. A prickly sensation was felt through my whole body and my brain, like pins being stuck into my skin. I left the ground and slowly ascended. When the tips of the trees were passed, I could see the lake. I went up about 50 meters, feeling a terrible 'vacuum' sensation in my stomach. I moved my right hand, nervously, and felt that the light was 'solid', like glass . . . I kept on moving upwards. A gate opened above me, I entered, and the light ray softly dropped me onto the floor of the ship . . .[16]

NOTES

1 Jacobs, David M., Ph.D., *Secret Life: Firsthand Accounts of UFO Abductions*, Simon & Schuster, New York, 1992.

2 ——, *The Threat*, Simon & Schuster, London and New York, 1998.

3 Mack, John E., MD, *Abduction: Human Encounters With Aliens*, Simon & Schuster, London and New York, 1994.

4 ——, *Passport to the Cosmos: Human Transformation and Alien Encounters*, Crown, New York, 1999.

5 Letter to the author from Enrique Castillo Rincón, 8 February 2000.

6 Castillo Rincón, Enrique, *UFOs: A Great New Dawn for Humanity*, Blue Dolphin Publishing, PO Box 8, Nevada City, California 95959, USA, 1997, (ISBN 1-57733-000-5) translated by Hugo A. Castro from the Spanish original edition, *OVNI: Gran Alborada Humana*, published by Enrique Castillo Rincón, San José, Costa Rica, 1995.

7 Ibid., pp. 1–7.
8 Ibid., pp. 9–10.
9 Ibid., p. 13.
10 Ibid., pp. 20–1.
11 Ibid., pp. 24–31.
12 Ibid., pp. 31–2.
13 Ibid., pp. 35–6.
14 Ibid., pp. 37–8.
15 Ibid., pp. 38–47.
16 Ibid., pp. 48–53.

Chapter 5

New Dimensions

Enrique Castillo found himself deposited in an empty, hexagonal-shaped room, illuminated by light from an unseen source that made no shadows. A voice ordered him to undress. He took off his *ruana* (a kind of poncho) and hat but kept his trousers on, the sphere still in his pocket, reluctant to undress completely. 'You have to undress; it is necessary', insisted the voice. He did so, whereupon a blue-coloured smoke, smelling similar to lemon or lime, issued from the joint between walls and floor, filling the room in less than five seconds. (In the famous 1957 case involving the Brazilian abductee, Antônio Villas Boas, a greyish smoke came out of small metallic tubes in the wall, causing him to vomit. Castillo remained unaffected by it.) Seconds later, the smoke drained back through the same openings.[1] He was informed that this process disinfected him from whatever microbes he might have brought in.[2]

Castillo looked about him for an exit, but there was nothing to indicate an opening. The voice ordered him to get dressed. A door slid upwards 'or bi-parted horizontally' and his two escorts entered. Speaking in Spanish, one introduced Castillo to 'Krunula' (spelled phonetically, as are names of the other crew members). 'I extended my hand, but to my surprise, he only touched it slightly and bowed slightly in salutation.'

The other being then introduced himself. 'I am Cyril, Enrique . . . Don't you remember, in Caracas in 1969?'

It finally dawned on Castillo and he was overjoyed. Cyril explained that he was a crew member of the ship and that his real name was 'Krishnamerck'. He asked Castillo to follow him. They entered a large, rounded room, with translucent, geometric-shaped partitions in sections. 'Four projections from the floor above were visible, shaped like beams,' Castillo reports. 'There were two columns, which had the appearance of plastic. The chairs where we sat seemed leather lined . . . shaping themselves to one's body, and moving to the correct height for comfort. Several pictures decorated the walls, some representing strange animals . . . And there were space themes – stars, planets, and stellar routes . . .'

Four other crewmen – one the 'commander' ('Kramier') – sat in front of a large table, made of a transparent material 'like the white of a raw egg'. Two wore reddish-brown, and the others silver uniforms. Castillo was incredulous about Cyril's claimed origin. 'His features were slightly changed, with more prominent cheekbones and thinner, almost non-existent lips; when he smiled, he showed perfect teeth. His nose looked very straight, his eyes a little slanted and deep blue. His long hair reached to his shoulders and was truly yellow.' The others were similar.

> Their height and features were almost identical, with yellow hair and perfect skin, like a baby's. Their foreheads were ample and their chins straight. They had no wrinkles, blemishes, or moles. One of them turned his head and I could see the perfection of his ears. Without being athletic, their bodies were perfectly shaped . . . their hands were white and silky, the fingers a little longer than normal.[3]

ORIGIN

Replies to Castillo's questions, expressed either verbally or mentally, were often received telepathically. The crewmen claimed to be emissaries from the Pleiades. Castillo asked where that was. 'You say that it is 328 light years away from here, which is not true.[4] We are over 500 light years away,' came the response. Castillo later checked in books and found the figures of 328 or 410 light years.[5] In more recent years, astrophysicists tend to accept a distance of 400 light years. As mentioned in the previous chapter, the Pleiades (or 'Seven Sisters') is actually a cluster comprising between 300 and 500 stars, some 30 light years across. By astronomical standards it is young, about 50 million years old, and contains some massive bright stars.[6]

Castillo asked his hosts to describe their solar system. 'It is made up of three suns,' they replied. 'Two of them rotate around a larger sun. A total of 43 planets orbit around the three suns. We come from one of those planets, which are not all inhabited. We are still establishing colonies. We call our sun SHI-EL-HO, and we live on the fourth and fifth planets . . .'[7]

That even a few planets, let alone 43, might have developed in such a young cluster of stars seems ludicrous. That life might have arisen on those planets in the relatively short space of time implied here is equally unlikely, especially in a triple-star system, where the planets would have erratic orbits, either too close or too distant from the stars.[8]

'When did you leave your planet?' asked Castillo.

'We just left it,' came the astonishing reply. 'For you, it was millions of years ago, when your planet had not the conditions for intelligent life. For us, we just left.'

Bemused, Castillo asked if this had anything to do with Einstein's theories of relativity. Back came the response:

> . . . the speed of light is not 300,000 kilometers per second. It is closer to 400,000 . . . light slows down in the atmosphere, because of the electrostatic, electric, or ionized layers of the planet, the belt that you call 'Van Allen', and other fields not yet detected by your scientists, which have the shape of two apple halves.[9]

DISCOURSE

Castillo was invited to visit various interconnected sections of the craft. First came a circular-shaped 'relaxation room', with several cushions on the floor. In another room were large, slightly slanted flasks, which appeared to be hermetically sealed. Castillo learned that the flasks contained chlorophyll, a substance vital to their alimentary system, which they obtained on our planet and used in the preparation of their food.[10]

It is chlorophyll extract, which we take from forests and jungles . . . We eat, the same as you do. We are very fond of the fruit cultivated in the southern part of [this] continent – peaches, grapes . . . We 'borrow' the fruit from some of the farms, and then, by night, with certain ionizing rays, we speed up the growth of the fruit. A few hours later, the fruits are ripe for picking . . . We carry out a directed alteration of plant metabolism . . . Aboard our ships, we operate laboratories to process all of our foods . . . We need this type of food because we have stopped the process of mitosis [division of body cells]. We have a technique for keeping alive the cells, stopping the ageing process.[11]

In *Alien Base* I recount the experiences of Ludwig Pallmann, a German businessman who claimed to have been taken to an alien base in 1967 in the Amazon jungle, on the borders of Brazil and Peru. It is of interest to note that, as with Castillo, the aliens encountered by Pallmann claimed a keen interest in various terrestrial fruits, many of which they hybridized at their base.[12]

'We have technological and cultural exchange with thousands of inhabited planets,' continued the commander. 'We often also exchange raw materials . . . We do not explore your planet, because we have had bases here for thousands of years.' Other civilizations, however, did explore Earth, he declared.[13] The commander then explained that Castillo had been 'followed' for eight years.[14]

We are here carrying out a very special mission. We belong to a very developed civilization, sister to others, from which we have received specific orders regarding Planet Earth. From antiquity, we have contacted other men, belonging to various cultures. We have influenced their thinking through what you call 'Masters'. But not only on this planet, also on others; we have contributed to their scientific, cultural, and spiritual development. Besides, some of us have been 'born' here, or incarnated, if you prefer, since ancient times.[15]

We are here because we know about the calamities that will overrun Planet Earth – one of them, the Third World War. It is not far away; we know the date, but we cannot interfere . . . You must learn to live in peace and harmony, but you have to do it by yourselves, and that implies gaining a new level of conscience. Perhaps the greatest discovery that Earthlings will make, will be to know God . . . You believe in a completely mistaken concept of God.[16]

Castillo was taken via a spiral staircase to another floor, the third, where the control room was located. What appeared to be maps came out of the wall.

The control panel, with lights that blinked on and off, like neon signs, must have had something to do with the maps. These appeared to be marked with multicolored lights, representing zones. Some were well-defined lights, and others were without apparent function, picturing galaxies, nebulae, suns, and planets . . . The Commander located Planet Earth on a Milky Way quite different from what we know in pictures. A pulsing light distinguished the planet from other bodies, located quite a distance away.[17]

Castillo was astonished to discover that the craft had been in flight all the time he had been on board. He had felt nothing at all. 'They took me to a special panel, where a visor opened like the lids of an eye, revealing a concave screen. I sat in front of the visor, on a fixed chair. One of my companions, who was operating the controls, adjusted them and invited me to look through them . . . I moved them somewhat, until I could see with perfect clarity . . .' What he saw was his own house.

I was dumbfounded; it was a sort of telescope, incorporating a beam of light, capable of penetrating the roofs and walls of buildings. I could see my family sleeping, and the dog seemed to notice something, barking and moving about nervously . . . When I moved the levers the wrong way, a neighbor's house became visible . . . We kept on going at a steady speed. I could identify 68th Avenue, a major thoroughfare in Bogotá . . .

Cyril provided additional information.

Making our ships invisible, camouflaging them above your cities, thanks to a special vibratory field, we fly practically above your heads, yet you do not notice it. We fool your radars, creating confusion with our maneuvers. We handle our ships whatever way we want to. Those are the advantages of our technology. On the other hand, we have people on the ground, blended with the humans, who daily walk the streets and avenues of your large and small towns, as in my instance back in 1969. Many of us are among you . . .[18]

MIND-MACHINE INTEGRATION

Through a window 'embedded in a metal wall', Castillo observed the craft's propulsion system. 'In the innards of the ship, a group of three great diamonds or crystals rotated slowly around a vertical shaft extending from ceiling to floor, which turned also, in the opposite direction. The colors and shades of the shaft surface were like a kaleidoscope of pure crystal.'

'Those are crystals, not diamonds,' explained the commander. 'We call them "memory crystals"; they are programmable and receive information from the "main transducer" [the rotating shaft]. We also call them "living crystals". We obtain them on a certain planet, where they grow and reproduce.' The crystals also rotated around themselves, Castillo noticed, united to a base that also turned around the main transducer. He calculated the crystals to be around 70 centimetres in diameter. His request to increase the speed of the crystals was turned down flatly. 'It is not possible while you are here on board,' the commander explained. 'If we speed up the rotation for only two minutes, when you get off the ship, more than 200 Earth years will have elapsed.' Castillo became alarmed. What if such a thing should happen accidentally? The commander put his fears at rest.

That is not possible while you are on here on board. I am the one who commands the ship *mentally*, and we have thus reduced the possibilities for error. If something should happen to me, other members of the crew have authority to carry out the *mind-machine integration*, where the coupling takes place directly by means of mental impulses, to the 'transducer and crystals' program. The mental energy that we deliver is translated as *flight energy*. That is why we told you that 'we have just left'. For us, the time factor is not a problem; we live in a present that modifies the future. That is why the future is 'malleable' and cannot be predicted with certainty. Not so the past; that is already history and is unmodifiable.[19]

Directed to a ladder going up a walkway, Castillo arrived in a huge hall, at the centre of which rotated the 'kaleidoscope' or 'transducer'. Twelve crewmen were present, eight dressed in the reddish-brown uniforms, the others in dull-grey. Suddenly 12 chairs, similar to dentists' chairs, emerged from the floor, located in a circle around the transducer.

From the ceiling dropped 12 helmets, similar to motorcycle helmets, which descended onto the heads of each of the crew members, as soon as they sat in their chairs. The four with the different uniform sat precisely equidistant. They held hands in 'padlock fashion', each one holding the arm of the next, until the circle was complete . . . This ritual lasted perhaps one minute; then the helmets retracted up into the ceiling, the company stood up and released each other's hands, and the chairs collapsed into the floor . . . They said that I had seen them liberate their mental energy to the transducer, where it would be converted into *flight energy*![20]

In his controversial book, *The Day After Roswell*, Lieutenant-Colonel Philip J. Corso, who served on President Eisenhower's National Security Council staff, the sensitive Operations Coordination Board (later known as the 'Special Group' or '54/12 Committee'), and the US Army Staff's foreign technology division, claimed to have stewarded the transfer of alien technology acquired from the craft recovered near Roswell, New Mexico, in July 1947. Corso stated that the great rocket scientist, Dr Hermann Oberth, 'suggests we consider the Roswell craft . . . not a spacecraft but a time machine'.[21] Oberth speculated that 'This was a time/dimensional travel ship that didn't traverse large distances in space. Rather, it "jumped" from one time/space to another or from one dimension to another and instantly returned to its point of origin.'[22]

Also pertinent to Castillo's claims are Corso's allegations that the aliens recovered from Roswell 'used some form of brain-wave control for navigation', according to the scientists who examined the artefacts at Norton Air Force Base, California, and Wright Field, Ohio. 'There were no conventional technological explanations for the way the Roswell craft's propulsion system operated,' said Corso.

The craft was able to displace gravity through the propagation of a magnetic wave, controlled by shifting the magnetic poles around the craft so as to control, or vector, not a propulsion system but the repulsion force of like charges . . .[23] Among the artifacts we retrieved were devices that looked something like headbands . . . these devices were a very sophisticated mechanism for translating the electrical impulses inside the creatures' brains into specific commands. Perhaps these headband devices comprised the pilot interface of the ship's navigation and propulsion system . . .[24] The analysts at Wright Field believed that the sensors on the headbands corresponded with points on the multi-lobed alien brain that generated low-frequency waves, so the headbands formed an integral part of the circuit.[25]

Corso also claimed that raised panels on the 'flight deck' had indentations for the creatures' hands, speculating that these, too, were related to the pilot/craft propulsion interface.[26] Desmond Leslie, co-author of *Flying Saucers Have Landed*, written with George Adamski, the American contactee, told me that in the early 1960s Adamski had revealed to him in strict confidence that the spacecraft he flew in were operated by 'mental control'. 'It was a small platinum gadget fixed to the forehead,' said Desmond. 'George drew for my children pictures of these handprint things, similar to those described in Corso's book.'[27]

Only in recent years has a similar technique been considered for practical application in our own aircraft. In 1999 it was reported that researchers at the Defence Evaluation and Research Agency (DERA) in Farnborough, England are developing a method to help fighter pilots fly jets by thought power. As James Geary reports:

> DERA's 'cognitive cockpit' research program is intended to give pilots the ability to control key flight systems simply by looking at or thinking about the appropriate icons on a computer screen . . . This technology would not only permit hands-free operation of crucial functions, but also give pilots quicker response times during complex and often dangerous manoeuvres. Pilots inside a future cognitive cockpit may have electrodes embedded in their helmets to monitor brain waves . . .[28]

A MIXED BLESSING

At one stage Castillo was offered food. This consisted of something like a chocolate bar, its flavour similar to that of 'zabajón', a Colombian drink made of milk, eggs, sugar and anis-flavoured liqueur, then a food that he learned was made from four cereals, two of which exist on Earth – supposedly the 'manna' referred to in the Bible. Although the food sustained Castillo for 24 hours, the initial effect induced drowsiness.[29] He was escorted to sleeping quarters.

'Four beds appeared before us. Cyril told me to choose one . . . The bed was very soft and yielding, the surface leather-like. It conformed to the shape of my body as I shifted positions.' He was awakened by a 'mental order' from his hosts. 'Please excuse the way we have awakened you,' said Cyril and Krunula. 'We are going to give you some final information, because the time is approaching to drop you where we picked you up . . . a Third World War is inevitable. Men will have a four-year grace period to attempt to attenuate it, in accordance with your behavior. Only the mental state of mankind can ease its effects . . .'

With this doom-laden prophecy in mind, Castillo was taken again to the main control room, where through the wide window he watched the scenery change from large valleys covered with rich vegetation, to low, flat lands. This, Castillo was told, was 'Los Llanos Orientales' (the 'Eastern Prairies'). A particular area was flown over several times, so that Castillo could memorize it for the next rendezvous – 18 November 1973 at 20.00. He then was lowered via the light beam to the ground. His watch had stopped during the contact, but he guessed it was around 05.00. Two hours later, at sunrise, he headed back to Bogotá.

'From that moment on, my transformation was total,' Castillo reports. 'All my ideas about the world, life, and religion toppled, taking on new dimensions.' He found it difficult to discuss the experience with his family, particularly his wife, from whom he became estranged. Members of the group reacted emotionally to his report, some elevating him to the status of a biblical prophet, much to his chagrin. He also revealed his experiences at a public meeting. Some days later

Castillo reluctantly agreed to an interview with a journalist from the newspaper *El Tiempo*, Humberto Díez. The story was published in a series of articles over a four-day period. Enrique Castillo Rincón now became famous throughout Latin America. It was to prove a mixed blessing.

Among numerous letters Castillo received was one from Rear Admiral Daniel Gómez of Venezuela, who described in detail messages that supposedly had been transmitted by an extraterrestrial being from the Pleiades during meetings of a group similar to the one in Bogotá. 'Our messages were quite similar to those reported by the Venezuelans, in fact, almost identical,' said Castillo, 'and there had been no communication between the two groups.' Castillo continued to receive telepathic communications, which often caused severe headaches. His communicators forbade him to take any medicine and advised honey, coconut, nuts, fish and all foods rich in iron and phosphorus. The headaches stopped.

Following the articles in *El Tiempo*, caravans of UFO believers invaded the lakes surrounding Bogotá and the nearby state of Boyacá, hoping for a sight of the alien craft. 'People in Colombia began to assume the location had been at Guatavita Lake, a deep lake where primitive peoples used to make religious offerings,' said Castillo. 'Honoring the request of the ship's occupants, I have never mentioned the name of the lake or revealed its exact location.' People from all walks of life flocked to Castillo. 'Some of them mistook me for a spiritual master . . . as quickly as these people arrived, they also left, as soon as they realized that I was not.' [30]

CONTACT RENEWED

On 18 November 1973 Castillo made his way via an interstate bus to Villavicencio, capital of 'Los Llanos', thence by local bus to the nearby town of Apiay, where he hired a native guide to take him on horseback to the specified location, Fulanos de Tal.[31] At first reluctant to leave Castillo alone in such a remote location, the guide eventually left. At 20.00 Castillo steeled himself for the expected encounter. Nothing happened.

Hours went by. Finally, at 03.00, numerous illuminated

objects appeared, one of which detached from the rest and approached slowly in a zigzag fashion and performed an astonishing series of manoeuvres before landing on three supports about 60 metres away. The other lights disappeared. It was quite different from the previous craft, of a rather peculiar shape, around 7.5 metres in diameter and 3.5 metres high. A metallic ladder emerged, leaving a narrow, illuminated opening, in which a human-shaped silhouette could be discerned. Castillo started to run towards the craft, but a deep voice ordered him to stop, then beckoned him to approach slowly. It was Cyril.

> He invited me to walk up the six steps of the ladder. When I extended my arm to greet him, he stepped back and motioned me to stop between the last step and the door . . . A very bright blue flash of lightning shone briefly, covering my whole body for several seconds. My hands and clothing fluoresced, and I assume my face did, too. It was a little annoying and gave me a feeling that was hard to describe . . . I understood that the blue light was part of another cleaning or sterilizing system, quite different from the [previous] one.

No explanation for the delay was given, although Castillo sensed that he was being 'tested'. On board were two other very different beings, with 'avocado-shaped heads', dressed in one-piece, ample overalls. They smiled constantly. 'I got up to greet them, but they just bowed, without extending their hands . . . These little men were bald, with pale brunet skin, seemingly completely coated with an oil film, so shiny were their heads. They were about 1.5 meters tall, well-proportioned, with large normal eyes, normal ears, Greek nose, and prominent jaw. They [wore] short sleeves that exposed their shiny arms.'

The beings, declared Cyril, came from Mercury. Incredulous, Castillo commented on Mercury's immense temperature contrasts, precluding the possibility of life as we know it. 'You would be astonished', answered Cyril, 'at the civilizations that have flourished there.' Castillo was indeed astonished.[32]

THE MOTHER SHIP

Via a spiral stairway Castillo was taken to the second level, which he found rather cramped.

> We entered the navigation room, which was covered by a transparent dome . . . outside of the ship I did not notice the transparency of the dome and figured that it was like one-way glass.
>
> The room seemed disconcertingly simple. The controls were located on a semi-oval table with a few buttons and other instruments. A medium-sized screen was embedded at the center. Two chairs were in front . . . The stellar panorama unfolded before us, under a breathtakingly starry sky. The dome gave the impression of metal fused to glass . . . What seemed like a huge diamond with many facets was located at one side of the control table. At its base, several needles pointed at strange symbols . . .

Cyril announced that the craft was on its way to the 'mother ship'. One of the other beings took Castillo to a closet on the first floor and gestured to him to put on a uniform, which stretched to fit him perfectly. Then, from the control room, a gigantic craft came into view, appearing to Castillo like a 'flying whale'. A hatch opened, from which came intense light.

> No sharp movements were felt. Our ship entered the opening snugly, moving up through it until it reached its parking spot inside. Our ship's transparent dome [opened] automatically, permitting the insertion of a ladder that dropped from above into the control room. Cyril climbed it quickly, asking me to follow him up a ramp or ascending corridor. [He] walked rapidly, taking long strides, until we reached a level, metallic hall, with some . . . labyrinthine passageways leading elsewhere. I noticed an emblem in high relief, of a winged serpent holding [what looked like] an egg . . .

Upon a metal table were samples of rocks, soil, sand, seeds and fragments of vegetation. 'The samples were classified and separated by partitions and labeled by lettering or symbols utterly meaningless to me,' Castillo reports. 'In front of the table was a half-moon-shaped special chair, where I sat. It was built so that it could turn from side-to-side and also slide upon a track.' A door opened and Cyril entered, accompanied by four others, whom he had encountered during his first trip.

In the majority of accounts involving trips aboard space-craft, seldom do contactees report the need to go to the toilet. There are a number of exceptions, one being Howard Menger[33] and another Enrique Castillo. Cyril accompanied Castillo to a room with a partition, explained the procedure and left him alone. 'Pushing a lever, something emerged from the wall with a "funnel", shaped like a lotus flower at its end,' said Castillo. 'I urinated there and felt a suction or vacuum. An amber liquid carried away the waste . . . When done, a delicious scent emerged from the funnel. Upon leaving the room, the contraption disappeared back into the wall.'

In the hall, Castillo claims to have encountered yet another thoroughly unbelievable being, a giant of a man no less than three metres tall. 'His features were remarkably similar to those of a common terrestrial. All was proportional in size. His skin was grayish, his hands, hairy, with normal fingers, shaped at the tips like spatulae. He dressed in a dull gray uniform . . .' His origin? Why, Jupiter, of course! 'There are great lakes there, made of water,' said Cyril. 'Other lakes are of liquid methane. The inhabitants live in cities furnished with tremendous technology, which makes them very safe.'[34]

The idea of humanoids actually living on Jupiter is preposterous. Although 'tremendous technology' conceivably might protect the inhabitants from the elements of this, the largest planet in our solar system, the surface is not even solid: basically, Jupiter is a giant ball of gas. Assuming some truth in the account, I think it more likely that Cyril was referring to Jupiter's moons (of which there are sixteen), rather than the planet per se, because, following this statement, he is reported to have said: 'This race comes specifically from a satellite moon, where we also have bases. Thus, I can tell you that there are two inhabited satellites.'[35] In *Alien Base*, I published, for the first time, the story of 'Joëlle', a friend of mine who claimed a series of contacts with human-type extraterrestrials in 1963–4. They, too, stated that they had bases on Earth (some in South America) and on two moons of Jupiter.[36] Although water-ice covers the surface of several of Jupiter's largest moons – Ganymede, Europa and Callisto – this hardly endorses Cyril's 'great lakes of water', however.

By all accounts Castillo is regarded as an honest man who questions everything that happened during his contacts. I told him I did not believe in his Jupiterian giant (smelling appropriately of methane!). 'Did this really happen?' I asked. 'Is it possible that you added certain fictional things?'

'Not at all,' he replied. 'In all honesty, it is absolutely true. I have told my story just as it happened, without exaggerating or inventing anything.'[37] I remain incredulous.

At one stage, when Castillo took out his Parker pen to jot down a question, Cyril asked to show it to the others, eliciting considerable interest. Castillo then was asked to pick up a small tube, about 12 centimetres long and 12 millimetres in diameter, connected to a thin flexible cable and some plastic-like paper. 'Draw whatever you want to,' came the instruction. He decided on a butterfly. After the first few strokes with the strange pen, which ended in a small sphere, a full-colour image of a butterfly appeared, just as he had imagined it. 'It was incredible; the little pen interpreted my thoughts with astounding fidelity [and] it was three-dimensional.'[38]

There followed a lengthy discourse, during which Cyril elaborated on his predictions relating to a Third World War, prophecies he conceded (perhaps conveniently) were 'difficult to place in time'.

> The great war will be preceded by a shorter one . . . At first, no nuclear weapons will be used . . . Pay much attention to environmental changes, the ozone layer, the weakness of your leaders, and their lack of credibility, the loss of religious values, which the 'religious' claim to have, the growth of crime, and the lack of countermeasures against it. No government on Earth will be able to win the battle against crime and insecurity . . . We cannot intervene directly [but] we can subtly implant ideas in some people's minds, placed in certain positions.

'But can't you show up more frequently, in the eyes of the people?' asked Castillo. 'Or at least initiate a direct contact with the leaders of the planet?'

'We will answer these questions for you in some other way,' replied Cyril. 'Come, follow me.'[39]

HUMAN REACTIONS

The two boarded another craft, identical to the one in which they had arrived on the mother ship, and were joined by the other two, smaller beings. The craft left the mother ship and slipped into space. 'We are going to answer your first question, why we do not contact people in general,' said Cyril. 'Watch carefully.'[40] The craft approached an area near where Castillo had been picked up.

It must have been about 05.30. In the farms of the plains, many people get up early to feed their animals and milk cows. The small craft made a circle over some people below. There were two men milking cows in a small shed behind a house. They saw the bright light and jumped up, the cow kicked one and knocked over the pail of milk, and both men ran like they had seen the devil. We shot up rapidly behind some clouds where they couldn't see us. Then the farmer came out and the two men pointed up, moving their arms excitedly. A woman came out, drying her hands, and a child of about eight years, and they all looked up but couldn't see anything.

'Yes, we have caused panic, but these people are farmers,' said Castillo.

'Now we will try an experiment with slightly different people,' rejoined Cyril. The craft headed towards a highway. Various types of transport passed, then a car approached, with no sign of any other traffic for miles around. The craft positioned itself about 300 metres above the car.

. . . Through an electronic apparatus, I could see that inside the auto were two men with suitcoats and loosened ties. One was driving while the other sat at his side, talking. In the rear seat another man had his collar turned up and was sleeping. The gentlemen seemed to be cultured middle-class people, from their dress and [the] appearance of their car. We descended in front and hovered alongside the road. They were so surprised to see us so unexpectedly that the two in front opened their doors to exit, running. The other, knowing nothing of what was taking place, fell off the seat when the driver hit the brakes. He stuck his head out the window and yelled something, because I saw his mouth open. When he saw our craft . . . he got out running and tore his coat trying to go through a barbed-wire fence.

'Do you think that answers the question?' said Cyril.[41] 'We are going to answer the other question, as to why we don't contact directly the leaders and governmental heads of the Earth.' The craft ascended to a great altitude and within a short time arrived above the African continent, where it was afternoon. 'The leaders talk about lovely things, referring to human rights, and especially to children, and to hunger around the world,' Cyril continued, 'and fill the hearts of the people with hope. But the sad reality is different. Look at the observation screen . . .'

> In an African country that I could not identify [I observed as] a long line of women, children, and old people waited for handouts . . . Children with their swollen bellies were eating some of the food, while swarms of flies crawled over their bodies and faces. Pregnant women looked absentmindedly at their offspring, debilitated by hunger. At an ambulance of the Red Cross International, two doctors and two nurses attended the sick . . . The line was respected, thanks to the help of some members of the army . . . All was desolation and ruin.

'The spiritual and political leaders, not only of Africa, but of the whole world, take advantage of this situation,' Cyril went on, 'basing their promises on clear examples such as this one you have seen. We do not contact those we don't trust . . . concerned with only their power and prestige.'

As the sun set on the sad scene, Cyril stressed that only radical changes could ameliorate the situation, echoing what has repeatedly been voiced by terrestrial observers. Although many individuals and organizations did all they could, fighting for effective birth control, education and so on, he stated, 'They face the opposition of the caste system in the more backward countries, and of deeply engrained religious dogmas.' Cyril also declared that 'to accelerate human evolution' our political systems would, in many years, eventually have to be replaced, as would dependence on specific religious organizations.[42]

RETURN

The craft returned to the mother ship. A ramp underneath opened slowly. Docking was accomplished in a manner different from the previous occasion. 'While entering, all controls in our small craft were off,' Castillo observed. 'A strong suction or pull controlled our direction and speed . . . During the whole trip, I didn't feel any movement, but now, a rhythmic swaying was noticeable. A mild electric shock was felt.' This, Cyril explained, was due to an electromagnetic field for 'cleaning' the craft. They arrived in a very large hangar.

During the next few hours Castillo claims to have seen a robot, with some human features, and – for the first time – women, with tight-fitting suits and decidedly feminine features. 'Their golden hair framed the most beautiful faces I had ever seen,' Castillo enthused. 'As tall as the men, perhaps 1.75 meters, they swayed their incredibly beautiful bodies while walking. They approached our table, but nobody stood up, as if gentlemanly manners did not exist.' One woman greeted Castillo in rather poor Spanish. They stayed for about two minutes then, with a slight bow, departed through sliding doors.[43]

Castillo retired to some sleeping quarters, which included an individual cubicle with a 'capsule-bed'. He noticed that there were no sharp 90-degree intersections between the ceiling and walls. Awakened by Cyril nine hours later, he joined the commander and some of the other crew members for a lengthy discourse. Among subjects raised was the silence of governments regarding the extraterrestrial presence. 'The miserly minds of some politicians and organizations have profited by this forced silence,' claimed the commander, 'capitalizing in their favour on the time factor, in order to obtain superior technology and progress never dreamed of before, through investigations into genetic engineering and medicine.'

Some governments, military, and scientific groups have already achieved considerable progress in this direction . . . Some 'crashes' of 'explorer ships' belonging to other races have taken place here on Earth, from where the lifeless bodies were extracted. On other occasions, living crew members have been captured and kept captive by the military of some of your governments, and subjected to merciless interrogations, forcing them to reveal formulae and knowledge on several scientific specialties . . . developments such as exist on Earth in the fields of electronic technology, computers, medicine, genetic engineering, and science in general do not normally develop in such a short time. Therefore, it must be imported.

Escorted by Cyril back to one of the small craft and accompanied by the two smaller beings, Castillo was returned to an area not far from Bogotá. He had been away for about 26 hours.[44]

ENTER THE VENUSIANS
Castillo and the group continued to communicate telepathically with an assortment of entities, including Cyril. With the help of Karen and a new medium from Cali, some 'Venusian' beings, with silly names like 'Orhion' (suspiciously similar to George Adamski's 'Orthon') came through. 'I could not understand how they could be Venusian,' Castillo reports, 'if scientific data from space probes showed that there is no life on that planet. Was it a trick . . .?'

At the end of December 1973, as a demonstration of their powers, the beings promised to remove the smog from Bogotá, surrounding the city with low, dark clouds and an electric storm with rain and wind, from 10.30 to 13.00. Castillo took the chance of revealing this information to Humberto Díez, the journalist. On the predicted day the weather was perfect, causing some disillusionment among the group. But by 10.30 a strong wind started to blow. 'Within 15 minutes,' reports Castillo, 'the sky became completely overcast, and powerful lightning bolts and thunder echoed over the city . . . Rain poured, flooding the streets.' At precisely 13.00 the rain stopped. 'They had come from a base somewhere on this planet,' Castillo claimed. 'They had had to "close" the city in order to hide the [three] ships while they carried out the cleaning of the air by means of gigantic "aspirators", which removed the smog.'[45]

Whoever they were and wherever they came from, the extraterrestrials apparently had delivered as promised, with a demonstration of biblical proportions. It will be recalled from Chapter 1 that a demonstration of the aliens' ability to control local weather was given to the meteorologist, Rubens Villela, a demonstration he found thoroughly convincing. 'I was a witness of such events in Limeira, Brazil, in November 1978,' he told me, 'when some abnormal clouds and wind gusts appeared for no apparent reason.'[46]

ENTER THE AMERICANS

In February 1974 two North Americans, accompanied by a Latin-American interpreter, met Castillo, by arrangement, in Bogotá. The Americans expressed great interest in his contact story, which they had learned about in the newspaper articles, and asked Castillo if he would accept an invitation to visit Washington, DC, for a few days, all expenses paid, to participate in a series of tests to determine the veracity of his story and to compare it with other cases they had studied, with the professed purpose of proving his statements in public. Castillo readily consented. He was told not to discuss the matter with relatives or colleagues.

Two days later, having explained to his wife and friends that he had to make a business trip to Managua, Castillo was collected by the Americans (minus the local interpreter) and driven to El Dorado Airport, where they boarded an Avianca flight to New York, thence another flight to Washington. 'No one asked me for a ticket, only some type of identification for my escorts with some authority who let them pass immediately,' said Castillo. 'Everything seemed to have been arranged beforehand, without the need to present passport or visa.'

Castillo's escorts asked him occasional questions about his profession, family and pastimes. 'I answered them in lousy English, and they spoke in lousy Spanish. To a degree, I was pretending, because I could understand more English than they suspected. This proved useful during the test in Washington . . .'[47]

NOTES

1 Castillo Rincón, Enrique, *UFOs: A Great New Dawn for Humanity*, p. 53.
2 Article by Fabio Zerpa, *Cuarta Dimensión*, (mid-1970s), translated by Wendelle C. Stevens.
3 Castillo Rincón, op. cit., pp. 53–8.
4 Zerpa, op. cit.
5 Castillo Rincón, op. cit., p. 58.
6 Mitton, Jacqueline (ed.), *The Penguin Dictionary of Astronomy*, Penguin Books, London, 1992, p. 301.
7 Castillo Rincón, op. cit., p. 62.
8 Sneath, P. H. A., *Planets and Life*, Thames & Hudson, London, 1970, p. 126.
9 Castillo Rincón, op. cit., p. 58.
10 Zerpa, op. cit.
11 Castillo Rincón, op. cit., p. 59.
12 Good, Timothy, *Alien Base*, pp. 301–25.
13 Castillo Rincón, op. cit., p. 61.
14 Ibid., p. 56.
15 Ibid., p. 59.
16 Ibid., p. 61.
17 Ibid., pp. 59, 61.
18 Ibid., pp. 63–4.
19 Ibid., pp. 64–5.
20 Ibid., p. 66.
21 Corso, Col. Philip J., with Birnes, William J., *The Day After Roswell*, Pocket Books, New York and London, 1997, p. 90. Copyright © 1997 by Rosewood Woods Productions, Inc.
22 Ibid., pp. 223–4.
23 Ibid. p. 100.
24 Ibid., p. 98
25 Ibid., p. 196.
26 Ibid., p. 109.
27 Interview, June 1998.
28 Geary, James, 'Think about it', The Communications Revolution, *Time*, vol. 154, no. 15, 11 October 1999, pp. 22–3.
29 Castillo Rincón, op. cit. p. 63. (A number of contactees and abductees have been given a similar 'chocolate bar'.)
30 Ibid., pp. 66–74.
31 Zerpa, op. cit.
32 Castillo Rincón, op. cit., pp. 76–80.
33 Good, op. cit., p. 184.
34 Castillo Rincón, op. cit., pp. 80–3.

35 Ibid., p. 83.
36 Good, op. cit., p. 251.
37 Letter to the author, 5 October 1999.
38 Castillo Rincón, op. cit., p. 84.
39 Ibid., pp. 85, 86.
40 Ibid., p. 86.
41 Zerpa, op. cit. See also Castillo Rincón, op. cit., pp. 86–7.
42 Castillo Rincón, op. cit., pp. 87–9.
43 Ibid., pp. 91–3.
44 Ibid., pp. 95–8.
45 Ibid., pp. 103–4.
46 Letter to the author, 10 November 1999.
47 Castillo Rincón, pp. 110–11, 113.

Chapter 6

Vortex

On arrival at Washington National Airport, Castillo and his escorts were met by two men in a Cadillac. During the journey, to an undisclosed destination, Castillo was constantly distracted by his escorts, to prevent him from looking out of the darkened window too often. 'We took a turnpike and traveled for 40 or 45 minutes, until we turned onto a narrow and lonely road,' he wrote. 'The car stopped in front of a great iron gate. We waited for a few seconds until a security guard authorized the admission. We advanced then on a gravel road, until we reached a large, old, English-style house, surrounded by gardens and hidden behind tall trees.'

Two doctors and a nurse greeted Castillo warmly. The escorts left and he was ushered into a small room, where an interpreter was called in. Castillo was asked for his full name, age, place of birth and whether he had served in his country's army.

I showed him my military card and explained the reasons why I had not served in the army. I had recently been married, and for this reason . . . I was given a second-class card, or so-called reserve . . . I also showed him my citizenship certificate. They inked the index fingers of both hands and imprinted them on the identification card, which had my name already on it. Then they made me sign the document and leave the name and address of my wife, in case of emergency. In the same document I had to authorize the tests on a voluntary basis. They took my picture with a Polaroid camera. I was asked to get rid of my watch, a silver chain with a charm that hung around my neck, my wallet, and my passport. Everything was placed in a plastic bag, then into an envelope with my name and arrival date. They told me that the whole lot would be returned at the end of the tests.

After these preliminaries Castillo was taken upstairs. The second floor had a beautifully appointed library and numbered bedrooms, one of which was to be his for the duration of the stay. 'The room had a telephone, private bath, a table with a typewriter, paper, ballpoint pens, pencils, a tape recorder with new tapes, a TV . . . and a small refrigerator, which contained some fruit, milk, several kinds of cheese, butter, soft drinks, wine, and beer. The nurse showed me two push-buttons, one for the kitchen and one for the nurse on duty.'

Following a rest, Castillo submitted to another series of questions. The nurse came to his room, together with a Dr Smith and a Dr Ramírez (conveniently common names). The latter spoke good Spanish, but with an American accent. This time, questions were more rigorous. Dr Ramírez asked about Castillo's medical history, whether there had been any mental illness in the family, about his children, marriage (which had deteriorated completely), whether he smoked and drank alcohol (he did neither), his general tastes, friends and about his religious beliefs. The interview lasted one and a half hours. Castillo asked if there were any books on UFOs in their library for him to read: he was lent a copy of *Flying Saucers Have Landed* by Desmond Leslie and George Adamski.

The following morning, breakfast was brought to Castillo's room by the nurse. 'I had not paid attention to her before. She had beautiful black hair, a pretty face, and spoke an excellent, fluid Spanish, similar to Dr Ramírez. She must have been Cuban or Puerto Rican . . . She said her name was Eva Douling.'[1]

THE TESTS

After breakfast came a polygraph (or 'lie detector') test. Dr Smith, Dr Ramírez, and a US Air Force doctor awaited Castillo in the first-floor office. 'The door opened and two men entered . . . One must have been in the military [but was] wearing just a white coat over his civilian clothes. From the way he watched me, he must have been a psychologist. The other was dressed like a bank employee, in a business suit.'

Nurse Douling placed sensors on Castillo's skin at different locations, joined by wires to the polygraph. He sat on a chair, naked to the waist. Two tape recorders were started, each with two microphones. Following preliminary test questions, the interview began. 'I believe that Dr Smith was an expert on extracting information,' said Castillo.

He repeatedly played the fool's role and faked bad memory, asking the same questions in a different context, in an attempt to confuse me. More than once he became bothered by my answers and my cool disposition . . . He tried to break down my tolerance by asking rough, repeated questions, difficult to follow because of the language, until they were translated by Ramírez . . . There were questions such as how it happened, the date and hour of the encounter, where they came from, their technology and propulsion system, how they got here, age, beliefs, how they live, government, scientific development, etc.

Two hours later, the first examination completed, Castillo retired to his room. The next examination, under hypnotic regression, took place at 15.00. For this a hypnotist joined the team. He began by looking deeply into Castillo's eyes and giving orders; to no avail. A second attempt was made. 'A tick-tock mechanism, with a swaying needle to be followed by one's eyes, couldn't do it either,' said Castillo. Finally, one of the doctors asked Castillo to close his eyes. 'I felt his hand passing close to my face a couple of times, then I felt it sliding down my neck, searching for a specific point; he touched my forehead with his thumb, then he searched for my throat and pressed with his fingers. That is the last I recall.'

Dr Ramírez declared that although the results were satisfactory, it was not possible to volunteer an opinion until everything had been analysed. Castillo was patted affectionately on the back and left alone for the rest of the day.[2]

At 09.30 the following morning Castillo was asked to sit in a reclining chair and injected with sodium pentothal (the so-called 'truth drug'), its effects explained to him beforehand. 'Ramírez spoke to me . . . His voice sounded weaker and weaker, and I spun slowly, losing my strength, feeling weak and defenseless. Then, I woke up . . . I felt my lips dry . . . They gave me more water, and told me that I must rest.' Castillo slept for five hours. In the afternoon a second, short hypnosis session was conducted, followed by a final session at 16.30.

Castillo returned to Bogotá the following morning.

> My personal belongings were returned, along with an envelope [containing] 1000 dollars! According to them, it was a compensation for the working days missed in Bogotá. It was more than I expected, because I felt satisfied by the tests . . . They said that the results would be sent through the American Embassy in Bogotá. However, I am still waiting for them.
>
> Years later, I still have several doubts . . . What were the true identities of those obscure agents who could take me and return me to Bogotá, with arrangements . . . all so well coordinated?[3]

It is not unlikely that the agency responsible for Castillo's trip to Washington was the Central Intelligence Agency (CIA), whose long history of involvement in UFO investigations is documented in my book, *Beyond Top Secret*. According to the American journalist Warren Smith, the CIA believed that the aliens were deliberately confusing those they contacted. 'The past several years has produced some incredibly wild contactee reports,' Smith was told by a CIA source in the early 1970s. 'We believe the extraterrestrials are testing our ability to withstand psychological warfare.'[4]

VENUSIAN CONTACT

Castillo's telepathic communications, many of them containing rambling platitudes, continued apace. Then, in July 1974, he was summoned for a meeting with the 'Venusians', at 05.00 one morning, near Bogotá. 'I expected them to be at least 1.70 meters tall,' he wrote in his chapter, 'The Venusians, Are They Venusian?'

> I had read George Adamski's reports, saying the Venusians were rather tall, 1.70 to 1.75 meters . . . all of the crewmen welcoming me were very much alike, all about 1.50 meters tall, but very human-like . . . Ourino, then Yaraka, Febo, Baros, Commander Yamaruck, and finally Orhion entered . . . The subject of the conversation was mostly the group and the results of the

information received . . . They said that they belonged to the same stellar organization as the Pleiadians, only that these were much more advanced in many fields. There were exchange agreements between the Pleiadians and Venusians on undisclosed matters . . . From the few questions that I asked, they sketched a very grim picture for humanity's future. By now, it seemed clear that the time for their communications with our group was coming to an end . . .

Castillo had taken along a tape recorder, with which he captured what he claims was the whistling noise of the craft as it approached the landing site. The recorder ceased functioning when he began to approach the craft. The following day he played the recording to some members of the group. Later, the tape was stolen by one of the members, who tried to sell it for 20,000 pesos.[5]

THE VORTEX OF THE ANDES

On 23 December 1974 Castillo, then visiting Caracas, received a telepathic summons for a contact early the next morning. 'I was told not to bring a tape recorder or camera. The trip was going to last about five days.' He took a taxi to Colonia Tovar, a town high in the Venezuelan Andes, and walked to a ravine where the contact had been arranged. At 04.25 a craft appeared a few metres above ground level, 'swinging from side to side and projecting a tenuous light downwards'. Around six to seven metres in diameter, it landed about 40 metres away. A tripod slid down, then a ladder and a man stepped to the ground. It was Cyril.

'He informed me that we were to visit a base in the Andes, where we were to receive the information promised during one of the telepathic contacts some months before. Krunula and a stranger, whose name he told me but I have not been able to remember, were on board.' Twenty minutes later the craft arrived over a town in the middle of the high Andes of South America. 'Thousands of kilometers in such a short time,' Castillo remarked. 'And as usual, I could not detect a single motion or discomfort.

'Below were the majestic Andes, and, at the tip of one of the mountains, the arrangement of the buildings was clearly visible. Cyril told me the inhabitants called this place the Vortex of the Andes.' But what inhabitants? Cyril elaborated:

At the moment there are 318 people here, who for many years – even entire families – have been contacted and brought here voluntarily. Here they live, work, study, and learn. They are instructed about the great events that humanity will experience . . . Many of them will be trained to help when the moment arrives. Nobody will know who instructed them, and besides, nobody would believe them; it could even be dangerous for them. This place, at about 3200 meters above sea level, is located between two great mountains that give natural protection against blizzards and frosts, and is known as Alto Peru [Peru Highlands].[6]

Castillo later came to believe that the Vortex was closer to Bolivia than to Peru. (In an earlier account, he gives the location as between Marcahuasi and Machu Picchu, at an altitude of 4200 metres.)[7]

It was impressive to see how the disc flew closely between steep mountain slopes and then landed softly on a platform and slid into the mountain – perhaps through hydraulic means – penetrating in through a horizontal tunnel. After climbing down to ground level, we walked to an office, where I was asked to take off my sweater and shirt.

What surprised me pleasantly was the temperature, about 16 degrees Celsius, similar to Bogotá, where I had lived for many years. The next day I was able to verify this point. The people getting ready to give me a brief check-up were not extraterrestrial, just ordinary people, except that they used some devices unknown to me. The first test was routine: heart, blood pressure, reflexes, lungs, vision, hearing, etc. They asked me my city of origin and consulted a listing . . . They asked me to take off my watch temporarily [and] placed a yellow band on my left wrist, and the watch was moved to the right arm.

At the end of the examination, another [human] took me to the room where I was going to live during my stay. When I went out, somebody followed us quickly. Apparently there had been a mistake; they explained that the wristband's color had to do with the type of food that I should eat. Finally, I was taken to my temporary bedroom . . .

I rested on a simple but comfortable bed. I thought I was going to see a city of the future, but the buildings were wooden, sort of

'Canadian type' cabins, with smooth and well-cut but rustic beams and boards . . . The great rectangular cabin had two rows of bedrooms, on both sides of its central passageway.

Up to then, I thought that I was the only guest at the Vortex. When they announced breakfast, I had not slept. I was restless as to why I had been taken so far and to what mission I was to be assigned. It was 6.45 a.m., and I had been there almost two hours. The fellow who picked me up was surely of Inca origin. I followed him to the dining room . . . six more people waited there, having arrived before me. Others would arrive in an hour or so. These contactees came from nineteen different countries, and eleven were Latin. There was only one woman among us. There was an individual self-introduction; no names were given, just the countries of origin.[8]

NUTRITION AND ENERGY

All guests wore the coloured wristbands, some different, some of similar colours. 'Each was to eat from the trays marked with the same color as the wristbands,' said Castillo. 'Instructor number one (there were four) told us that the food had been prepared according to geographic zone. Their ionization was different, according to the elevation above sea level. This way it prevented illnesses from occurring.'

Food and drink, usually served buffet style (assisted by native Inca), included warm milk, herbal tea, fruit juices, broth, honey, bread, greens, potatoes, tomatoes and peppers, and various types of fruit. 'We saw fields cultivated with legumes, strawberries, and other fruits,' Castillo reports. Tropical fruits, including coconut, oranges and pineapples, were also available, causing him to wonder how they were provided. All the eating utensils were made of wood.

Some of the older visitors received oxygen on arrival. Castillo managed without, although at times he suffered from altitude sickness.[9] Outside, the temperature was 'bone-chilling'. 'We were able to see a great contraption projecting from the mountain, with fins and crystals. We were told that energy is thus captured for the whole community, and that there is another source for the appliances and lighting. One of the energy sources was used for powering a "magnetic shield" or camouflage of the base and its climate-controlled environment.'[10] This shield, presumably, prevented detection by aerial and satellite reconnaissance.

INSTRUCTION

On that first morning the instructor assigned to the new group explained the purpose of their visit. Each was to receive privileged information. 'We were to be very careful as to who would receive it, either orally or in writing,' said Castillo.

> The instructor told us that grave events were taking place in various fields, which would lead the planet to undergo, with its occupants, untoward experiences of several types. Our presence in that place had the objective of transmitting to the public, through various means, the occurrences that will take place and culminate in several momentous events. For personal reasons, I do not give out an account of the calamities announced by the instructors. They had information covering many years as to how the facts will unwind.

The instructors had received this information from the extraterrestrials, through 'adequate scientific means', they explained. 'We were not given all this information,' said Castillo. In cases of emergency, information would be imparted through personal contact. 'We were told that the withholding of certain information from us at that time was intended to protect us from any danger.'[11]

The instructors were not always terrestrial. Later that day, in a small living room, Cyril lectured to a group of seven Spanish-speaking visitors, including Castillo. 'It is up to you whether or not you divulge what we are teaching you,' Cyril began. All wrote down the dictation. Following a proselytizing, 'new-age'-flavoured preamble, he dictated his 'message to the world'.

> In 1958, the US Air Force admitted that the Strategic Air Command bombers had been hurled more than once against Russia, when the defense radar detected mysterious objects, which have never been identified . . . This information from the US Air Force makes it clear that nuclear war can start by accident

or error, through confusion of our ships with rockets from a foreign power against the US. It is positively known that our ships can initiate a war, when detected by the radar network, due to the degree of tension and fear between the different countries. Countermeasures have already been taken, both on the part of our ships and the governments of the countries who study the presence of our fleets . . .

The important aspect is that our ships are systematically making cautious appearances in the air spaces above all nations, especially those whose technological, military, and technical advancement are such that they are bound to observe us. We have done this for a long time, to create a clear indication of our presence among you.

The recklessness of the governments of two terrestrial countries has been obvious, when they have ordered their combat pilots to attack our space and scout ships, as soon as they are detected on their radar. This is highly dangerous for the crew members of your airplanes, because if they approach our gravitational field, their engines and controls become inoperative. In this way, several have lost their lives . . . They do not seem to understand that our orders are clear, not to harm their craft. Otherwise, at least 50 of their planes would have been destroyed.

We are aware that many high-ranking military personnel and scientists have been silenced under the pretense of endangering the security of their countries, if public statements were to be made. This is another serious mistake of those governments. If we had any ambition or desire to conquer this planet, we would have done it 300 years ago, when the population could not have opposed any resistance. Even now, it would not be difficult to do.

This phase is alternative: we shall continue making appearances, landings, contacts, all over the world, more and more frequently, as planned. You will be responsible for the education of the people in the different countries . . . using all means available. This is a difficult task, because you will be left to your own means [and] you will have against you those who do not take you seriously, and the dark machinations of the great established powers on your planet, hampering, creating doubts, and attacking you as promoters of this knowledge . . .

After many years of observation and analysis of your world . . . the conclusion was that humankind, with few exceptions, were a barbarian horde . . . from the deepest levels of their spirit, and utterly incorrigible. Nevertheless, because of the merit of the few, [we are giving] direct help to many men, instructing them. It requires in many cases their evacuation from this planet, to a special place where they will be provided with a new conscience, to be transmitted afterwards to their fellow men . . . The disappearances of such people from Earth have already begun . . . This procedure holds the key to the future of your planet.

Thus spake Cyril/Krishnamerck. 'While dictating,' said Castillo, 'he held in his left hand a gadget the size of his fist, which he operated with his thumb. It must have been a decoder or screen, perhaps an advanced kind of teleprompter, from which he read the text to be given.'[12]

A BREAK

That evening Castillo and four others were selected for a short trip in a 'scout ship', flown by Cyril. The group entered through the same tunnel they had arrived in that morning, boarded the craft, and sat on comfortable chairs around the upper dome. 'There was a concave screen showing whatever was underneath the machine,' Castillo reports.

The takeoff was impressive: the craft flew away, slowly at first, and then surged forward tremendously. We didn't feel any pressure or discomfort, though. Within a few minutes we were watching the high peaks of the Andes . . . There was a fabulous view of Lake Titicaca. I was finally able to see its so-famous shape, like a jaguar . . . We could see clearly a great city under the ship, which was changing position to let us see various different views. It was Lima, the capital of Peru.

We stared, open-mouthed, as the ship lost altitude, oscillating like a falling leaf in the wind. It stopped again, after 'skimming' twice over a section of Lima . . . The craft had several multicolored lights on, whose reflection reached the cabin. Now the lights flashed, in order to draw the attention of the people below. We saw several people getting out of their houses, going out on the streets, looking and pointing upwards . . . We watched clearly men, women, and children, and a police patrol car showed up . . . I thought it couldn't possibly be ignored by the press.

On returning to the Vortex, Castillo learned that another group had been taken on a different tour. He also learned that some of the other contactees had been given different kinds of information and instructions. 'They would act in a different way than us, penetrating at the executive level and very discreetly passing information, suggesting the possibility that we were being infiltrated by two different extraterrestrial societies, one dedicated to corruption, manipulation, and domination; and another one with the intention of helping, but while acting very discreetly.

'Even today, after all this time,' wrote Castillo in 1997, 'I don't think there is a single person who knows fully their complete plan.'[13] Once again, a conflict of interests between extraterrestrial parties, alluded to by some other contactees, such as Rubens Villela, is here indicated.

SERMON ON THE MOUNT
On Christmas Day 1974 Castillo and others supposedly were taken to meet a 'master of wisdom' who apparently resided some distance away from the cabins. As they came out of a tunnel, four shiny craft, about four metres in diameter, could be seen, 'suspended' some eight to ten metres above the ground. Lo and behold, in due course a man looking like the Jesus as fancifully imagined, dressed in a simple, short-sleeved robe and, of course, sandals, appeared out of a tunnel. Smiling, he addressed the assembled gathering. 'I am not who you believe I am,' he declaimed. 'My name is a thousand names.'[14] The 'master of wisdom' went on to deliver a flowery speech of such absurdity that I shall refrain from quoting any of it. Castillo, however, seems to have been captivated, although nonetheless confused by this and other experiences at the Vortex.

A SUBMARINE SHANGRI-LA
Castillo claims that his fifth, and final, physical contact wth the 'Pleiadians' took place early in January 1975, at the end of his visit to the Vortex. This involved a trip to an alien base located over 5000 metres down in the Mariana Trench, North Pacific Ocean. (The Mariana, or Marianas, Trench is the deepest trench on Earth: in August 1960 Jacques Piccard and Don Walsh descended in a bathyscaphe, *Trieste*, to the record

depth of 10,917 metres.) Castillo generously provided me with a synopsis of the chapter in his second book (prior to publication) in which this experience is recounted (in Spanish).[15]

A group of six, including an instructor and a woman named Eallyn, was selected for the trip. Cyril accompanied them. It was explained that the base they were to visit had been constructed conjointly with another race of extraterrestrials 'very many years ago'. 'We were taken via a subterranean passage, illuminated by a strange light which was let into the floor, covered in transparent tiles, giving the impression that we were in full sunlight,' Castillo recounted.

We continued along a passage about 100 metres long, with just two slight curves. Arriving at one of the bends we were confronted by a magnificent view and a fascinating spectacle. We had come out into a sort of artificial crater about 200 metres in circumference, set in the rounded top of the Andes mountains. Beside the exit from this remarkable tunnel, to the left, six craft hovered in the air silently, shining in the morning sun. They were all the same, circular, without rivets or seams and about seven metres in diameter and three metres high, burnished, metallic, with a small dome like an observation tower. They were perhaps some six metres from the ground, stationary, and with the permission of Cyril, we went up to them. Stretching our hands out underneath them as far as we could, we could feel nothing, apart from a slight sensation of something electrical on our arms, which also affected the hair on our head. No sound could be heard . . . it was as if they were suspended by an invisible thread.

Immediately, we were guided towards a craft which approached with a slight oscillation and landed some 20 metres from us, tripod landing legs having appeared from the underside. Cyril beckoned us to follow him. Steps came out from the side of the craft, allowing us to see the legs of a crew member who was coming out to greet us. His clothes were of a light mustard colour, with no insignia, close-fitting but allowing freedom of movement. He beckoned us to follow him on board. As gentlemen, we gave Eallyn the option of going first. Inside, another crew member offered us seats in a semicircular area, giving us a clear view of everything through a glass-like screen in the dome. One crew member returned and we remained on our own with Cyril and the crew member responsible for accompanying us to the base.

I noticed that the craft seemed to be made of burnished steel, cast in one piece. It must have been a strange alloy, because when I stroked it, it was so polished that I couldn't feel any grain in it. The craft started taking off slowly, almost vertically, and at the same time the glass-like screen drew back and the dome became like a large panoramic window. We could hear no sound nor was there any sensation of movement, and in a few moments we were hurtling towards a marvellous blue, cloudless sky . . .

Very soon the great mass of the Andes faded into the distance. A few moments later the sea appeared before us, as though from nowhere. No more than ten minutes had elapsed when Cyril informed us that we were over the Pacific Ocean, coming towards an area known as the Marianas Trench. He had been examining and interpreting a screen full of symbols. Various buttons and lights on an average-size panel showed us that their technology far surpassed our own avionics.

We now seemed to be going at a dizzy speed and looked at each other as one does when the inevitable is about to happen. Banking visibly, the craft began a perilous nosedive. We held our breath and prepared for imminent impact with the water. As we watched in amazement, the sea seemed to open up in a certain place just in front of the craft, at which point it slowed down and plunged into the waters of the Pacific . . . The initial darkness during our descent in the sea was suddenly illuminated and we then noticed that the water surrounding the craft was not actually touching it – there was a sort of resistance. Cyril, now reading our thoughts, explained that an energy field prevented the water from making contact with the hull of the craft, thus preventing it being crushed by the very high pressures to which it is subjected. 'We are now entering one of the deepest places on this planet, known to you as the Marianas Trench,' said Cyril.

Now the whole seabed was illuminated. We could make out an enormous dome. Was it a mirage? We didn't believe what was before our eyes. The craft had come to a standstill. It turned around and approached a part of the dome, settling gently across a large porthole that was opened . . . the water that had got in was rapidly absorbed, leaving the craft on a sort of hydraulic-type ramp, all covered in a transparent layer. We felt a momentary sensation of emptiness or vacuum. Cyril said there was no danger . . . The ship's door opened and we were instructed to go down slowly one by one. We were absorbed in gazing at the scene: strange trees and vegetation, walkways, lounges with glass walls, structures in what seemed like granite and metal, colours on the walls, pleasant lights, great ferns hanging from the roof and other unknown plants.

We followed the two cosmonauts towards a building. The floor on the seabed was covered in shiny little stones (manganese) . . . 'These depths are rich in various metals and there are some deposits which would be called precious stones by you,' said Cyril. We arrived at the entrance to the building and followed him to a large room or hall in which there were easy chairs, offered to us by two escorts who came to meet us. A viewing panel opened in the wall. An opening was revealed on another side of the glass wall, and a man appeared, seated. He was young. An abundant head of almost yellow hair reached down to his shoulders, like Cyril's and the other crew members'. But what really caught our attention was the radiant intelligence and force that emanated from his direct, kind-hearted expression. Unlike the others, he was wearing a light-blue, very simple overall. He had some insignia on the chest: I don't know what they represented, but by the way in which he was greeted by Cyril and the other man there was no doubt that he was a person of high rank. They told us he was head of the base.

The man 'addressed' the group, his words received telepathically in Spanish and, by Eallyn, in English. 'You've been brought here because your planet is threatened by dark forces, and at the same time by a possible cataclysm having great repercussions preceded by various calamities,' he began. 'Your presence here also has profound significance for us, which for the time being you are not to know about.' After listing the iniquities of earthlings, he continued:

For us, it would be very easy to get rid of this mortal plague, but it rests with you, when a new generation grows up with a superior knowledge on the basis of what it has learned and a new state of consciousness is established . . . These impending changes will be disastrous for the whole human race, affecting your organisms and the equilibrium of life itself . . . serious geological changes, more and more frequent earthquakes, tidal waves and hurricanes, flooding and drought as has never been seen before. This is together with a movement of the solar corona, which might increase these calamities. Scientists should observe this unusual and complex solar irregularity . . . we too are being affected in some way. We don't want to play at being

saviours, announcing these events openly. You must be prudent
. . . and should communicate this information first to your
rulers. The moment will eventually come when we will have to
appear before the whole planet, but you have to carry out the
changes yourselves . . .

'When we left the building,' said Castillo, 'we saw some large,
half buried ducts in the seabed. Cyril informed us that they
were connected to young marine volcanoes, from which they
extracted enough heat to use in the buildings of the marine
complex. It occurred to me afterwards that the air conditioning incorporated this system . . . We had been almost
two hours in that amazing place.'[16]

'We learned that we were the first to go there,' Castillo
informed me. 'There was a time, in 1946–7, when the aliens
were about to take a civilian and a military person to that base
– I don't know which country they were from – but it was
because of the underwater atomic tests then being carried out
in the Bikini Atoll, when they were on full alert. In the end, it
wasn't necessary to take them, for reasons I am not aware of.'[17]
(In 1946–58 the USA carried out 23 atomic- and hydrogen-
bomb tests – some underwater – in the Bikini Atoll in the
Marshall Islands, West Pacific Ocean.)

Others claim to have been taken to similar submarine bases.
Included in *Alien Base* is the remarkable experience of
Orlando Jorge Ferraudi, who together with another Argentine
witness was transported to a base in the Gulf of Mexico in
1956. 'We saw an immense sub-aquatic dome, similar to a
giant Eskimo igloo,' he reported, 'where buildings, people and
several [space] ships similar to ours, could be seen.' Two other
such bases had been built, one off the Uruguayan coast at
Barra de San Juan, and the other in the Bahia
Samborombón.[18]

CONDITIONING?

Following his return to Caracas, Castillo continued to
wonder – as he still does – about the real purpose of his
contacts with the extraterrestrials. 'What role do we – the
contactees – play, in this confusing panorama?' he asks. 'I

still do not know. What about the other twenty-three? Why were no names and addresses exchanged?'[19] Indeed. If Castillo's seemingly apocryphal experiences at the Vortex and the Mariana Trench have any basis in physical reality, why has not one of those others come forward to support Castillo, who for so many years has endured much ridicule and vituperation? Cyril is reported to have stated that those contactees who had been 'evacuated' from Earth had been 'provided with a new conscience'. Is it possible that *all* the contactees were subjected to some type of conditioning process, affecting their actions following release from the Vortex? Taken at face value, this statement implies formidable means of mental manipulation. A simpler alternative, of course, is that no one has come forward because Castillo is deluded or lying.

WHAT'S IN A NAME?

Another stumbling block to acceptance of Castillo's story is the vexed question of the 'Pleiadians', 'Venusians', 'Mercurians' and a 'Jupiterian'. The list does not end there. 'I have seen others from Orion, Orton, Yamaru, Yonica, Yaraka and other places,' he declared in an earlier report.[20] The aliens' supposed names (e.g. 'Krishnamerck', 'Yamaruck', 'Baros', 'Rondby') also lend an equally farcical tone, effectively stalling serious appraisal of Castillo's claims. 'These *are* their real names,' he insisted to me in 2000. 'I always associated [some of them] with Hindu names.'

As discussed earlier, I do not believe these aliens originate in the solar systems nor on the planets they name. *If* Castillo has spoken truthfully, it is likely that the named origins are part of an alien programme of deception for their own, and possibly the contactees', security. As mentioned earlier, in *Alien Base* I recount what for me is one of the most convincing contact stories, that involving my friend 'Joëlle', who told me that the extraterrestrials with whom she had ongoing contacts in England refused to reveal their origin, although they did confirm that they had bases within our solar system, including a number on Earth. They also explained that they do not use names as do we.[21]

Rubens Villela, the Brazilian contactee, told me that the equally silly names of the aliens with whom he communicated ('Kandrix', 'Hendrix' and 'Sandrix') were 'mere codenames', used by the aliens for purposes of identification. 'We're dealing with "absurd" facts,' concedes Villela. 'Puzzles, enigmas, charades – that's what we're confronted with in this subject. Contradictions seem to be part of the game – the light might lie behind them . . . '[22] In any event, Castillo's first son born of his third wife, Gloria, was baptized 'Orhion Yamaruck', following Orhion's successful prediction of his birth date![23]

EMBARGO

Castillo insists that his experiences were real, in the accepted sense of the word. 'They are not the product of hallucination, astral travel, or any other type of paranormal phenomena,' he declares. 'They physically happened . . .' He also insists that he is neither a mystic nor a religious fanatic. 'Neither have I considered myself a "chosen one" to save humanity, and I detest those "contactees" who pretend to have been appointed by some divinity to carry some message to the suffering and almost disgraced human race.' The teachings and messages contained in his first book, he said in 1997, 'should be taken only as a warning about future events, which are predicted to take place between now and the year 2011'.[24]

Despite Castillo's castigation of those contactees who spread false messages and prophecies, it has to be said that many of his own messages and prophecies are equally apocryphal, redolent of the evangelical teachings on which he was brought up. A corollary, then, is that much of this material originates in his own subconscious mind. Castillo holds a different view:

The spiritual and messianic teachings, having a Christian flavor, seemed to me to be intended as a means of gauging the reactions of humans when faced with news of a serious, impacting, possible event at a planetary level, because our religious beliefs are so entrenched. I believe they purposely touched the point of [these] beliefs, to estimate the reactions at planetary level, should they disclose that humanity was not created as taught by the religions,

121

and show that all humanity will have to drastically change their values and actions in order to survive . . .[25]

In a paper discussing the avoidance by extraterrestrials of open contact with Earth, Professor James Deardorff speculates that an 'embargo' has been implemented, to forestall religious and other repercussions. Any extraterrestrial communications with Earth, he believes, would progress over a very long time period, perhaps two or three generations, 'and in a manner designed to reach people whose value systems can accept the message they are likely to deliver'.

> The messages might, moreover, contain vague descriptions of extraterrestrial technological achievements that would read like magic or science fiction. They might even contain a few absurdities purposely added; these, along with the absence of any detailed instructions on how to achieve any technological breakthroughs, would help ensure that any scientists who happened to learn about the communication would regard them as hoaxes or fiction . . . the messages could be expected to contain some spiritual, or at least ethical, aspects which might further deter scientific enquiry . . . Government agencies, upon advice from scientists, would then take no actions, and the embargo would more or less remain intact.[26]

ANOTHER REALITY

Tempting though it is to dismiss Enrique Castillo's story on the basis of the sometimes ludicrous origins and silly names given, as well as the apocryphal and apocalyptic messages, it may be prudent to suspend disbelief while other factors are taken into consideration.

It is quite possible that Castillo concocted his stories of meetings with aliens and trips in spacecraft. He freely admits that, following the first dramatic sighting in Costa Rica in 1963, he read everything (in Spanish) that he could get his hands on, thus in time he would have learned about the more famous contact and abduction stories, such as those by George Adamski, Daniel Fry, Antônio Villas Boas, Barney and Betty Hill, Travis Walton and Eduard 'Billy' Meier (who in the 1970s began promoting stories of his contacts with

'Pleiadians'). Although Castillo's subsequent claims include similarities to those stories, however, this itself neither validates nor invalidates his claims.

The question arises of interpolation in Castillo's narrative. Although he is reported to have a prodigious memory, there remains a strong likelihood that he filled in missing gaps when writing his books; particularly, I surmise, when reporting speeches (with the exception of the dictation by Cyril). On the other hand a number of contactees have told me that, when the time comes to write something down, they become imbued with a vivid recollection of the words, as if somehow under the influence of the source.

'I have never been able to have proofs for what I state,' Castillo told me in 2000. 'Now, after all these years, there are times when I feel quite stressed, wondering if it was all a dream or a figment of my imagination.'[27] Most probably his narrative is a mixture of truth and fiction. Whatever the case, he has provided us with a fascinating story and one which I believe contains important new insights.

'I have not the slightest doubt that the events described by Enrique actually took place,' declares Carlos Vilchez, a Costa Rican researcher who, together with his brother Ricardo, investigated Castillo's claims for many years. 'This does not mean that I believe, or have to believe, that what the extra-terrestrials told him is true . . . the information received should be doubted and questioned in most instances, be it messianic, apocalyptic, or scientific.'[28]

'Those of us who investigate the UFO phenomenon are always in danger of taking at face value what the contactees say,' warns the distinguished scholar and writer, Salvador Freixedo, a former Jesuit, in his Foreword to Castillo's first book.

With the UFOs, we must remain aware that we are bordering on another reality . . . where the governing patterns that command our mind are not the same . . . It is to be expected that contactees make this sort of mistake, because they may have been over-exposed to the vortex of the events, and their minds may have been manipulated to make them see what is not really there . . . I do believe that all that Enrique Castillo relates, actually happened to him [and] that regardless of the intensity with which he had lived his experiences, his remarkable intelligence, his impressive memory, and his professional training as an engineer, those experiences had made him suspect that beyond the witnessed events there might be something deeply mysterious and disquieting . . .[29]

NOTES
1 Castillo Rincón, Enrique, *UFOs: A Great New Dawn for Humanity*, pp. 113–15.
2 Ibid., pp. 115–17.
3 Ibid., pp. 118–19.
4 Good, Timothy, *Beyond Top Secret*, p. 532.
5 Castillo Rincón, op. cit., pp. 138–143.
6 Ibid., pp. 172–4.
7 Article by Fabio Zerpa, *Cuarta Dimensión*, (mid-1970s), translated by Wendelle C. Stevens.
8 Castillo Rincón, op. cit., pp. 174–5.
9 Ibid., pp.175–6, 183.
10 Ibid., p. 176.
11 Ibid., pp. 175–6.
12 Ibid., pp. 177–81.
13 Ibid., pp. 181–2.
14 Ibid., pp. 183–6.
15 Castillo Rincón, Enrique, *OVNI: Gran Alborada Humana* (Tomo II), 2000.
16 Castillo Rincón, Enrique, 'Un Sangri-La Submarino', 24 January 2000, translated by Margaret Barling.
17 Letter to the author, 8 February 2000, translated by Margaret Barling.
18 Good, Timothy, *Alien Base*, 1998, pp. 223–8.
19 Castillo Rincón, *UFOs: A Great New Dawn for Humanity*, p. 187.
20 Zerpa, op. cit.
21 Good, *Alien Base*, pp. 248–56.
22 Letters to the author, November–December 1999.
23 Castillo Rincón, *UFOs: A Great New Dawn for Humanity*, p. 173.
24 Ibid., pp. xiii–xiv.
25 Ibid. p. 140.
26 Deardorff, Dr James, 'Possible Extraterrestrial Strategy for Earth', *Alien Update*, ed. Timothy Good, Arrow, London, 1993, pp. 151–63; first published in *Quarterly Journal of the Royal Astronomical Society* (27/1986), London.
27 Letter to the author from Enrique Castillo Rincón, 8 February 2000.
28 Castillo Rincón, op. cit., p. 249.
29 Ibid., pp. ix–xi.

Chapter 7

An Atrophied Culture

At 03.30 on 5 February 1978 Julio Fernández, a 30-year-old Spanish family businessman, set off by car with his dog Mus, an English pointer, to go hare-hunting in an area due west of Madrid, near the town of Casavieja, in the province of Avila. For some unaccountable reason he took a road that led in the opposite direction, heading north-eastwards along the Barcelona road towards the province of Soria. And thereby hangs the tale. Thenceforth, Fernández's journey became surreal.

At about 04.30 Julio stopped to drink coffee and an anis at a wayside bar known as the Hostal 113, beside the highway on the outskirts of Algora, near Guadalajara. A strange waiter served. He was tall and fair, wearing rubber gloves and what looked like a wig! During the 20-minute stop, no other customers came into the bar – unusual even for that time of night. Also, a smell of pine pervaded the establishment, which Julio assumed to be a detergent. Subsequent checks showed, however, that the Hostal 113 had not been open at the time and no one matching Julio's description of the waiter worked there. Some would adduce the scenario described as a 'screen memory' planted by the aliens.

At 05.45 Julio left the bar and drove on, half an hour later passing Medinaceli. Suddenly, he 'knew' that he had to be at a certain location 15 kilometres further on, and put his foot down on the accelerator. At that point his conscious recollection stopped.[1] What follows is a synopsis of a lengthy, richly detailed story, which emerged from over a year of hypnotic regressions conducted by José Luis Jordán Peña, a psychologist, Ana Mozo, a hypnotist, and Dr Jesús Durán, a psychiatrist specializing in clinical hypnosis, all of whom were impressed by Julio's sincerity and the authenticity of his story. I have based my synopsis of this – one of the best-investigated yet paradoxically one of the least-known cases – on the definitive report by Antonio Ribera, the distinguished Spanish investigator and author, translated by Gordon Creighton, with some amendments provided for me by Ribera.

QUASI-HUMAN BEINGS

According to Julio's recollections, he was driving his car (a Seat 127) down the road when for no accountable reason he suddenly braked. From this point on the car seemed to act of its own accord, reversing, then coming to a halt after having entered backwards a narrow dirt trail which started at the right side of the main road.[2] Then the engine stopped, the lights went out and the radio-cassette player ceased to work (Julio had been listening to a tape of the singer, Jorge Cafrune). It was as though the electrical current had been completely severed: the new battery no longer charged and the plugs no longer sparked properly. Mus growled so, as a precaution, Julio took his Winchester single-barrel, semi-automatic shotgun out of the boot and loaded it with its maximum of five cartridges. It was then that he caught sight of two quasi-human beings coming down the track, finally halting only one and a half metres from him. As Ribera reports:

> They wore seamless one-piece pastel-green overalls that reached to the feet [and] gave off a very faint luminosity [with] no zip-fasteners nor openings and gathered at the waists . . . The overall was sufficiently tight-fitting for their muscles to show . . . No fibres, no thread, and no designs were to be detected in it. The material was smooth and did not rustle when it moved. Their heads and shoulders were covered by [pale] yellow cowls or hoods, leaving only the face uncovered . . . Their hoods, like their [five-fingered] gloves . . . were made of a texture resembling satin-stitch, very fine and fitting the parts of the body closely.

The 'men' had extremely broad shoulders, with powerful dorsal muscles showing prominently, narrow waists, and they seemed athletic. Among features that set them apart from ordinary human beings were the exceptionally long arms and hands, large crania and very large eyes. Julio felt a sense of peace and calm envelop him – a sensation reported in other cases. When they addressed him he at first thought they were using speech, but later, realizing that their lips did not move, he assumed they communicated mentally with him. They 'asked' him to calm down and to follow them. Julio obeyed, taking along his dog and the gun. The aliens walked with a majestic, elegant and rhythmical gait.[3]

THE GREAT DISC

'It was a bit like Karl Marx beholding God,' Julio explained to one of the investigators, describing his reactions on seeing the aliens' craft. 'I, who had been a sceptic till then, now found myself at 70 metres from an extraterrestrial craft.'

The huge craft had been concealed behind two hillocks in the bottom of a small valley, though hovering four metres above ground. It was an awesome sight. Shaped like an inverted soup plate, of a matt, silvery, metallic colour, it appeared to have a diameter of about 60 or 70 metres and a height of some 15 to 20 metres (Plate 11), from the lowest part to the top of its dome (cupola).

Where the cupola joined the great disc he observed what seemed to be a ring about 15 metres wide which was emitting flashes of light of different colours, always in an unbroken sequence of blue, green, red and yellow. The ring gave the impression that it was rotating from right to left (counter-clockwise) but this was a false optical effect . . . Up above, almost at the top of the cupola, he observed a series of dark, vertical rectangles, which eventually proved to be the windows of the control cabin.

Temporarily ignoring Julio, who had paused to take in the breathtaking sight, the occupants pressed ahead so that he had to run to catch up. Arriving underneath the central area of the craft, Julio noticed its completely smooth surface, as though moulded in one piece, with no rivets or fittings. At this point, he became aware of a powerful odour of pine, or possibly ozone, a smell also detectable on board. Julio's gun and knife 'levitated' upwards into the craft.

A smooth, metallic cylinder then emerged silently from the centre of the disc, stopping just above the ground. It was about four metres in height and 2.5 metres in diameter. A door, sliding upwards, opened in the descended cylinder's wall, revealing a small compartment lit by a strange light, 'coming from everywhere', of an absolutely pure whiteness which Julio found thoroughly disturbing, although it did not hurt his eyes. By now frightened, he hesitated before stepping through the door into the shaft. He found himself in a cylindrical compartment, the walls of which were of the same finish as the exterior, while the ceiling looked like burnished glass or plastic. So reluctant was the dog to follow its master that Julio had to drag him in. What was now an interior elevator rose silently, stopping at an entrance to a corridor, where the party alighted (Plate 13). Further along was another corridor, with two metallic doors, about 2.5 metres high.

> These doors were very finely fashioned, and he could see no hinges, handles, or latches on them. The whole appearance of the place was the most clinically aseptic that could be imagined . . . There were no internal angles. The walls were continuous with the ceiling, being joined by a gentle curve.
>
> Continuing along the circular passage, he suddenly came to a small ladder . . . it did not seem to him logical that people with a technology capable of keeping a craft floating weightless four metres off the ground should require a ladder in order to pass from one level to another!

As Antonio Ribera points out, this apparent anachronism turns up in other close-encounter and abduction cases (examples of which are cited in my book *Alien Base*). 'In our own Space Age technology,' explains Ribera, 'we too have "antiquated" gadgets still co-existing beside the most sophisticated advances of our Science.'

The ladder looked like the steps of a swimming pool, with a very shiny finish and a cylindrical handrail. The semi-cylindrical steps were set at intervals of about 40 centimetres. One of Julio's hosts led the way, scaling the steps in two jumps with phenomenal agility. With some difficulty, carrying the dog under his right arm and with the gun over his shoulder, Julio followed. He noticed that the railing felt exceptionally cold, a singularity also reported by the American policeman, Herbert Schirmer, during an abduction aboard a craft in Ashland, Nebraska, in 1967.[4] At the top of the ladder, which led up to a room through a circular hole, was another individual who, like the others, assured Julio that he had nothing to worry about. Again, it was the odd interior lighting which caught Julio's attention.

> There was not the slightest bit of shadow. All colours could be seen evenly. It was a white, bright, pure world . . . where there was no darkness and where, when you looked at someone's skin, you could count the very pores themselves . . . It inspired a feeling of peacefulness, though in this the structure of the room played a part too.

'One might here postulate,' wrote Ribera, 'the existence of a technology based upon molecular excitation and producing a uniform luminescence possessing no points of origin.'

THE FLIGHT DECK

The 'flight deck', as it turned out to be, was about 15 metres wide and five metres high (Plate 12). Interestingly, unlike Julio's shoes and the claws of his dog, the steps of the crew members made no noise on the floor; again, a curiosity noted in other such cases. In the centre of the flight deck stood a kind of console, the description of which correlates well with the little-known 1951 South African contact case involving a British engineer[5] and that of some other contact accounts. In shape it was like a desk or a bureau, Julio reported. 'It also had some resemblance to an electronic organ. It was about 2.5m wide and, standing on it, set in metal footings, was a transparent glass screen. The control-table itself was standing upon a circular platform of the same white material as the rest of the floor.'

Elsewhere on the flight deck stood three other, smaller consoles, about one and a half metres wide, set around the circumference of the room, in front of which were strange, high, conical seats, with the pointed part towards the bottom.

(Herbert Schirmer reported two triangular-backed seats set in front of a console and a large visiscreen for exterior viewing standing on top.) Also set close to the surrounding wall was a large, square panel, about four metres square, leaden greyish in colour, and a rectangular table of a metallic, blackish-blue sheen. Set around the dome at intervals of about one and a half metres were rectangular windows made out of what to Julio looked like smoked glass, but through which he observed the countryside perfectly, in colour, even though dawn had just arrived.

PHYSICAL EXAMINATIONS

Meanwhile, Mus had been around the flight deck, sniffing at everything, including at least one of the aliens, who reacted in a surprised manner. Concerned lest his dog should urinate, Julio called him to heel. 'The sound of the name "Mus" evoked great surprise among the entities,' Ribera continues in his report, 'all three turning around with a faint expression of amazement on their poker faces. The vocal means of communication cannot have seemed strange to them, because Julio discovered in due course that they themselves used speech sometimes. [It was] as though this particular sound may possibly have had some meaning in their own language or was somehow familiar to them.'

On asking where his hosts originated, Julio received an unintelligible mental response, including the expression 'three, seven, squared'. After this the aliens indicated that they would like to examine the dog and take blood samples from him. Julio agreed. Mus was carried to the rectangular table and blood from his paw was precisely, carefully extracted with a fairly normal-looking syringe of about 10 cc capacity (Julio had received veterinary training for three years). The men then communicated to Julio that they wanted to examine him and placed him behind the screen on the rectangular table. After a few minutes he was given to understand that was all to be required of him.[6] But in subsequent recollections – which proved harder to recover and which clearly he found very disturbing – Julio said that numerous samples had been extracted from him, including blood, semen, urine, cerebro-spinal fluid, synovia (a viscous fluid lubricating joints and tendon sheaths), saliva, and gastric and intestinal juices. He believed that two women, similar facially to the men, were on board at the time.[7]

CENTRAL CONTROL

Politely ordered to sit on one of the seats at the central console, Julio did so. He expected the conical seat to collapse, because the tapered end was inserted in the floor, but it seemed solid, rocking a bit. The seat itself was square, while the armrests had rounded edges. Next to Julio sat one of the crew members who, having raised the left armrest, nimbly fingered several silvery buttons. The seat began to revolve along a track in the floor. The crew member's long arms reached easily to the controls on the central console. 'He was fingering the buttons and moving the switches with a speed and an assurance that were simply marvellous . . . all without looking,' Ribera relates. 'He put Julio in mind of a first-class typist, from the speed and precision with which his long, fine fingers darted to and fro, the actual palm of the hand remaining meanwhile motionless.'

At the sides were nine levers, set on each side in three rows, which were black and delicately shaped, terminating in what looked like nickel-plated handles. 'Above them on each side were nine truncated cone-shaped red buttons . . . with a central depression. The automatic pilots [so assumed by Julio] were hemispherical, about 2 cms in diameter, and seemed to be flashing continuously . . . changing colour in sequence.'

CRISIS MANAGEMENT

Julio continued to sit beside the crew member, his dog and gun at his side. Suddenly, a brief, piercing whistle was heard, producing a commotion on the flight deck. The tallest of the three crew members quickly headed toward one of the console units and all three studied the remote viewing screens in front of them. An image appeared on the screens of an older-looking man. At this point the crew members began talking among themselves, their telepathy with Julio interrupted. The man on the screen, who seemed to be a superior, spoke first, then the others conversed with him. The language sounded harsh to Julio: later he described it as if it were a mixture of German and Korean. As Ribera reports:

> They seemed to 'spit out' the words as they were talking, and some of the sounds were like coughs. They never modulated their speech; the words seemed to come up out of their stomachs [and] did not seem to be produced by the vocal cords but to be thrown out by the diaphragm [and] from time to time they emitted a little cry as though they were choking. Among the sounds that Julio recalled under hypnosis there were many strong consonants, Ks and Rs and Ps, all pronounced very harshly [and] also many vowels and diphthongs, like AU or UE, which sounded just like outright barking.

The image disappeared from the viewing screen. Julio found himself back in telepathic communication with his hosts. Hectic activity ensued, as crew members started desperately pushing buttons. The central platform began to rotate anticlockwise, halting when the control console came in line with what Julio assumed was a 'computer'. Another whistling sound could be heard, from which point Julio seems to have 'blanked out' and it could have been that the postulated second physical examination, described earlier, took place at this point. The reason for the crisis was not communicated to Julio. The next event he initially recalled was another piercing whistle, followed by a brief reappearance of the superior's image on the screen.

MISGIVINGS

The crew members showed interest in Julio's gun and, passing it around among themselves, asked him about its use. He explained that he used it for hunting animals.

'Do you hunt because you need to?' they enquired.

'No, because I enjoy it,' he replied. At this, the tallest of the three made a gesture of disgust. Julio, who of course had unloaded his gun, showed them two of his cartridges, opening one of them to display its contents. They asked if they could keep the cartridges and deposited them into a metal cylinder.

A heavy smoker, Julio lit a cigarette. The men asked if they might take one away for study and deposited it into the same cylinder. Julio then was asked how Earth society functioned. 'He told them that there are two ideological blocs here, and explained about our systems of government,' Ribera reports.

He was amazed that people so well informed and so intelligent as they were should ask such simple questions. They obviously knew their way about in external matters and so must surely know, if not everything, at least almost everything about us! As a matter of fact his admiration for them began to abate somewhat at this point, and meanwhile he was starting to have some misgivings about them. He did not know whether they were perhaps 'taking the mickey out of him', or what they were up to.

DEPARTURE

Julio was escorted to the lift cylinder, the metal door rose and he was back outside, in bright sunlight. He staggered back to his car, where Mus, immediately bolting from the cylinder, awaited him. Julio assumed that he must have just awoken from a very vivid dream, but on checking Mus he was bothered to notice what looked like a needle mark on one of his paws. The car engine now worked and Julio headed directly back to Madrid, without bothering to look for the great disc. At about 13.00 he pulled to the side of the road a few kilometres from Torremocha del Campo, Guadalajara. To bring himself back to reality he did some hunting, managing to take home over a dozen quail. According to Julio's later recollections, it seems that he may have returned to the craft for another 'trip' prior to this, although details could not be recovered.[8]

PHYSIOGNOMY

Julio's hypnotically induced recollections are rich in data, particularly those relating to the physiognomy of the cosmonauts. As Antonio Ribera relates:

The extremely long hands looked ... feeble and bony, very fragile, like the hands of pianists. Their immensely long, fine fingers [were] thin and knotted – there was nothing but tendon and bone to be seen beneath the skin [and] their fingernails were short and clean and normal . . . Their heads were also different from the human head. The forehead went straight up for a good distance and then into a great high curve; it protruded more than our foreheads do, and was also much bigger. One of their most typical features was a prominence over the eyes, very massive . . . As for the area of the temples, the entities had the parietal bones very much developed, their size and degree of convexity being considerable, the head almost a huge globe. He likewise observed no ears, these being presumably covered by the hoods. [There were] no eyebrows, eyelashes, or traces of beard or hair.

The face was 'bony', with a long, thin nose and high cheekbones. The mouth showed as a mere streak, likewise very thin, in place of lips. Among outstanding features was the 'cone-shaped' chin, described as 'enormous, projecting outwards and downwards and ending in a point'[9] (Plate 10). Interestingly, in the 1960s the contactee George Adamski revealed to my friend Lou Zinsstag a photograph in profile of 'Orthon', the spaceman he claims to have met first in the Californian desert in 1952, showing a long and thin nose – and a markedly pointed chin.

In her commentary on the physiognomy of the extraterrestrials allegedly encountered by Julio Fernández, Dr María Teresa Pérez Alvarez hypothesizes that the longer the chin, the more developed the race. 'The chin is in fact a relatively recent addition,' she comments, 'even in Neanderthal Man . . . the chin was small. The chin appears in fact to have a relationship with man's erect posture, and its development, it seems, helps to confer on him his sense of *directionality*. In the present case of Julio's entities, it could be, as it were, a sort of counter-balance, to offset the tremendous volume of the cranium, although this of course is only a hypothesis.'

Dr Pérez also comments that the size of the aliens' crania suggests more than five times the cranial capacity of *Homo sapiens*, indicating very high development.[10]

The eyes of the cosmonauts, said Julio, were quite unforgettable, 'like two huge beacons projecting from the face'. As Ribera reports: 'The eyelids were oval in contour and did not terminate in an angle or a fold, as they do in humans.

The iris, gigantic, was double the size of the normal iris of a human eye, and was of a pale blue, almost transparent, shade. The pupil seemed to be extremely dilated, and this gave them a hypnotic gaze as though in a kind of permanent state of fright or shock (though – paradoxically – it had a tranquillizing effect).'

The skin colour of the aliens was extremely bluish-white, typical of those who seldom go out in the sun, giving them a 'Nordic' caste. Julio believed that they had superior night vision to us, owing to their ability to walk so rapidly and gracefully in the dark, forcing him to take an average of one and a half strides to their one.[11]

The extreme dilation of the eyes, says Dr Pérez, suggests 'a habitat where the light is soft and mellow, or simply does not hurt the eyes, and this fits in again with the reported absence of any eye-lashes, the function of which is to serve as shades or awnings, and it fits in too with the low amount of pigmentation in the iris, and also with the parchment-like colour of the skin'.[12]

A PERFECT WITNESS?

Regrettably, I never met Julio Fernández. He was killed in a car crash in 1992, coincidentally near the site where he claimed to have been abducted. The police report states that he was already dead when his car crashed,[13] so presumably he suffered a fatal heart attack. He had led an interesting life, as a keen sportsman, a Tae Kwon Do black belt, a photographer, mountaineer, explorer and, of course, as a hunter – his main passion. Until his abduction experience he held no interest in UFOs or parapsychology. As to the validity of his story, Antonio Ribera points out that the psychological tests carried out on Julio by the reputable experts revealed:

an IQ higher than normal, together with a very well-balanced personality, perfectly integrated and without a trace of the psychopathic. Julio is not a mental defective nor a concoctor of tales nor a mythomaniac. On the contrary. He is a very realistic person, very objective, and, above all, incapable of lying. Such were the results revealed by the psychometric tests carried out on Julio by the meticulous and sceptically minded Jordán Peña, who in the course of his professional duties has done hundreds and hundreds of psychometric laboratory tests of this kind and whom it would be impossible to deceive. And this goes for the hypnotist, Dr Jesús Durán, who did not believe in the existence of UFOs until he met Julio.[14]

Not once was any contradiction found in any of the numerous statements given by Julio under hypnosis.[15] The investigators sensed, therefore, that Julio was describing real events. And to Julio the aliens were palpably real; they were neither robots nor were they projected images. With sunglasses and beards, he believed, they should pass as natives of Scandinavian countries.[16]

AN ATROPHIED CULTURE

Among the interesting items of information imparted telepathically to Julio by the cosmonauts, both during *and* after his alleged abduction, was that other, shorter beings were coming here who were less evolved ethically. These others, it was explained, 'are engaged in probing and "programming" the minds of those humans whom they have contacted or kidnapped . . . And relations between the two groups of visitors are not precisely of the best.' Yet again, a conflict of interests among alien species regarding Earth is indicated.

Asked by Julio why the cosmonauts did not seek out eminent scientists of Earth with whom to establish these strange relations, they responded that the greatest of our scientists 'does not come up to the level . . . of their most modest technicians'. What they are seeking are the 'warm human qualities' that have atrophied in their race which evidently have been lost 'throughout the course of the centuries of a harsh and difficult self-imposed evolution, in a cold and hostile environment'.[17] 'They didn't have a Beethoven' was how Julio expressed it. 'In us,' believes Ribera, author of several books on the subject of aliens,[18] 'they see – and they admire – what they had centuries ago and what they have now irremediably lost . . . they are superb biological machines, frigid and perfect, but robotized, retaining merely an archaic sense of humour as a relic of their lost humanity.'[19]

A corollary, then, if we compare a typical abduction scenario, is that Julio was contacted specifically for the purpose of 'humanization' of the aliens. If so, he is not alone. Ed Walters, for example, is one of a number of abductees who claim that aliens (of the shorter, bug-eyed species, at least) are also fascinated by human emotions. He says that during an abduction they clamped a headset on him, then stimulated his memories so that the various emotions engendered could be transferred directly to the creatures.[20]

Assuming some validity to these accounts, I do not discount the likelihood that Earth is being exploited for its human – as well as other – resources.

'Your world is marvellous,' Julio was informed by the cosmonauts. 'Its biological richness is unbelievable. There are very few worlds like it. We ourselves don't know of a single other one like it. It is a veritable mine, a well-nigh inexhaustible mine of many of the things that we need, and that we do not have: water for one. Unfortunately you yourselves have already begun the process of destruction of this world. It is a story that has been repeated on many other occasions: it happened in our own world once, centuries ago . . .'[21]

NOTES

1 Ribera, Antonio, 'The Soria Abduction: or – The Hunter Hunted: Part I', *Flying Saucer Review*, vol. 30, no. 3, May–June 1984, pp. 7, 8–9, translated by Gordon Creighton.

2 Letter to the author, 20 April 1999.

3 Ribera, op. cit., pp. 9–11.

4 Good, Timothy, *Alien Base*, pp. 271–3, 402.

5 Ibid., pp. 90–7.

6 Ribera, 'The Soria Abduction: Part II', *Flying Saucer Review*, vol. 30, no. 4, July–August 1984, pp. 2–10.

7 Ribera, 'The Soria Abduction: Part III', *Flying Saucer Review*, vol. 30, no. 5, September–October 1984, pp. 2–8.

8 'The Soria Abduction: Part II', pp. 7–10.

9 'The Soria Abduction: Part I', pp. 10–11.

10 Pérez Alvarez, Dr María Teresa, 'Some Anatomical and Morphological Conclusions from the case of Julio F—', in 'The Soria Abduction: Part III', pp. 4–5.

11 'The Soria Abduction: Part I', p. 11.

12 Pérez Alvarez, op. cit., p. 5.

13 Letter to the author, 15 August 1998.

14 'The Soria Abduction: Part I', p. 8.

15 Ibid., p. 7.

16 Ibid., p. 11.

17 'The Soria Abduction: Part III', pp. 6–7.

18 See, for example, *Secuestrados Por Extraterrestres* (1981) and *Encuentros Con Humanoides* (1982), published by Planeta, Barcelona, and *Abducción* (1998), Ediciones del Bronce, Barcelona, which contains a chapter on the Julio Fernández case.

19 'The Soria Abduction: Part III', p. 6.

20 Walters, Ed, and Walters, Frances, *UFO Abductions in Gulf Breeze*, Avon Books, New York, 1994.

21 'The Soria Abduction: Part III', p. 7.

Chapter 8

The Creature of Pretare

MOULDED 'MARTIAN' PHOTOGRAPH DENOUNCED BY THE CARABINIERI

He moulded in clay a 70cm-tall 'Martian' with the miserable appearance of a foetus, quite scary and with three-fingered hands, showing a photograph of it all over the place, causing alarm among the inhabitants of Arquata del Tronto (Ascoli Piceno) and arousing the curiosity of the press and TV. But the brief moment of glory for Filiberto Caponi, aged 23, and a resident of the small district of Arquata del Tronto, has come to an end, with a charge of spreading false rumours and disturbing the public peace. The Carabinieri worried about the unusual consequences, from telephone calls in the night by people frightened by a strange animal's noises and especially about the invasion of journalists trying to find traces of the material used by Caponi for sculpting the puppet, or other evidence of what might have been a miraculous Polaroid photo of the 'Martian' caught walking in the streets of Pretare. Filiberto, interviewed by *Visto* and *I Fatti Vostri* and already contacted by numerous journalists from abroad, has been charged under Article 656, and is risking up to three months in jail or a fine. It seems that he has confessed the truth to the Carabinieri, yet he is still going around stating that he really did see a 'Martian' . . .

Thus stated the Italian National Press Agency (ANSA) in its news release of 9 November 1993. The story, which caused a stir in Italy although not elsewhere, was soon dismissed as a hoax and forgotten. But not by those involved.

In November 1993 my friend Bruce Renton, a reporter who had written for *The Economist* and *Il Messaggero*, among others, telephoned me from Rome, where he lived, to tell me that he had watched a television talk show on the channel

RAI-2 called *I Fatti Vostri* (Your Affairs), in which one Filiberto Caponi, together with his father and grandmother, were interviewed by the famous television personality, Giancarlo Magalli. Excitedly, Bruce informed me that a series of six colour Polaroid photographs had been shown, some clearly depicting what appeared to be a bizarre creature of origin unknown, photos taken by Filiberto outside the family home in Pretare di Arquata del Tronto between May and October 1993. Suspecting a hoax, I asked Bruce for his opinion. He replied that the photos looked genuine and that the family seemed sincere. 'I think you should come over and meet them,' he added. 'I'd be glad to make arrangements and act as interpreter.'

A luncheon meeting was arranged for 3 February 1994, at the Foreign Press Association in Rome. Filiberto was accompanied by his father, Bruce by Jasmin Sagna, a photo-journalist. After that memorable first occasion, I had further meetings with Filiberto and his family in Italy. What follows is taken directly from Filiberto's own account of this amazing case, which I asked him to write, translated by Bruce Renton (who died in 1998) and his daughter Yasmin, and from my own extensive research, including interviews and corre-spondence with Filiberto conducted between 1994 and 1999. In my view not only is this an important case, it is also one from which much can be learned; not least about the reaction of a small community to reports of an alien being in its midst.

FIRST ENCOUNTER

Filiberto Caponi is a professional painter and ceramics artesan who lives with his family in Pretare di Arquata del Tronto, a charming village in central Italy in the province of Ascoli Piceno, resting on the slopes of Monte Vettore, a mountain in the Apennines range which rises to some 2000 metres. The story begins on the night of 9 May 1993.

'It was about 11.30 p.m. and I was returning home by car from a nearby village,' said Filiberto.

As I was about to park the car in the garage I heard a very strange cry. At the time I did not attach particular importance to what I heard, even though in a village like Pretare the usual silence of the night is often broken by the cries of nocturnal animals, or by cats and dogs in the surrounding countryside. I got out of the car to open the door of the garage.

Once outside the car, the sound became clearer. It seemed not to belong to any usual animal. I had parked the car in the garage and was closing the shutter door when I was literally overwhelmed by that cry or 'lament', which was getting closer and sounding very strange. On the road in front of me there was little light though enough to establish that nothing was there. My curiosity aroused, I decided to walk further down the road.

The further I walked the louder became the cry, until I came to the corner which stood between the wall on my right and a house where the dim light of a street lamp created a dark corner. There I noticed a whitish, spherical shape. The cry came from that very spot. My first thought was that it was probably an animal trapped inside a small bag and that its cry sounded so strange because it was distorted by the echo which can be caused by an enclosed space, for example in a plastic bag. I decided to set free whatever creature was trapped in there.

I stretched out my arms towards this spherical shape, though as a precaution I decided first to give it a gentle push with my foot, fearing that the animal could either bite or scratch me. It was at that instant that my life changed completely. The moment I touched it, the 'bag' leapt up into the air, emitting a terrifying scream. I was dumbfounded. What had seemed to be a small ball had suddenly leapt up and stretched itself like an elastic band. It jumped so vigorously that a small rock set in the ground beside it rolled away. I feared that the 'thing' would fall over me so all I could do was move back a little, keeping my eyes fixed on the creature, which fell back on the ground and ran down the road at an alarming speed.

Though it had its back to me, I discerned a humanoid shape, in the sense that I noticed a head, small arms, and long legs – from which hung white bandages – and the soles of its feet. The creature's back was curved and on it was a strange brownish bundle which seemed to deflate. There was no hair on the head, which seemed to have stains on it that made it look spotted. It moved rapidly, oscillating swiftly from one side to the other. It thrust its legs forward and its short arms hung by its side as though atrophied. It ran headlong into a stone wall, as if it couldn't stop. After the impact, it got up, relying solely on its legs, jumped over the wall, screaming, and disappeared into the countryside. I was left standing there, incredulous and frightened by all that had

PLATE 1 Edgar D. Mitchell, Apollo 14 lunar module pilot and the sixth man to walk on the Moon. Via his contacts in the military and intelligence community, Dr Mitchell has learned that the US Government has covered up the truth about UFOs for over 50 years. (*NASA*)

PLATE 2 Taken from an aircraft 10,000 feet above Lake Cote, Costa Rica, on 4 September 1971 during a cartographic survey by the National Geographic Institute, this enlargement (original format shown in box) shows what appears to be a metallic disc that had just left, or was on the point of entering, the lake. Scientific studies ruled out conventional explanations. (*Collection B. Thouanel*)

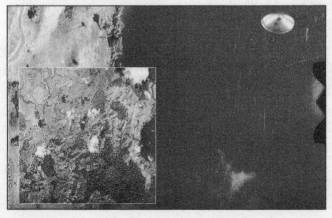

PLATE 3 Captain Graham Sheppard on the flight deck of a British Airways Boeing 757 ('City of Lisbon') on a scheduled flight from London to Milan, September 1992. (© *Timothy Good*)

PLATE 4 Sheppard beside the Cessna 172 in which he became mysteriously displaced during a flight from San Juan to Mayagüez, Puerto Rico, in March 1993. (© *Timothy Good*)

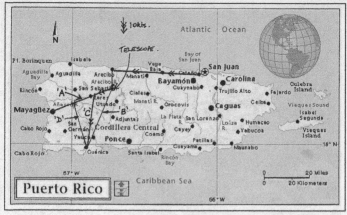

Track 'A'	Flight Plan
Track 'B'	45 degree track error – unlikely
Track 'C'	60 degree track error – probable
Track 'D'	90 degree track error – unlikely

PLATE 5 A map of Puerto Rico annotated by Sheppard to show the probable track of the Cessna during its unexplained 'lateral displacement'.
(© *GeoSystems Global Corporation*)

PLATE 6 An aerial view of the Sierra Bermeja, Puerto Rico, looking south-west. Sheppard was flying several miles to the east of this position when he realised he was unaccountably over the south coast instead of the west coast.
(© *Timothy Good*)

PLATE 7 An aerial photograph taken in 1998 of the US Air Force Tethered Aerostat Radar Site at Lajas, south-west Puerto Rico. (© *Timothy Good*)

PLATE 8 (*Below left*) Enrique Castillo Rincón, the Costa Rican engineer who claims extensive contacts with extraterrestrials, including flights in spacecraft and visits to alien bases in South America and the Pacific Ocean.

PLATE 9 (*Below right*) Rubens J. Villela, the Brazilian meteorologist, explorer and former CIA communications-monitoring specialist. Villela was one of many witnesses to a UFO sighting in Antarctica in 1961. Years later, he had further sightings and claims to have communicated with extraterrestrial beings.

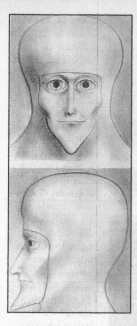

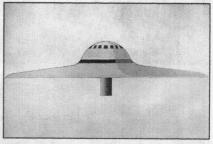

PLATE 10 (*Left*) Drawings of one of the humanoids encountered by Julio Fernández in the province of Soria, Spain, in February 1978. (*Maite Álvarez López*)

PLATE 11 (*Below*) The craft in which Fernández claims to have been taken aboard. He estimated its diameter at between 60 and 70 metres.

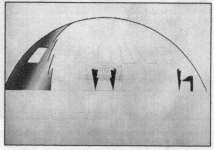

PLATE 12 The flight deck, about 15 metres wide and 5 metres high, with a console, viewing screen and bizarre conical seats.

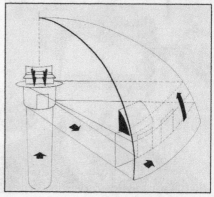

PLATE 13 Arrows show the direction taken by Fernández and the humanoids when boarding the craft via a circular elevator, which led to the lower deck then flight deck.

PLATE 14 The Caponi family home in Pretare di Arquato del Tronto, Ascoli Piceno, Italy, outside which Filiberto Caponi took six photographs of an unknown creature between May and October 1993 (see plates 17 to 22). (© *Timothy Good*)

PLATE 15 Antonia Perla, Filiberto Caponi's grandmother, who was present when Caponi photographed the creature on 9 October 1993. (© *Timothy Good*)

PLATE 16 Filiberto Caponi, Rome, January 1999. (© *Timothy Good*)

PLATES 17 & 18 The first two photographs of the creature (Photos 1 and 2), taken by Filiberto Caponi on the night of 23/24 May 1993. 'The first photograph was not clear because of distance and darkness,' Caponi explained. 'The second one portrayed a creature in the act of walking, with its right limb raised.' Overnight, the Polaroid prints mysteriously transformed, 'creating a kind of bas-relief, as if the flat figure had transformed itself into a three-dimensional one.' The thin bands of bluish light around the raised images are reflections created when the author made these first-generation copies: they do not appear on the original prints. (© *Filiberto Caponi*)

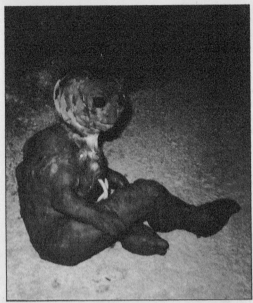

PLATES 19 & 20
These two remarkably detailed pictures (Photos 4 and 5 – enlarged) were taken on the night of 19/20 August 1993. 'This time there were no bandages on its legs [and] from the sternum emerged the two inexplicable tubes...I had the impression it was suffering, because the skin seemed to be entirely burned.' Moments after taking the first photograph, Caponi moved to his left and took a second one, as the creature remained motionless.
(© *Filiberto Caponi*)

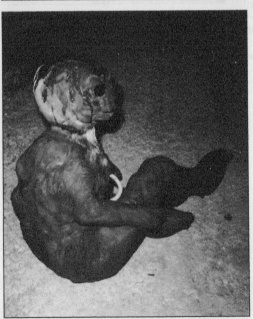

happened. I stood there for about 10 minutes, staring at the wall, then went back to the car to drive around for a while, listening to some music in the hope that it might help me to recover.

My head was full of all kinds of theories to explain what I had seen. It might have been a monkey, a clown on the run from a nearby circus, an animal escaped from a laboratory, or a dwarf. As I continued listening to the music, absurdly pretending nothing had happened, those images kept coming back to me, perhaps a normal reaction in someone who cannot rationalize what they have seen. After 15 minutes, I decided to drive home. I was afraid the creature would suddenly jump out of the darkness, but nothing happened. I wondered if it was terrified of me, considering the way it had run off. I tried to identify with it, thinking that it was having the same thoughts as I was, which meant we were both frightened by the encounter. Perhaps it was I who was the strange creature of the night!

Although it was late, Filiberto knew that someone in the family would be awake. His mother, Domenica, opened the door.

I tried to look as normal as possible, but as soon as I walked in she noticed that I looked quite pale and that my voice trembled. My mother knows when I am concealing something. She asked if my pallor was due to a car accident, but I tried to reassure her that it was only the cold which had affected me. Except for my grandmother (Antonia Perla), all the others were awake: my father (Luciano), my sister Antonella, and my brother-in-law Giuseppe. They all began to notice my trembling voice and goose pimples. I was so bombarded with questions that I finally decided to tell them a little of what had happened.

I tried to play down the story, saying that I was frightened only because an animal had darted across the road while I was driving. Everyone seemed satisfied with my explanation – except my mother. Seeing her still worried, I decided to tell them what had really happened. My mother was the only one willing to believe me. The others tried to convince me that it was just a trick of the light or my imagination. To prove the point, Father took a torch and asked me to accompany him to the place where I had seen the creature. While I was inspecting the wall over which it had jumped, Father stood in the corner between the wall and the house, staring at something on the ground. He bade me to come over.

When I came to the spot, I noticed a white bandage on the ground, soaked in a reddish substance which looked like blood. Father asked if this could be part of the bandage in which its legs had been wrapped. It looked like an ordinary medical bandage, the kind used for first aid. We decided that the next morning we would go into town and take it to a medical laboratory for analysis. We wanted to be certain about the composition of that reddish substance and so track down its origin. Fearing an infection, we avoided picking it up with our hands and used a little stick. We decided not to bring it into the house and as a precaution inserted it under an old washing machine that had been left against the wall of a neighbouring house.

SECOND ENCOUNTER

Filiberto was unable to sleep that night, the image of the creature haunting him. Suddenly, at around 04.00, he heard the scream again.

> I jumped out of bed, opened the door and ran out, shouting that the creature had come back. I could hear its hurried footsteps on the cobbles as the scream moved away in the distance. I started running to try and catch a glimpse of 'him', but it was useless. It was now 04.15 and I wondered what I was doing in the middle of the street, in my pyjamas, chasing 'nothing'!
>
> In the meantime, my father had been looking out of the window and had seen me in this state. He called me back, saying that he'd heard the scream but had seen nothing. So we stationed ourselves at my parents' bedroom window from where we could look down onto the road. My mother was very frightened and stayed in bed. Father now confessed that the sound had shaken him and that he was beginning to see the story in a different light. After half an hour, he returned to bed. At the very moment when he told me to do the same, we heard that scream again. I flung the window open and looked out on to the street and saw the creature cross the road quick as lightning and disappear under the archway. I turned round and saw my father standing behind me with his eyes fixed in the direction where the creature had disappeared. I asked if he had seen anything. He said he had, if only fleetingly, but that didn't matter because that brief moment was enough to convince him. So now I had another witness.
>
> My mother heard the creature as well, but stayed in bed, frightened. When told about our sighting, she said innocently that

maybe the creature was coming back for its bandage. By this time, everyone else in the house was awake and we stayed up until dawn.

AFTERMATH

Later that morning Filiberto, together with his father and sister, prepared to go down to the town to have the bandage sample analysed. When Antonella went to retrieve the bandage, it was nowhere to be seen. 'I turned the old washing machine upside down but there was no sign of it,' said Filiberto.

Maybe a dog or a cat had been attracted by the smell of the blood, or substance, and had carried it away, yet that was impossible because they would have had to turn the washing machine upside down to get at it. Suddenly we remembered my mother's words: 'What if the creature had really come back for its bandages, perhaps because it had understood that this was the proof of its existence?'

I felt angry, disappointed and deceived. The proof we had was gone. I realized that my father's and my own testimony would not be enough to convince public opinion, especially in a village like mine, where most people are reluctant to believe such stories. We decided therefore to keep it to ourselves, treating it as a personal experience to be shared only with the family. We returned to our normal lives but often our thoughts turned back to that episode.

My behaviour changed completely. I became more and more restless and bad-tempered, probably due to the insomnia, which never abated. I thought that perhaps I was the only one to have touched a creature which had come from God-knows-where, but I daren't tell anyone for fear of ridicule. Every night before going to bed I would look out of the window in the hope of seeing it again. Every noise in the night made me jump out of bed and look out again, but there was no trace of it anywhere. I began to think that it would never come back. This thought left me with a terrible feeling of emptiness. I started keeping everything inside and creating a barrier against the rest of the world. You cannot live with certain experiences if you cannot share them with anyone. I asked myself if that was the price I had to pay for having been in a sense privileged, or chosen. But for what purpose?

Five days after the second encounter I woke up, got out of bed and instinctively looked out of the window. It had happened at other times too, as if something had beckoned me to get up. This gave me the idea of trying to take a photograph of the creature if it appeared again. Giuseppe had a Polaroid camera and thought it would do, especially as my chances of seeing the creature again were minimal.

On various nights I waited in ambush with the camera, near the garage where the first encounter had taken place. I would lie in wait from about midnight to 1 a.m., cold and frightened, though my curiosity was stronger than anything. I remember one night when my heart jumped as I heard the noise of someone or something approaching. I had the camera ready but put it down once I realised it was only a fox crossing the road.

THIRD ENCOUNTER

On 23 May 1993 the silence of the night was shattered again by the now familiar scream of the creature. Filiberto awoke abruptly.

I jumped out of bed, grabbed the Polaroid, ran towards the door, unbolted it and flung it open. The sound of footsteps treading on the road was almost unreal: I realized it was approaching but I still couldn't see anything. The excitement of seeing it round the corner was overwhelming. I wanted to shout, to wake someone up, yet I couldn't; and besides, I would probably have frightened the creature. I aimed my camera in the direction of those hurried footsteps, though they were not as fast as they had been the first time. This time it wasn't running, but walking quickly. The creature positioned itself in the shadow of a street lamp which hung underneath my balcony, so that I couldn't see it clearly. I thought that when it caught sight of me it would run away, but it just carried on walking in that funny manner. I took a few steps in its direction to get a better picture, but it seemed not to notice my presence. I was overcome with excitement and joy, and it was at that moment that I took the first photograph, even though I realized the creature was too far away and concealed by the shadow of the balcony. When the flash went off, the creature stopped abruptly and turned round, then carried on walking at the same pace. I had the impression that it could only see but not hear, because it didn't turn around at the sound of my approaching footsteps. Also, it could not really see the outline of my body since it was walking with its head bowed. The creature noticed me only when the light of the flash had lit up the surroundings.

When the Polaroid photograph had developed itself, I realized that the distance had been too great and I threw it down without waiting for it to dry. I wanted to take a closer picture. This meant catching up with the creature and trying to take a photograph of its face as well as its body, and I had to take advantage of the fact that it wasn't running but walking. I was afraid and hesitated for a while before running after it, but I had to do so because I might never again have another chance like this. I didn't know how it would react nor whether it had an aggressive nature. I caught up with it. Now there were only two metres separating us, yet the creature did not turn round: it really did seem as though it couldn't hear me. I wanted to stand in front of it but the fear of overtaking it face to face was too strong, so I stopped. My thumb, which had been as rigid as a piece of wood from excitement, managed to press the button on the camera. At this second flash, the creature timidly turned towards me, so that I managed to see a little of the face but not enough to understand what it really looked like.

With the photograph in my hand I ran faster than ever, shouting at the top of my voice that I had done it: I had managed to immortalize the creature in my photograph! I was so excited that I ran into a wall and hurt my hand. In the meantime my father awakened and was looking out of the window, asking why I was in my pyjamas again, screaming and running like a madman. I picked up the first photograph that I had dropped on the ground and walked into the kitchen without looking at either one. I wanted to see them with my family, under a good light. I put the two photographs under the light of the chandelier, but they hadn't developed yet: all that was visible was the outline of the creature. To see them develop under my very eyes made it all the more exciting. After a few minutes the photos were completely dry and one could see the creature clearly. Father came downstairs and looked at the pictures incredulously, while Mother shouted upstairs, asking what had happened. We went up to her room and my father, without saying a word, put them on the bed. My mother hesitated for a moment, but as soon as she picked them up she dropped them on the sheet, refusing to look at them. They both asked how I had managed to take them. After explaining, I calmed them down by emphasizing that we were not dealing with a dangerous entity.

The first photograph was not clear because of distance and darkness: one could distinguish only an outline. The second one portrayed a creature in the act of walking, with its right limb raised. The sole of its foot was visible as was its small head, slightly overshadowed by the 'bundle' on its back. Small arms were attached to the brownish trunk, which seemed a little more bloated than when I first saw it.

These photographs created almost as much excitement as the actual sight of the creature. My mother began to cry with emotion whereas Father just beamed tenderly. We wanted to wake up my grandmother, but then thought it would be better if we showed her the pictures in the morning. What had happened was extremely important, yet my father believed the photographs might cause complications in our lives. I didn't understand him at the time. My happiness was such that I wanted to telephone my sister and everybody I knew, but at that hour it was hardly a good idea and, besides, we needed to think carefully before disclosing such an event.

I put the photographs in a wooden box that I was making and placed it beside my bedside cabinet. We all went to bed, even though for me – and I suspect my parents – it meant another sleepless night.

A STRANGE SEQUEL

Over lunch next day Filiberto's grandmother was brought up to date. 'Initially, she thought we were joking,' explained Filiberto, 'then she associated everything with some kind of esoteric or mystical phenomenon. In short, she believed it was a ghost. I decided to look at the photographs in the light of day and, at the same time, convince my grandmother, so I went to the bedroom to fetch them.'

As I entered the room, I immediately noticed that the lid of the wooden box in which I had put the pictures was curving, as if the wood was undergoing some kind of contraction. I wondered if the wood had not dried properly, causing it to shrink, but why was it happening at that very moment? After all, the box had been there for a long time. Also, glued to the lid of the box was a piece of thin cardboard covered in cloth on which was a drawing I had left unfinished, and the strange thing was that it did not detach itself from the lid as would have been normal had it been contraction, but curved itself with the wood, even though the wood was much thicker.

Alarmed, I lifted the lid. The moment I did so a strange smell, similar to that of burned plastic, filled the room. Looking inside, I could see that the photo on top seemed to have changed, and when I lifted it I noticed that the second photograph was stuck to the first. The outline of the creature was raised, creating a kind of bas-relief, as if the flat figure had transformed itself into a three-dimensional one. Terrified, I let the photos drop to the floor and shouted to the family. They did not immediately realize what had happened, but then father picked up the pictures and could see the transformation they had undergone. My grandmother reacted hysterically, telling us to throw them away at once because she was convinced this was the work of an evil spirit. My mother thought the same, but father tried reassuring us by saying that it was probably just a chemical reaction.

We examined the top photograph. Unable to see the condition of the lower one, we separated them carefully. As we did so, we realized that the second photograph also had undergone a change. Both pictures seemed to have swollen in proximity to the outline of the figure. At the centre of the figures the layer on the surface had risen, creating a hole which, however, did not penetrate to the back. It seemed as if the image of the creature wanted to rise on the clearer picture – the one on top. It was even more obvious because, apart from creating a relief of itself, it had also slightly broadened, leaving only the part where the head was visible unaltered.

We also noticed that underneath the lid, near the curvature, was a dark circular stain, and the piece of paper which had been placed between the two photographs was slightly burned with a hole in the middle. Strangely, the other objects in the box had not been damaged. It looked as if a beam or source of heat had cut through the lid, the two photographs and the little piece of paper between them. This seemed the only possible explanation, but what kind of beam was it?

We all now were agreed on one point: If it had been inadvisable to reveal the photographs, it was now out of the question to say anything at all about the events either; at least, not until experts had been called in. We put the photographs in a plastic bag and cleared the box of all the other items. While doing so, I found a torch, which made me think that all this could have been due to the chemical reaction from a leaked battery, given the pictures were not yet dry when I put them in the box. Ultimately, though, I did not believe this to be possible because, hard as I tried, I couldn't reconcile it with the fact a chemical reaction could have taken place only on the image of the creature.

RUMOURS

Two days later Filiberto overheard a conversation between two women in the village who, while hanging out their washing, were talking about strange screams in the night. One said that the spirit of an old woman who had recently died was wandering around the streets at night. Filiberto found an excuse for joining in the conversation.

I knew both women, and they explained to me how they had heard the screams moving very rapidly, and that others had heard the same. I parted from them, feigning mere curiosity.

The most absurd rumours were going around the village, though some attributed the screams to drunkards or animals. I was sorely tempted to explain to everyone just what those screams came from, even though I realized that my explanation would have been regarded as the most absurd of all, especially if I couldn't support it with proof. I had to remain silent, but in case I decided to show the photographs to someone, I started buying specialized magazines in which I found the names of various organizations and UFO centres. Among these was the National Ufology Centre in Rome, and I promised myself to go there as soon as possible.

Ten days later I visited Carlo, a friend of mine, in his studio, for reasons connected with my work. As soon as I entered the room he greeted me with a strange expression – 'Hallo, elf!' This seemed peculiar and I asked him why he called me that. He said it was quite spontaneous and there was nothing wrong in saying that. At that time I was particularly susceptible and wondered if maybe he knew about my story and had associated the definition of 'elf' with that strange creature. Eventually, pressed by the need to confide in a friend, I decided to tell him everything, making him swear not to tell anyone. He listened to me carefully. I thought he wouldn't take me seriously, but on the contrary, he was very upset by both the story and at the state of shock I was in. Carlo had also overheard certain conversations in the village but thought them fanciful.

Unexpectedly, Carlo's brother suddenly turned up at the studio. The expression on his face immediately betrayed the fact that he had been eavesdropping. Now it was three of us who knew the story, so there was nothing left but to ask him to keep the secret to himself. He confided that for a while now he had heard of a family in the village that had been hiding a deformed child, letting him out only at night. I pointed out that it couldn't possibly have been a child, even though it had a humanoid shape, because a child could not run in that way and I did not believe that nature could conceive genetic mistakes of that kind. He persisted that for some time he had been suspicious of a certain family in the village. It was true that this family was particularly introverted and socially isolated; that they hadn't been out for years, and that this would only serve to encourage such an absurd theory.

The two brothers asked if they could see my photographs. I explained that it was not appropriate and that in any case it was probably a mistake to have confided in them. In a small village, no matter how hard you try to keep a secret, it is bound to come out sooner or later. I hoped, however, that the very weirdness of my story would dissuade them from disclosing it. After all, my reputation was at stake.

FOWL DEATHS

Following his meeting with the two brothers, Filiberto left the studio and on his way home called in at the village café-bar, a regular meeting point for the locals. There he overheard a conversation between two elderly men discussing an abnormally high number of deaths among the local chickens, which they attributed to some fierce 'beast'. Apparently, this beast had killed dozens of chickens. At this point, a third person joined in the conversation, claiming that 20 chickens had been killed in one night alone. They were found piled on top of each other with no trace of wounds or blood. This last statement puzzled Filiberto.

Theories began to crowd my mind. Was this the creature's doing? And if so, maybe it killed the hens to drain them of their liquids, like blood and water. In other words, it was a kind of vampire. To be certain of this, one had to examine the carcasses, but they had already been buried, and I didn't know where. So I went to the owner of the henhouse. He must have thought it odd, but he did tell me that he had buried them in the ground surrounding the henhouse, without showing me precisely where. He couldn't understand my sudden interest in his poor hens, so I made an excuse saying that they could be given to an organization that collected food for starving dogs. He said that was inappropriate considering their unusual death: were it not so, he would have eaten them himself.

I said nothing and reached the place he had pointed out to me.

The plot of land was much too vast for me to start digging without making a mess. I did notice, though, that the only access to the henhouse was a small open window, quite high up, so that the animal that killed these hens must have entered through there. The creature I had seen was quite small, about 70 centimetres high, so it could easily have come in through the window.

If my suspicions were well-founded, and the creature was the cause of these deaths, it obviously did not belong to this world. I am well acquainted with the behaviour of animals in this area and none has this strange habit. The slaughter of hens continued, but some had been strangled and others taken away; at least, that is what the owners said. So the situation began to complicate itself again. I was angry: it seemed that every time I reached a conclusion, someone or something would undermine it.

THE STORY LEAKS OUT

The following evening Filiberto went to the café-bar. 'A tomb-like silence reigned, which was most unusual,' he reported. 'It felt as if everyone was expecting something from me.'

One of the men asked me to step outside for a talk. I could never have imagined that he was acquainted with my story, and this upset me a great deal. Obviously one, or perhaps both, of the two brothers had been unable to resist the temptation of blurting out everything. So now the mechanism anticipated by my father and me had been set in motion. I attempted to deny everything but the man knew of the existence of the photographs and demanded to see them. I did my best to defuse the situation by dismissing the story as a joke or wild rumour.

That evening, Filiberto met Carlo and accused him of leaking the story to others in the village. At first protesting his innocence and blaming his brother, he later admitted to having confided in a friend.

The following day various villagers approached Filiberto, bombarding him with questions and begging to see the photographs.

I realized I had to stop the villagers and others from invading my house, so I told them I no longer had the pictures as I'd sent them to a research centre – which I had planned on doing in any case.

The news spread quickly, even to nearby villages. Many claimed that it was all a big farce, while others took it very seriously. In a way, I hoped people would believe it was a joke, but there was always someone who wanted to get serious about it all and turn it into a confrontation.

I discovered that the story had spread even to the nearby town of Ascoli Piceno. Over and over again I was stopped in the street by people who knew me and who expected an explanation that I couldn't give. It became practically impossible to walk down the street in Pretare, so that for a time I was obliged to give up going out altogether.

IL MESSAGGERO

In late June 1993, tired of rumours and unwanted attention, Filiberto decided to contact *Il Messaggero*, an important Italian daily newspaper, only to discover that they already knew about the story and were sending a reporter to Pretare to investigate.

I told them it was preferable to get the true version of the story from me, thus avoiding a frivolous article dealing with ghosts and elves. We made an appointment for 28 June. Accompanied by my mother, I went to the editorial offices, taking with me the box containing the photographs.

The reporter who met us did not know about the existence of the photographs, and was astounded when he saw them. As I suspected, he had thought he would be dealing with a fairy tale which he had planned to entitle 'The Elf from Pretare'. Now he agreed it was a much more interesting story – a real 'scoop' for his newspaper.

Before starting the interview I explained that even I could not say what the creature was, and that I would stick to an objective version, with the photographs as proof. I hoped that publishing the photos would arouse the curiosity of someone who dealt seriously with such phenomena and who could provide a logical and scientific explanation for these events, thereby satisfying public opinion. I wasn't certain if I was doing the right thing by disclosing my story, yet there was nothing else to do. Anyway, in time people would forget, and my family and I would find peace again.

On 1 July 1993 the article – under the headline I HAVE SEEN
E.T. – appeared in *Il Messaggero*, together with photos of
Filiberto displaying the Polaroids, and his mother. Copies
sold out rapidly. 'The story was related accurately – with the
exception of one word,' said Filiberto. 'At the point when, on
that 9th May, my mother gave me a glass of cold water to
recover from the shock, the editors changed the "glass of
water" into a "glass of mulled wine". Also, the Polaroids,
printed in black and white, were so small that one could hardly
distinguish them, whereas the photos of mother and myself
took up most of the page.'

Following publication of the article, Filiberto received a
letter from the Italian Centre for UFO Studies (Centro
Italiano Studi Ufologici – CISU), based in Turin. CISU
asked for Filiberto's notes, drawings and copies of the
photographs, explaining that these would be used for
scientific purposes, and that one of their members would visit
him as soon as possible. Filiberto sent CISU a detailed report,
with drawings of the creature seen from different angles.

I did not send the photographs because there were no copy
negatives, and it was too risky to send them to a centre I knew so
little about. They took an extremely long time to answer. Perhaps
they wanted to see how events would evolve before replying or
coming to see me.

After this first exposure in the press, I was bombarded with
letters and telephone calls from writers, magicians, children,
ordinary people and those who had had encounters themselves.
What really pleased me was the fact that these people seemed very
happy about what had happened to me, because they regarded this
as proof at last for the existence of some kind of extraterrestrial
being. Finally, I too began to convince myself that I had
experienced a close encounter with an alien.

I also received letters from fanatics and sects. These worried
me somewhat. Some claimed that this phenomenon was the
beginning of an era of evil, represented by the 'little devil',
whereas others claimed it was a sign from heaven. A magician
wrote to me saying that I would see the creature again and that we
would communicate telepathically, as it was the only form of
communication possible to aliens. This aroused my curiosity and
I began to wonder if the creature had probably spoken to me but

that I had not been capable of receiving its message. Perhaps I should have tried to speak to it or tried to make myself understood with gestures, to establish a relationship of trust between us. On the other hand, I would have gone mad if I had taken into account all the strange theories expounded in those letters.

Going out became a problem, not just for me but for my family and friends. It was the price I had to pay for appearing in the newspapers. All those friends who used to approach me on the street to question me were now themselves being approached by people who hoped to get some information on me and on the places where the 'alien' had visited.

The telephone calls Filiberto received were from friends, relations, or simply curious people – with the exception of one anonymous caller with a strong Florentine accent who, after a brief conversation, hung up, refusing to give his name, for reasons that he promised to divulge in due course.

Chapter 9

Dead or Alive

One afternoon late in June 1993 two friends, Carlo and Professor Aleardo F., arrived excited at Filiberto's studio to tell him about two sightings of a strange creature in Pescara and Sulmona (60 and 100 kilometres respectively from Pretare), which had been widely reported in the media. The professor said that both he and the rest of the village were now more inclined to believe Filiberto's story.

During a training flight from Pescara airport on 15 June 1993, five members of the fire brigade (Vigili del Fuoco), flying an Agusta/Bell 412 helicopter, were surprised by the sight of an unusual aerial object which joined them at their flight level of 600 metres. Although a collision seemed imminent, the object made a rapid manoeuvre and avoided the helicopter. Captain Vincenzo D. took over control from a trainee pilot and executed a left turn. His report follows:

> The object appeared to me and the crew as about 1.30 metres in height, like a small diving-suit or space-suit with a little sphere or globe on top that could have been the head, about 50cm in diameter, with two large and easily visible oval-shaped 'eyes'. From the top of the 'trunk' slightly protruded what looked like two 'bags', beneath which were 'legs', of a yellow–ochre colour . . . We continued on a left turn, with the object always keeping to our right. After a few moments, it turned, then flew around our helicopter twice before darting away at an estimated speed of 300–400 k.p.h. As it turned, I could see a kind of antenna or aerial coming from the top of the head.
>
> We radioed Pescara airport and asked if they could look in our direction and try and see where the object went, but it wasn't possible. The controller contacted the Carabinieri, but they couldn't find anyone else who had seen it. The object was flying

against the wind without any adverse effect, and from the way it moved, it seemed it was showing interest in the helicopter.[1]

On the afternoon of 20 June 1993 Giuseppe Zitella, a 49-year-old former non-commissioned officer of the Italian Air Force, together with members of his family, encountered a strange creature in a wheat field at Pettorano sul Gizio, near Sulmona, in central Italy – about 100 kilometres south-east of Filiberto's village, Pretare. Signora Zitella noticed something in the sky near a row of poplar trees which looked like a child's balloon, of the sort made in the shape of a doll or animal, that seemed about to land. She alerted her husband. As Zitella approached the object to pick it up, he realized that the 'balloon' was some kind of creature.

'It was 80 centimetres high with brown legs attached to the round head,' reported Zitella. 'It seemed to be all covered by black plastic, and on the legs I saw a V- or U-like sign. It didn't say anything. It looked me in the face. I have no doubt it was alive.' The creature had two black eyes and what looked like an antenna coming out of its head. As soon as Zitella attempted to touch it, the creature leapt two metres in the air (as happened in the Caponi case) then made two or three more leaps, hovering between each leap in mid-air as it moved away, then, as if propelled by a mysterious energy, it rose perpendicularly and flew off backwards. Police and scientists, some reportedly from the National Research Council, investigated and found burned areas at intervals of 10–15 metres, where the creature had touched down, in the wheat field.[2]

'After listening to these incredible stories,' said Filiberto, 'I told them I had never seen the creature fly nor had I seen the antenna nor the inverted U- or V-shape, but that some of the other details corresponded to my own experiences.'

There were more reports from this period, in the same part of Italy, succeeding one another, which made me think that something important was about to happen. The hypothesis that these were extraterrestrial creatures seemed more likely now. Was it a coincidence that the sightings occurred so close to the Adriatic coast?

I resented the fact that people were only now starting to believe me now that they had heard of the other sightings; however, I did care about what others thought, because my credibility was in question. So I tried to put myself in others' shoes, trying to experience this story as an outsider, with both the perplexities and the ignorance that people have with regard to UFOs. Although I had never seen a UFO and was no expert 'ufologist', I gradually acquired a vast amount of knowledge on the subject, reading books and collecting all the articles concerning the events that took place in Sulmona and Pescara and many others that followed.

THE CREATURE AGAIN

One evening late in June 1993, Filiberto joined his friends and neighbours at the village club to watch a film on television. Some left during the interval, but Filiberto remained with three friends, including Carlo, the brother in whom he had originally confided his story. After the film, Filiberto and Carlo left the club. Filiberto describes what happened next:

> We were walking down the road and talking when Carlo suddenly stopped, pointing fearfully in the direction of a big gate from behind which came that deafening scream I knew so well, a scream that echoed in the silence of the night. With a stunned expression on his face he asked me if it belonged to the creature. I said it did, and asked him to stay calm and do as I told him, explaining that the scream meant that the creature had never left our village, and that with a bit of luck we would see it tonight. Now, after one long month, I was tracking down that creature again, ironically in the company of the person who had divulged the news of its existence.
>
> Silently, we moved in the direction of the gate, behind which was a large garden with tall plants obstructing our view. As the scream drew nearer, we reached the gate and decided to climb over. I went first and told Carlo to follow, but he grabbed my leg and pulled me down again, begging me not to go. I tried to calm him down, telling him there was no danger. My thought at the time was that if Carlo could see the creature too, then we would have another witness. I told him that maybe we could catch the creature and help it, if needed, but Carlo ran off to get the couple who had stayed behind at the club, while I waited.

They all arrived a couple of minutes later. The girl, on hearing that metallic-sounding scream, began screaming herself, pleading with her fiancé not to go near it and let it be – whatever it was. He told her to keep quiet or she would frighten the creature away, but by this time its scream was barely audible. So he and I climbed over the gate while the others waited at the end of the road. All of a sudden the scream returned, loud and piercing, heading in our direction. The girl screamed again, begging us to come down because that 'thing' was coming towards us. Her boyfriend turned back and as soon as he had climbed over the gate – to which I was still clinging – he grabbed some stones and started throwing them in the direction of the scream. I begged him to stop, but it was too late: the scream was already vanishing in the darkness, leaving us in complete silence. We waited for 15 minutes in the hope of hearing some other signal. Nothing happened, so we walked back to the village square to talk about it.

The couple confessed to Filiberto that they had never really had much interest in the 'ET' story, but after this experience they saw everything in a new light. The group wondered whether it was now time to turn to the police who, strangely, had never become involved with the affair, though they must have read about it in the newspapers. The group decided otherwise. 'That little creature was neither dangerous nor aggressive,' said Filiberto, 'and one hardly needed the intervention of the authorities who probably would have launched an "alien hunt", turned against me, confiscated my photographs, and God knows what else. So it was best to wait for the CISU, or other research centres, to pronounce their verdict on the creature and on the mysterious distortion of the photographs, thus quenching, I hoped, my terrible thirst for knowledge.'

DILEMMA AND CONTROVERSY

'During our conversation,' Filiberto continued, 'my friends picked up on the fact that I was still in possession of the photographs. This was unfortunate because it meant that once again my house would be flooded with people, disrupting the peace we'd had until that evening.'

> After that night I thought about trying to catch this creature. After all, there was nothing to fear as I was convinced it was harmless. But what if I succeeded? I could never let it be known: the authorities would seize it and dissect it on a laboratory table, or perhaps keep it locked up in a cage. On the other hand, were I successful in capturing it, such an act might be interpreted as an act of aggression, thus compromising any possibility of a 'friendship' developing between us.

Filiberto's conviction that people should know more about the story grew stronger, yet he found himself continually surrounded by controversy.

> Many accused me of having fabricated the whole story in order to get money and publicity. There were a few, however – mostly those who had heard the screams in the night – who believed me and who claimed they had the right, as inhabitants of the village, to see my photographs. Others took the view that if any of this were true, the authorities and experts would have intervened. I responded simply that stories like mine did not necessarily need confirmation from others (though it would have been useful) and that the photographs, my integrity of character (which had never been questioned before) were sufficient proof of the story's authenticity. I decided to show all the material I had to anyone who wished to examine it. This time, at least, I didn't have to hide anything from anyone.

'MAZZAMORELLI'

Although people were disconcerted by the picture of the little creature, most did not associate it with that of an alien; rather, they believed it depicted an elf, known in the local dialect as a *mazzamorello*. As Filiberto explains:

> In local tradition, *mazzamorelli* are small creatures that live in the forest undergrowth. Each mazzamorello supposedly carries a stick to hit anyone who tries to steal his gold-filled 'pendulum'. Many villagers consulted books in the library on mythology and folklore. The mazzamorello became the endearing official name for my little friend, though I felt that what needed to be pursued was the theory of non-terrestrial creatures – or at any rate of creatures not belonging to any known species. All this talk of a sub-human species was absurd. Elderly people would leave my

160

house in a hurry, convinced that 'the spirits' had altered those photographs.

STOP

On 10 July 1993 a reporter from the weekly magazine *Stop* turned up unannounced at the Caponi house and requested an interview. 'I was told that if my story was related in the right way and accompanied by the photographs,' said Filiberto, 'it might be published by other magazines, and that I could make a lot of money.'

> Until that moment, I had never given much thought to the possibility of making money with my story. So far, I had only lost money because people visited my house so frequently that I had lagged behind with my work. Every time someone came, I had to tell my story, even though it had already been published. The journalist, Leonida Barezzi, told me I was the only person in the world who had managed to photograph an alien.[3] All the archives were full of photographs of flying objects and luminous spheres, but not of aliens, he said. So there seemed nothing wrong in making some money. I had given my story freely to *Il Messaggero*, after all, and they had made a real 'scoop' out of it.
>
> We showed Barezzi the photographs. After examining them carefully he threw them on the table and asked us why they were damaged, blaming us for ruining such crucial documentation. We were dumbfounded. I explained that the photos had 'burned themselves' in mysterious circumstances – as had already been reported by *Il Messaggero*. He apologized, admitting that he had read only the beginning of that article. Now the idea of payment for the article evaporated. Barezzi pointed out that one could not sell damaged photographs as proof to any magazine. However, I agreed to the story being published. *Stop* had a good circulation, though it was rather cheap-style: I would have preferred to have the story appear in a scientific review.

Filiberto refused to part with his precious Polaroid photos, but agreed to Barezzi's request to make a sketch of the creature's profile. The article, accompanied by photographs of Filiberto and his family and the places where the creature had been observed, would be published on 17 July 1993.

THE LUNATIC FRINGE, THE CURIOUS AND A MIRACLE SEEKER

A few days after the interview for *Stop*, Filiberto received another telephone call from the anonymous man with a Florentine accent.

> He asked me whether there had been any further developments and if the 'men in black' had been following me. I told him that I had seen no such 'men in black'. As before, I insisted that he introduce himself, or I would not speak with him again. He replied that he could not give me his name because he suspected my telephone was bugged. He also advised me not to publicize the story because it would trigger the intervention of various detective agencies, especially those of the United States. The 'men in black', he claimed, were none other than Pentagon agents whose job was the gathering of UFO information for the purpose of keeping it secret. I was somewhat disturbed by all this, yet I couldn't bring myself to trust someone who wouldn't even introduce himself. Then he told me of an experience he claimed to have had with an alien creature.
>
> He begged me not to attempt to capture the creature, as he had done: his own attempt having left him partially burned. Sounding on the verge of tears, he pointed out that any creature that feels threatened is naturally going to defend itself. He also assured me that I would see the creature again very soon. In any event, I was supposed to look out for big, black cars with tinted windows and men dressed in elegant dark suits. I explained that if my phone was bugged, his call could be traced anyway. He responded that he was speaking from a public phone, and before hanging up gave me further cause to worry about these men in black: apparently they were connected with the disappearances of many people who had been in contact with aliens.
>
> Was I to take him seriously, or was he just a lunatic? What perplexed me was his apparent disinclination to recollect fully what had happened to him, as if he had been terribly traumatized by the experience. When I had questioned the authenticity of his story, he did not become defensive, yet he seemed offended, describing burns that covered most of his body after the scuffle with the alien.

Two days later Filiberto was called by the spokesman of a group of young men in Florence who dedicated themselves to the study of extraterrestrial phenomena on a purely private basis. Many in the group supposedly had undergone experiences with aliens and bore the 'signs' on their bodies. The anonymous Florentine caller, it later transpired, was a member of this group.

The Caponi residence was besieged by all manner of curious people: those who simply wanted to meet Filiberto and see for themselves where the creature had been seen, those who issued dire warnings (such as the anonymous Florentine) and, in one case, a young man paralysed from a car accident who turned up in his wheelchair in the middle of the night. 'After waiting in vain for a miraculous encounter with the creature that he hoped would make him walk again,' said Filiberto, 'he and his friends thanked me and left.'

SEARCH PARTIES

The following evening some of the villagers in Pretare decided that the only way to give any credibility to the story about the creature was to launch a search party. Reluctantly, Filiberto agreed to accompany them. At about midnight the group of ten set off, but returned having found nothing. This did not deter other villagers and soon the number of search parties grew steadily. Filiberto became concerned.

The village was practically empty between midnight and four in the morning. Everybody, it seemed, would go into the surrounding countryside searching for the creature. Only later did I find out that this had also already happened in neighbouring villages. Since publication of the *Messaggero* article, I discovered that strangers in the area had told the journalist that if the creature really existed they would capture it – dead or alive. Evidently, the search had escalated into an all-out 'war' against the creature. Nobody was certain of its existence yet all seemed desperate to find it, lured probably by the idea of appearing in the media and possibly making money out of it.

Meanwhile, the article in *Stop* appeared. Its headline – I HAVE SEEN THE MONKEY-MAN THAT HAS LANDED ON EARTH – angered Filiberto, who had yet to adjust to the fact that such sensation-mongering headlines are the lifeblood of the pulp press. 'I had cautioned the journalist not to attribute names too easily to something that even I could not properly identify,' he complained.

> As for the rest, however, it was clearly expressed and entirely factual, and referred to the sightings in Sulmona and Pescara. In the latter part of the article, where the nightly expeditions were described, the creature was correctly portrayed as 'a wounded animal uttering cries in the night, the like of which had never been heard on Earth, inspiring both tenderness and fear'.
>
> The goal of these expeditions, the article continued, was to find the alien, dead or alive. The participants were described as ravenous hunters armed with weapons as well as cameras. Later I learned that some of them even carried guns. All this frightened me, because if anyone had been injured I would have been held responsible and this would have attracted the attention of the local authorities, who so far had not become involved.

During ensuing days Filiberto received an increasing number of telephone calls from cranks, cultists and sectarians, including one from the anonymous Florentine. 'I warned you, but you would not listen,' he told Filiberto, then hung up. Meanwhile, the villagers prepared for yet another night-time expedition, this time with a hunting dog called Dick. Because of his concerns about the authorities – particularly the Carabinieri – Filiberto objected, but the villagers persuaded him that there was no harm in going out for a 'summer night stroll'.

> Towards midnight, we picked up our torches and headed for a country lane which led to the gate of a large garden. Our group, comprising ten people, suddenly came to a halt. There was that unmistakable scream again. It was so close that we were rooted to the spot. Dick, our dog, started barking and leapt over the gate then over a stone wall, finally disappearing into the bushes. We could hear Dick whining – the sort of noise hunting dogs make when they detect game – it mingled with the creature's scream as if the two were fighting. By the time one of the men had decided to jump over the wall, the dog was hurled violently over it, landing on his back. We jumped over the wall, but the scream already had receded. We shone our torches over the area but there was no trace of the creature. One of our group, recently returned from Kenya, said that among the animals of Africa, he had never heard such a

sound. We checked the dog to see if he was wounded but, though rigid with shock, he seemed all right.

This last episode set me thinking again. That creature was still in the vicinity and something had to be done. The news of what had happened that night spread throughout the village, and now there were many who claimed to have heard the scream. Perhaps now they could understand the analogy I had made to them when I said that a Catholic believes in God even though he has never seen Him, though he has seen all the works of His creation. In the same way, it was evident that the scream could not be attributed to a terrestrial creature.

THEORIES

Every night before retiring, Filiberto would spend time either standing outside the house or looking out of his bedroom window, sometimes staying up until three in the morning in the hope of some sign of the creature.

The creature could have been out there at any time and could have chosen any moment to establish some form of contact. I considered it an intelligent creature because it could not have been a coincidence that the bandage had disappeared from under the washing machine or that the photos had altered in that peculiar way. All this was proof of its existence, so it was clearly trying to destroy the evidence I had collected. This possibly meant that it had come to Earth on a secret mission – perhaps to collect data – but that something had gone terribly wrong. That, I reasoned, was why it ran around at night, screaming to attract my attention. This was one of the many theories that crowded my mind.

I began to ask myself whether my encounter had been a coincidence. If it were not, it wouldn't have run off in that way. Or had I maybe been chosen for some obscure reason? Perhaps its screams were the only means of communicating its predicament to its fellow beings. Or were they just cries of pain? This last theory might have explained the bandages wrapped around its legs, but who had wrapped them and where had the bandages come from? Perhaps it was impossible or dangerous to contact its fellow beings. Whatever the case, it was obviously in great difficulty. In all probability it had been abandoned or, worse, had suffered injuries resulting from a crash of some sort, perhaps one involving whatever craft had brought it here, though in the latter case, somebody would have found debris.

165

These thoughts left me with a certainty: the creature was in difficulty, and it was suffering. My greatest hope now was that one day it would come back to me so that I could help it; after all, I was the only human it had ever encountered, so far as I knew. I also wondered where it found food or shelter. If it were really needy, I hoped it would take a risk by trusting me. I started by leaving some food and water outside the house, but my two cats and some stray dogs scoffed the lot. I also scoured the countryside for metal fragments of the 'spaceship', but to no avail.

THE NIGHT OF SAN LORENZO

Every summer a major meteor shower known as the Perseids occurs, typically from 23 July to 20 August, peaking on the night of 12 August, when up to 100 meteorites (or 'shooting stars') may be seen in an hour. On the eve of Filiberto's birthday on 10 August 1993, known in Italy as the night of San Lorenzo, 'the night when wishes come true', Filiberto and some friends went to a nearby hill to look for shooting stars. The shower that night was not so spectacular as they had hoped, but Filiberto took advantage of the occasion to wonder at the heavens.

We have lost our capacity to observe what is around us, let alone what is above us. The infinite blue that lights up with the sun and the dark blue that glitters with the stars at night – life's secrets that are largely hidden to the world of science. We know so little of the universe, yet the universe knows all about us and all humans that have lived on Earth. It has seen the birth of life and the evolution of Man. It has witnessed our history and will probably view our demise, like a hidden camera that has filmed our lives. Man, so obstinate in his desire to find his roots on Earth, does not even suspect that we might all – like the little creature – originate from that living mechanism, the universe. We are nothing but a microscopic part of that immense organism . . .

NOTES

1 *L'Indipendente*, 30 June 1993; *Il Centro*, 22–7 June 1993; *Il Tempo*, 23 June 1993, *Il Messaggero*, 23, 24 June 1993, and numerous other sources, cited in Fiorino, Paolo, 'Umanoidi Volanti? L'ondata italiana di segnelazioni dell'estate 1993' ('Flying Humanoids? The Italian wave of sightings in Summer 1993'), *UFO: Rivista di Informazione Ufologica*, no. 13, December 1993, pp. 1–3.

2 *Il Messaggero*, 25–9 June 1993, and other sources, cited in Fiorino, op. cit., pp. 3–4.

3 Photographs of alleged aliens have been taken in many countries, including Italy, e.g., the well-known series by Gianpietro Monguzzi in the Italian Alps (1952); in the USA by Howard Menger (1956), Carroll Wayne Watts (1967) and Jeff Greenhaw (1973); and in the UK by Jim Templeton (1964) and 'Philip Spencer' (1987).

Chapter 10

Face to Face

On 10 August 1993, Filiberto spent the late evening of his 24th birthday watching the second, particularly exceptional shower of meteorites forecast by the news bulletins. This time he decided to be alone, sitting on a bench behind the Caponi house. As before, he was consumed by an intense desire to see the creature again. 'That creature had changed my way of living and thinking. It had deprived me of the solace of sleep, with the result that I walked around red-eyed, like a zombie.' He watched some shooting stars, then became aware of a presence, as if something was watching him from the grass underneath a nearby wall. Suddenly, the creature appeared right in front of Filiberto.

Cautiously, I approached it, hoping that this time it would not run away again, leaving me in such mental turmoil, with all my questions unanswered. At last, I was close enough to look it in the face for the very first time . . . It had big, black, almond-shaped eyes, which appeared immobile in their sockets, making them shine like plastic. There were no eyelids and the light reflecting in the retina resembled the magnified eyes of a fly. There was also a small protuberance with two small holes, very probably the breathing apparatus. On the lower part of the face, the mouth seemed to be missing, yet from time to time it opened and closed at lengthy intervals, revealing no teeth but only small gums.

This time it made no sound, so I decided to try and open a dialogue, but all that came out of me was a tear, probably a reaction to the impotence I felt when faced with this incredible situation.

On its back was a brown lump. Short arms protruded from its sides. The legs were very long and still covered in bandages. The feet were chunky and had only two toes. Its little arms hung by its side as if it could not control them properly. On the extremely small hands only the thumb was visible, the fingers seemingly clenched in a fist. The skin on the face was wrinkled, although the top and the back parts of the head were smooth, as were the arms. Its mottled complexion – comprising various shades of brown – gave way to white patches at the back of the neck and on the chin. There were also marks on the cheekbones.

I raised my right hand in greeting but failed to elicit any reaction from the creature. It seemed distracted by its surroundings, and kept on staring at the houses and seemed particularly fascinated by a street light attached to an upper storey of our house. I must have seemed as strange to the creature as it did to me, yet obviously it considered me less interesting than the street lamp.

What particularly aroused my curiosity was that 'bundle' which covered most of its body. It seemed to serve no purpose other than as an article of clothing, though its peculiar shape seemed to indicate that it had some other function. It was rather like a partially inflated balloon.

I decided to try to immortalize the creature in another photograph. This meant that I had to rush back to the house to fetch my camera, hoping that the creature would not flee in my absence. I started to move slowly backwards as far as the back door of the house. Once inside, I rushed to my room to get the Polaroid. Before going outside again, I looked out of the window to ascertain that the creature was still there. It was, and still gazing at the street lamp. I came down the stairs very slowly, because I was so overcome with emotion that for a moment I thought I would faint. My heart was pumping and I was almost gasping for breath.

I got within three or four metres of it and took the photograph (realizing that it might have been out of focus) and not wishing to go any closer for fear of startling it. As soon as the flash went off the creature arose, curving its back and almost burying the nape of its neck in it. It started to run very quickly, beating its feet heavily on the ground, then vanished beneath the old archway at the top of the street. I was left there with the camera dangling from my wrist.

Filiberto's disappointment at not having taken more photographs was more than compensated by the quality of the one Polaroid picture he did take, which clearly showed distinguishing features (Photo 3). He spent most of the remaining night contemplating the face of the creature, which reminded him of a tortoise. He decided to tell nobody about this latest episode until the evening of 16 August 1993, when combining a celebration of his birthday with that of his brother-in-law, Giuseppe Pontani. After dinner, Filiberto surreptitiously placed the photograph beside Giuseppe's plate. 'He immediately stopped eating and his eyes popped out of his head,' said Filiberto.

> Without a word, he passed it around the table. They demanded to know more. Their astonishment grew and they now concluded that the creature must be an alien.
>
> Grandmother went on insisting there was an evil influence around and advised me to avoid the creature if I saw it again. This was not an entirely unexpected reaction, as she was very fond of me, and Pretare was a village where tales of the supernatural were rife. I reassured her because I had noticed that for some time she had been locking herself in her bedroom at night, something she had not done before. I convinced her there was nothing to fear.

This time, it seemed that the creature did not intend to destroy evidence of its existence, as the photo remained intact. Filiberto warned the family to keep silent about the episode.

A day or so later, two of Filiberto's friends told him that they had been sitting in a secluded part of the football stadium at night when they noticed strange formations of red and green spheres descending from the sky, then rising up again, shooting off at right angles and disappearing at high speed with a hissing sound. Meanwhile, increasing numbers of villagers reported terrifying screams in the night.

CLOSE UP

During the evening of 19 August Filiberto's sister, Antonella, told her brother that she had heard strange thumping sounds outside the house. He looked out but could see nothing. After spending the evening with friends, he returned at about 23.30.

> Before going to sleep, I went to my studio to prepare work for the following day, as was my habit, and to sweep out the dust that had been made by the clay. I was about to tip it in the grounds of an abandoned house nearby when I noticed something on the ground. The creature was there once more, and it blocked my exit.

This time there were no bandages on its legs. For an instant, I thought it was another creature. I rose slowly to my feet while the creature stood immobile, so that I was able to examine it in detail. It looked different. The face and head, as well as the small arms were the same, but the rest definitely seemed different – the creature appeared to be much smaller. Something was dripping from its head and it moved slowly, then stopped every few minutes. What was most disconcerting was that from its chest emerged two white tubes. The creature seemed to be changing before my very eyes. Then I understood what had happened: it was not wearing its habitual spherical 'helmet'. For the first time, the creature was showing itself completely naked; this was why it appeared to be smaller than before.

Its legs were very long and slender, revealing visible muscular tissue and developed calves. There was a large lump on each knee that was particularly accentuated on the right leg. Both legs were laced with small veins and capillaries. The back also struck me as curious because it was curved with two humps, one behind the other, terminating in a third very small hump. It was a great shock for me to see the creature like this. That part of its body which had looked like a strange semi-inflated balloon was now extremely narrow in the front and much wider on the hips. The skin was very wrinkled and rugged, especially at the joints and on its back, which now seemed to be pointed. From the sternum emerged the two inexplicable tubes, white and rigid. The skin appeared to be brown, with areas of red and violet, becoming white in what was only a hint of a neck. There also were yellow patches and no visible ears.

Regarding the creature's skin coloration, some correlation is provided in an encounter which took place in Orocovis, Cordillera Central, Puerto Rico on 26 March 1995. Jaime Torres, the witness, described the creature he encountered as having a large head, no hair, elongated eyes, tiny mouth and – of particular significance here – different skin shades on its back and side, including brown, yellowish-orange and purple.[1]

Filiberto's account continues:

Even though the creature appeared to be smiling, I had the impression it was suffering, because the skin seemed to be entirely burned. It was so quiet that it seemed to be seeking help, and its expression moved me so much that I smiled back. This was the only communication between us.

I looked around to see if the 'helmet' might have been left somewhere, but saw nothing. After our exchange of glances the creature gazed at the street light and seemed to have no desire to look elsewhere. I found its position unusual because it was seated in a human-like manner, despite its external appearance. I thought I should photograph it in this new posture, so once again I had to return to the house to get my Polaroid. It was the same ritual all over again – almost as if the creature wanted to be photographed. I felt as though I were a photographer who had been given the incredible chance to do an exclusive feature on an alien. Slowly, I retraced my steps to the studio, while the creature continued staring at the light, which evidently held a great attraction for it, as though there was something reassuring about it.

Once inside, I made great haste, fearing to find the creature gone. When I stepped outside it gazed at me for an instant, then looked towards the illuminated window of my workshop, on my right. It was at that moment that I took the first photo. While continuing to stare, its reaction was to close its mouth. I placed the first photo on the ground, then, moving to the left, took a second photograph, as the creature remained motionless. Later I realized that it was not only attracted by the light from the window, but also by the movement of the cat behind the glass. It rose abruptly on its feet, assuming the same position as previously, as though this were a preliminary movement without which it could not run.

PHENOMENAL PHOTOGRAPHS

Filiberto was left with that familiar feeling of being in a dream from which one is about to awaken. He constantly looked at the photos to reassure himself that it was impossible to photograph a dream. They were truly phenomenal, showing the creature in great detail (Photos 4 and 5). 'It seemed incredible that a simple Polaroid could have produced such extraordinary photographs,' he said.

Nobody would be able to dispute their authenticity because there were no negatives, therefore no pre-existing opportunity to alter the images. No one would be able to call me a madman or a visionary any more.

It was a remarkable feeling; the knowledge that I was the only person who could furnish proof of the existence of aliens. However, this feeling was tempered by doubts about the reactions of people on seeing the images of the creature. I wanted desperately to show them to my parents, but this time the images were too powerful. I had to prepare my family, especially my mother, who is particularly sensitive.

Filiberto lay awake all night, puzzling over the pictures and trying to find some answers to the creature's unusual features. What, for example, were those white tubes? 'It would have been a rare opportunity for scholars,' he wondered, 'to discover why those white tubes came out of the chest. My theory was that they were not part of the body. They looked to me as though they had been applied, perhaps to filter our air which probably was different from the creature's.'

HOPES AND FEARS

Although in following days Filiberto made every effort to keep this last encounter secret, his behaviour betrayed him. Sometimes he became so absent-minded that he was unable to follow conversations.

Each night, before retiring, he checked the photographs (which remained unchanged) and the Polaroid, which had fallen to the ground the last time he used it. Although the camera (which belonged to Guiseppe) was not damaged, Filiberto was anxious that it should function perfectly in case the creature returned again. His hopes were diluted with apprehensions.

I knew I had strong proof of the presence of an alien – or, at any rate, of a strange being that seemed to reveal itself to me. I also knew it wasn't dangerous; on the contrary, I began to feel tenderness towards it, though I did not know whether these were the first stages of a dialogue between us. I was afraid that it would want much more than mere contact. This fear was based on my knowledge of abductions by aliens, with sometimes terrible consequences for those abducted: I was terrified that the same might happen to me. If the creature had such intentions, I felt powerless to thwart them.

If ever it did come to a real dialogue, I would ask it all about distant worlds, extraterrestrials, the price of butter on Mars, and about all the mysteries of the universe, such as: Where did it come from? What were its habits, its religion, its God? If its intention was to study a human being then transport him or her to an unknown planet, why hadn't it already done so? Perhaps, though, it was trying to accustom me to its presence. I would have to do the same to accustom people to its presence if I decided to publish these photographs, which were far more disconcerting than the earlier ones.

I was both afraid and fascinated. I worried that the creature's thoughts were the same as mine: I was studying it and it was studying me, that was my impression. Then I began to feel remorse because I should have helped it somehow, instead of just observing and photographing it. Maybe it would not come back to me because of that.

It was not long before Filiberto's sister, Antonella, came across the new photographs. Reluctantly, Filiberto told her about the incident, agreeing that the rest of the family should be informed.

The family was very confused, especially my mother and grandmother. My father and brother-in-law, on the other hand, simply discussed our possible course of action. We were all agreed that it was necessary to release information about the event, but also that it had to be done in the right way.

Grandmother was screaming and begging me to leave the creature alone. She threatened to supervise me personally every night and to make sure I went to bed instead of wandering around all night, running the risk of encountering that creature and getting involved in some terrible adventure. I tried to reassure her that I was certain the creature was harmless.

Meanwhile, although less frequent, the night expeditions to hunt down the creature continued. 'I didn't take part in them any more,' Filiberto explained, 'knowing too well that nobody could succeed in the way I had because it was the alien that decided when and by whom to be seen – and it seemed to have chosen me.'

INITIAL TELEVISION EXPOSURE

At the end of summer 1993, as the tourist season finished, Pretare returned to normal. No one bothered any longer to look for the alien. In October Filiberto was approached by a television news station which wanted to do a feature about his story. He did not mention the new pictures, so the crew filmed the burned photographs while Filiberto related his story and answered questions. Afterwards, locations of the encounters were filmed. When the feature ran, it was interrupted intermittently by images from Steven Spielberg's film *ET: The Extraterrestrial*, including the famous scene where Elliot and ET are riding a flying bicycle. 'These inserts, mixed with the interview, might have been effective,' said Filiberto, 'but they were not in keeping with my story. Yet the report, which was broadcast several times, provoked great interest, particularly among children. They believed me to be Elliot and wanted to be introduced personally to ET!'

A few days later a villager told Filiberto that he had seen the creature, which he described as similar to a bald monkey with a limp. He had seen it only from behind, however. Nevertheless, Filiberto was overjoyed. 'Finally I had a witness whom I knew well and considered reliable. I asked him to help me convince people in the village that the story was true, but he answered curtly that he didn't want to make a fool of himself: he had a family to consider and couldn't afford to go out on a limb. Later, we heard that he had denied everything, saying it was only a joke. Everyone had always known him as a serious man, so we could not understand the reason for his withdrawal.'

Surprisingly, no one from any of the UFO groups had yet visited Filiberto. After the television exposure, the Italian Centre for UFO Studies (CISU) wrote to Filiberto, enclosing money to cover the costs of mailing the two 'burned' photos, which they needed for analysis. 'I explained that I couldn't risk losing the pictures,' said Filiberto, 'but I invited them to come to Pretare. They put me in contact with one of their members who lived close to me. I spoke with him on the telephone, but he never seemed able to come and visit me.'

Filiberto received more telephone calls and letters from people asking to be cured, as well as from others claiming to receive messages from extraterrestrials by teletext, messages consisting of incomprehensible formulae. 'I devoted most attention to the letters from children. They were still amazed at the fact that ET had come out of the screen, and wanted to meet it. I didn't want to disappoint them so I answered that ET had gone back home, but that one day they would all meet it.'

THE HIGHEST BIDDER?

When Filiberto decided the time had come to have the new photographs published, he contacted Leonida Barezzi, the journalist who had written the piece for *Stop* magazine. Sounding excited at first, Barezzi seemed to lose interest after receiving Filiberto's sketch of the creature. He promised to contact a well-known Italian researcher, the producer of a documentary on animals, before coming to examine the photographs. Weeks went by. 'After many calls both to his office and to his home, I finally reached him,' said Filiberto. 'He explained that neither his magazine nor others wished to write about the story. He advised me to forget all about it, then hung up. Why had he lost interest?'

Filiberto considered taking his uncle's advice to sell the photographs to the highest bidder. 'I didn't want to do it only for the money, but also to show the world that there was irrefutable evidence of extraterrestrial life. I considered delivering the photos to the authorities, but worried that they would almost certainly confiscate them.'

A SECOND MATERIAL WITNESS

One night in the middle of September 1993 the Caponi family retired to bed rather late, Filiberto and his father later than the others. Suddenly the familiar scream was heard. 'We had just opened the window when the screaming stopped,' said Filiberto, 'but the creature was still moving through the bushes.'

My father wanted to see him clearly at all costs, and he was leaning out dangerously, but the creature remained hidden behind the vegetation. We expected him to show himself sooner or later. My father had just told me to hurry and fetch the camera when a trail of light illuminated the trees in the direction of the nestling leaves.

It was almost like daylight. Father stepped backwards, crouching down under the windowsill, covering his head with his arms. I did the same. We thought it was some kind of meteorite falling rapidly in our direction, but it proved to be a beam of light – a flash of light that blinded us for a few seconds. We were terrified. When the light receded, everything was quiet again. A few minutes later, I recall Father exclaiming: 'He's gone!' But it turned out he was wrong.

On the evening of 9 October 1993 Filiberto went to bed early. At about 02.00 he awoke suddenly, apparently without motivation, and could not get back to sleep. On returning from the bathroom, he half opened the window to take a look outside. It was raining.

I noticed something on the same spot where I had photographed the creature for the first time. I flung the window wide open and could see that the creature had come back.

It was right there, standing in that funny way and watching that same street lamp. I turned the light on and at the same moment the creature raised its head and spotted me. I took my camera at once, but this time I didn't only want to photograph it, I wanted someone else in the family to see it. I had to be very quiet; shouting would have frightened it. I also had to be very quick, because I didn't know how long it would stay there.

Grandmother slept in the room next to mine. I hesitated at first to wake her up because of her fear of the creature, but decided to take the risk because there wasn't time to go upstairs to wake my parents. I entered her room, fortunately unlocked that night, and awoke her gently. I begged her not to be afraid, explaining that the creature was outside and that I wanted her to see it because she too would then realize that it wasn't dangerous. She tried to persuade me not to go out but to call someone for help at once. I was afraid she would cry out so I told her not to make any noise and to hurry. I took her by the arm and helped her stand up, covering her mouth. I regretted treating her like this, but had no other choice.

We reached the window. The creature was still outside. Grandmother couldn't see it well as she was still sleepy and her sight wasn't so good. The creature hadn't moved far away; it was still watching the street lamp. I grabbed my Polaroid and pulled Grandmother downstairs. She was still begging me to call for help, which annoyed me because I feared the creature might escape and I would lose the chance of having another eyewitness.

I was afraid of how my grandmother would react at seeing something so unusual for the first time. Her reaction was totally unexpected. When she saw the creature she stopped trembling and talking, hesitated a little, and then smiled to the being. 'He's so small – he's a darling!' she exclaimed. 'What is he looking at?' She was speaking so tenderly, as if talking to a child. She told me to leave it alone and to not do anything, but I wanted to photograph it again and touch it gently. I asked her to intervene only if the creature became violent, but she said something about letting sleeping dogs lie.

In the meantime, the creature darted quick glances at us from time to time. I was afraid it would be gone any minute so I told Grandmother to go upstairs and look through the window to see what direction it would take. She insisted I let it alone and grabbed the camera which was around my neck, trying to stop me. I walked towards the creature, which was standing, completely naked, four to five metres from us. I noticed for the first time that it had no visible sexual organs.

When I came closer to it and took the photo it gave me another look, then turned its head towards the light. I left the photograph inside the camera, covering it with my left hand to protect it from the rain. After a moment's hesitation, I stretched my right hand towards the creature without touching it. Grandmother intervened, running toward me crying out not to touch it. I waved her away and tried to silence her. Now the creature was slowly retreating, watching her. She began whispering, telling me to come back and saying that she was afraid not so much of the creature's appearance but of its unknown motives. Dangerous though it might have been, I was determined to get closer. I waved to Grandmother to go upstairs and she hurried away.

I stretched my hand towards the creature again. This time I was so close I could have touched it, but at that very instant it bent and retained that position for a while, opening its mouth from time to time, apparently irritated by the raindrops that were falling from its chin. For a moment, I thought it wanted me to touch it, but just as I was about to touch its skin it ran away.

I ran home screaming to my grandmother to look out for the creature because I had already lost sight of it. While running I heard her telling me that it had hidden under the old arch. She begged me to come back, but I was determined to catch it, frustrated at watching it run away every time. I went under the arch, ignoring my fear of running into it in the tunnel, and aware that he might use the darkness to attack me. Finally, I was out of the tunnel and in front of a gate. In the light there, the creature was nowhere to be seen.

I pulled the photo out of the camera and put it in my pocket without checking it, then climbed, panting, over the gate and into an open field. There was a tomb-like silence, apart from the falling raindrops. I was overwhelmed by the excitement. I looked around hoping to see it, but to no avail.

I was sure this would be the night of contact or dialogue, but I had lost the creature once more, just when I had got so close and could have touched it. I wondered what I had done wrong. It had let me come so close, but that wasn't enough for me. I wanted the answers: What was it? Where did it come from? Why had it chosen me and then escaped? I felt desperate as I made my way home.

Filiberto arrived home, soaked with rain, at about 03.00, to learn that his parents had been looking for him, having been alerted by Antonia, the grandmother. His mother was in tears. Reassuring them all, he showed the new photograph. Fortunately, it had developed perfectly.

Filiberto felt that the time had now come to make the whole story and the photographs public, although he wondered if anyone would pay attention, amid the media devoting so much attention to the prevailing economic and political conditions in Italy. Italian government had become a contradiction in terms, with arrests of famous politicians and industrialists almost on a daily basis. 'Unlike in many other countries,' Filiberto explained, 'the UFO and alien subject stimulated very little interest in Italy, even prior to this particular crisis, and when the media did publish anything it was always done sarcastically and superficially. I was determined to try everything possible to bring this important story to their attention.'

I was now in possession of six photos and the time had come to show them to someone, even if I had to go to the press in person. I was no longer the only witness, because my grandmother had seen the creature too, even though I had forced her to do so. The others in my family felt somewhat left out of the picture. My father especially was frustrated because he had seen the creature only vaguely on 10 May. Grandmother's attitude changed completely. She was calmer about the situation, finally realizing that 'the nice little creature' wasn't some sort of ghost, though she continued to urge caution with regard to its intentions.

GIUSEPPE SEES THE LIGHT

On the evening of 13 October 1993 Filiberto's brother-in-law, Giuseppe, was driving back from work on his way to Pretare when he saw an intensely bright yellow sphere on Monte Vettore, a light that ascended, then slipped away. Ever sceptical, he dismissed it at the time. On his arrival home his embarrassment was evident as he related the sighting to the others.

The following morning Giuseppe's wife, Antonella, told Filiberto that her husband had not slept all night. He had woken up suddenly and startled her, standing beside the bed, but said nothing when she asked if he had had a nightmare. In the morning he finally admitted that he was on the point of falling asleep when an intense light illuminated the room. Dazzled and alarmed, he jumped out of bed. At first he thought he was just exhausted after a hard day's work, but the light was too intense and lasted for quite a few seconds, then it disappeared in a peculiar manner, concentrating itself in a ball near the window before flashing away quickly. Antonella saw nothing because she was under the blanket.

Filiberto wondered if all this might have been more than coincidental. 'I was reminded of what had happened to me and my father, of the beam of light that had fallen right in front of our house. I was sure the creature was still in the neighbourhood. That dazzling light appeared to be connected in some new way with it. My brother-in-law changed his sceptical attitude after this experience.'

Filiberto and Giuseppe now resolved to take the photos to Rome and show them at several editorial offices, with the minimum delay.

NOTES

1 Martín, Jorge, 'What Are the Creatures seen in Orocovis, Morovis, and Naranjito?', *Evidencia OVNI*, no. 6, 1995, pp. 16–17.

Chapter 11

Full Exposure

One Monday morning in mid-October 1993, Filiberto and Giuseppe drove to Rome to visit the main newspaper and magazine editorial offices. Having made no prior appointments, they were prepared for some difficulties. What they had not anticipated was the reaction of those editors they were able to see.

On arrival at the office of a famous monthly review, Filiberto was asked by the editor's secretary to explain the purpose of their visit. 'When I produced the photos, she took one glance at them and literally jumped out of the chair,' said Filiberto. 'She seemed disgusted and begged us to take "that blasted thing" away from her immediately.' Nonetheless, she did arrange a meeting with the editor.

> We briefly told him our story, explaining only the most significant points. He observed the photos very carefully one by one, arranging them in chronological order. After summoning an assistant, he asked us in a rather serious tone if we knew the creature's origin and identity. We couldn't answer except with hypotheses; the most incredible one about the alien being the most probable one. Fifteen minutes later his assistant came in and picked up the photos. After a quiet word with the assistant, the editor explained that they couldn't possibly publish the photos because theirs was a mainly political review, and advised us to try a different sort of magazine. If anyone did publish them, they added, it probably would lead to many problems. They warned us to be careful, because we might be interfering with some top-secret government experiment or with something that could disturb and scare people. They advised us to inform the authorities, before some magazine blew our story out of proportion.

Filiberto and Giuseppe were disappointed. Giuseppe felt that the editor's advice should be heeded, but Filiberto wanted to try elsewhere.

I didn't think that going to the authorities was such a good idea: they surely would confiscate the photos or classify me as a mythomaniac or who-knows-what. They must have known about the story by then, and the fact that they hadn't appeared on the scene yet made me very suspicious. It was out of the question to go to some small, third-rate magazine because it would ruin the story from the start. There weren't many respectable reviews that would know how to reproduce the story properly. We had to find the good ones. So we found another editorial office and succeeded in talking to the editor. Our photos astonished him, but he acted exactly like the former one. We spent the day in the offices of various newspapers and magazines, but it was always the same – they couldn't take the photos or the story. It was my impression that something or someone held them back, or perhaps they simply suspected a hoax. Still, we didn't ask for money and were willing to show the photos to their experts for brief analysis, and all those who did examine them found them to be authentic.

It was unbelievable that nobody wanted to publish these photographs. The press, even the broadsheets, did not hesitate to publish the most banal articles, yet refused to write about this unique and proven case. True, the image of the creature might scare someone of a particularly sensitive nature, but it was certainly less scary or disgusting than all those reports on violence, murder and genocide in Bosnia, for example.

THE ITALIAN NATIONAL PRESS AGENCY

Filiberto and his brother-in-law eventually succeeded in making an appointment with the Italian National Press Agency (ANSA), whose photographic expert, Renato Bianchi, seemed genuinely astonished by the pictures. He promised to discuss the case with his editor, expressing confidence that acceptance by this most prestigious agency would confirm the authenticity of the photos and story.

Bianchi said it was a very important story but that we must be cautious. The story probably would be announced on the national television news then repeated by all the media. It was necessary, he said, to leave the original Polaroids with the agency at some point, though he understood that we couldn't part with the photos before some sort of guarantee was given.

Five days later Bianchi telephoned me. I noticed at once that his tone was different. He sounded confused, explaining that the agency could not accept the story because it was not their policy to involve themselves in such cases: they could not afford to have the problems that would surely arise if the story were published; however, he invited me to Rome again because he felt that something odd was going on. He couldn't accept the fact that such a story wasn't going to be published. The world had waited so long for evidence of the existence of other intelligent beings in the universe and now that it was finally possible to produce it, nobody wanted to write about it – not even the 'yellow' press.

We returned to Rome four days later, this time with my mother and sister. Renato now looked worried. He confessed that something else was now bothering him. One morning, while going to his office, he was stopped in the street by two men. They didn't identify themselves, but asked him to give them information about me and my experiences. The excessive interest of the two men scared him. He replied that he didn't know much, that I had come to him seeking help to publish the story. The men advised him in an abrupt manner to drop the matter, and that went for me too, because it was not our business, or else we'd all get ourselves into serious trouble.

There was more to it. Bianchi hurried to the office to check if the photos were still there and ran into two of his colleagues. They repeated more or less the same thing as the men in the street had. Bianchi knew these colleagues well; they worked with him side by side every day. Angered, he asked them bluntly whom they were representing. They answered that they were members of some religious sect, an answer he found incredible. As journalists, he explained, they had professional obligations not to suppress information nor to put pressure on a colleague who was only trying to do his job, without at least giving him a credible explanation.

'MEN IN BLACK'

Renato Bianchi told Filiberto and Giuseppe that he was still keen to publish the story and photographs, even if it meant that he would have to bypass the agency and approach some tabloid. He had the idea of putting the matter in the hands of his son, Alessandro, a former police officer and now a well-connected photojournalist. Bianchi phoned his son from the office and arrangements were made for Alessandro to come to Pretare. 'It was agreed that he would take my original photos and give us a personal document signed by him and countersigned by me and Giuseppe,' explained Filiberto.

He would promise to return the photos after publishing them, and not use them for his personal benefit. He would also request my written permission to publish the story, because I was to give the interview and there could be no misunderstandings.

When the call was over, two men, one of them bearded, rushed into the office, startling us. They didn't say a word. One of them started rummaging through a card index while the other busied himself on the computer. We assumed they were employees of the agency doing their usual job, but Bianchi gave us a sign that it was not like that, by treading on my foot under the table and shaking his head. We understood it was necessary to change the subject, so Bianchi started talking about something innocuous. The two men showed no signs of leaving so we acted as naturally as possible, thanked Bianchi and left the office, with the Polaroids safely in my pocket. Bianchi pretended to say goodbye.

We left the building and headed to the car, where my sister and mother were waiting. The man with the beard was following us at a short distance. He seemed to want to make us understand that we were his quarry, because when we turned round he stared at us in a threatening manner. I was scared, especially since I had the Polaroids in my jacket pocket. He continued following us, so we ducked into a crowded bar, but he wouldn't give up, following us into the bar and continuing to stare at us. After drinking our coffee we hurried out of the bar, leaving him stuck in the queue in front of the till.

The Caponi family left their car in the underground parking lot and walked to the nearest restaurant to have lunch. Filiberto immediately telephoned Bianchi and asked about the two men in the office.

He told me they were the same colleagues who had threatened him, but he hadn't expected that one of them would shadow us. He didn't know who the two previous men were – those who had

185

not identified themselves. He was very worried about them, so he advised me to hold on tightly to the photos. If someone tried to shadow us we should call him immediately and he would call the police.

After lunch, we were walking towards the parking lot when we noticed two men wearing elegant, dark clothes. They were standing on both sides of the parking entrance as if waiting for somebody. There was another man there, dressed the same way, walking up and down in front of them with a mobile phone in his hand. All three wore dark sunglasses. The car parked near the entrance was dark blue, with dark-tinted windows. I think it was a Lancia Thema limousine. I noticed unusual initials on the number plate, the blue CD [Corps Diplomatique] initials, and a little flag that looked like the American one. I noted down the number plate and found out later that the car was used by the American Diplomatic Corps.

Had it not been for their odd attitude we wouldn't have paid any attention to these men. Now I was alarmed. My feelings were almost the same as when I had seen the odd creature for the first time, only these fellows didn't look harmless. I recalled those anonymous phone calls warning me of strange men wearing black uniforms, an indication perhaps that they were members of some organization (such as the FBI or CIA). Whoever they were, their way of dressing was certainly effective, giving them an air of absolute authority. They looked like celluloid gangsters.

What were we to do? The rest of the family stood still, staring at each other, clearly very worried. I decided that if the men stopped me I wouldn't put up any resistance and would hand over the photos. Then I had a brainwave. Ordering Giuseppe to do exactly as I said, I told him to go to the underground car park and to tell us, in a loud voice, to wait for him outside while he got the 'stuff' (meaning the photographs) from the car. Once he got there he was supposed to unlock all the doors so that we could get into the car and drive off quickly. Giuseppe did exactly as he was told, pretending to ignore the men who were staring at him. Meanwhile, I told my mother and sister to rush into the car.

I knew their plan was to get hold of the photos. My plan was to delay them as long as possible, making them believe I did not have the Polaroids with me, but that Giuseppe was going to collect them. The most dangerous moment would be when he came out of the car park. And it was just at this point that the three men made their move. One of them put his mobile phone in his pocket and adjusted his tie, just as Giuseppe shot out of the car park. We all jumped in. I looked behind to see that the other two men were running towards us.

We got stuck in the traffic, so that the two men easily caught up and had a good look at us. By now, my mother and sister were terrified and urged Giuseppe to get away as quickly as possible. We managed to overtake the traffic, but by this time the man with the mobile phone had jumped into the Lancia and came after us with a screech of tyres. Giuseppe told me to keep an eye on the car, which continued to follow us. We were genuinely worried that these men might even open fire on us. Fortunately, Giuseppe knows Rome well, and after 20 minutes of wild driving we finally felt safe enough to stop the car and recover from the ordeal. Mother urged us to drive on, fearing that the men might appear again.

'We were a normal family who had emerged from an absurd and disquieting situation,' Filiberto commented. 'My plan had worked, thanks to the fact that we have always been a united family. But we would have to be even more united if we now had to live in fear that the "men in black" might reappear.'

VISTO

Filiberto related details of the incident to Bianchi, who said he had no intentions of dropping the matter. In the meantime, his son Alessandro had found a magazine, *Visto*, which was interested in doing a feature on the story. Alessandro came to Pretare on 19 October 1993. 'As a former policeman, he understood what was going on,' said Filiberto.

To save time, he said he would look after the photographic part while the interview would be conducted over the telephone. He signed a document stating that he would pass only copies of the original Polaroids to *Visto*. I felt I could trust him.

After I had given the interview, the journalist pointed out that it was in the magazine's interests to do a convincing article, but added that the photos would not appear on the cover nor on the first page, in order to avoid any censorship by the authorities – or by the 'men in black'. This had happened with other stories unrelated to aliens, they told me.

Visto purchased the photographic rights from Alessandro.

The fee having been divided, Filiberto was left with 200,000 lira (about £80). The four-page article – headed I AM A FRIEND OF ET AND I WILL PROVE IT – appeared on 28 October 1993 (issue no. 43), together with an enlargement of the creature, sitting naked on the ground, spread across two pages, and another showing the creature apparently standing up. Some of Filiberto's sketches also were included. In the last part of the article, Dr Roberto Pinotti, vice-president of the National Ufology Centre (CUN), reminded readers of the case involving Giuseppe Zitella, the retired air force officer who encountered a similar creature in June 1993. The reaction in Pretare was mixed, as Filiberto explained:

> My fellow villagers were somewhat irritated that I had told nobody about the last photos, but I did not want to make the same mistake as when I had confided in my friend Carlo. Their resentment was soon overcome by the fascination of these last Polaroids, though many were disillusioned by the unpleasant appearance of the humanoid. Elderly people, in particular, thought that the powers of evil were at work and that the devil was about to show himself. Others, however, found it rather sweet, and expressed a certain tenderness towards the creature, which had now become a sort of mascot for the village.

RIVAL FACTIONS

Almost immediately after the *Visto* article appeared, Filiberto and his family were approached by various national UFO groups. Filiberto was told to keep the press at bay when they started to invade the village – or at least until the ufologists themselves had invaded the village. 'It became a competition between the ufologists and the journalists to see who could get the story of those last disconcerting photos,' said Filiberto.

Three members of the National Ufology Centre interviewed Filiberto and examined the Polaroids carefully. Chief investigator Gianfranco Lollino declared that he was particularly baffled by the strange 'burned' prints. Radiation readings taken at the sites where the creature had appeared proved negative. One of the investigators made the obvious connection that since Filiberto's work included sculpting, and that he enjoyed Steven Spielberg's films, he might have created the creature himself. 'I agreed that it would not have been difficult for me to construct such a model,' said Filiberto, 'but pointed out that I certainly would have made it rather more attractive. I also explained that I was not desperate for money and could earn that by my daily work, without resorting to trickery.'

According to CUN, the little creature might still be in the area. Perhaps, they surmised, it had escaped from the aliens – or even the Americans – who were trying to recover it. In any event the group made clear their intention to capture the creature before anyone else did! CUN warned Filiberto not only about the 'men in black' but also about the potential appearance of low-flying white helicopters. As it happened, prior to the warning Filiberto had been on the roof, mending the chimney, when a white helicopter passed so low over the house that nearby trees bowed in the downdraft from its rotor blades. He gave little thought to the incident and later learned from other villagers that the helicopter belonged to a petroleum company conducting geological research in the area. Some time later, however, a military jet overflew the village at extremely low altitude, alarming local people. Filiberto assumed this was related to NATO operations connected with the crisis in Bosnia, although, perhaps becoming slightly paranoid after CUN's dire warnings, he did wonder if the military was looking for a trace of the creature, or a piece of wreckage from its supposed craft.

CUN continued its investigations in ensuing months. They concluded that the creature corresponded in some respects to other cases and descriptions, but was anomalous regarding its legs. Although it had limbs similar to those of a man with particularly developed calves, the feet could be classified as those of an animal, since they resembled the hoof of a horse.

Meanwhile, members of another group, the Rome Centre for UFO Studies, headed by Massimo Fratini, introduced themselves to Filiberto and proceeded to conduct their own investigation. On the question of the creature's morphology, there was a difference of opinion. Fratini, a radiologist, maintained that the feet were not necessarily of (terrestrial) animal origin and therefore could not be compared with horses' hooves solely because they terminated in a bifurcation; rather, the foot was composed of one large toe and a second, smaller toe, joined together. Filiberto also pointed out that the structure of the foot showed a sole similar to that of a human being. 'I said that we were talking neither about a man nor an animal but possibly a hybrid creature, not produced by man,' he added. 'To explain it away as a genetic experiment performed by man was even more absurd than the hypothesis of it being an alien.'

The Rome centre voiced the opinion that if the creature was alien, it might have been undergoing some form of mutation, perhaps as a result of adaptation to the Earth's atmosphere. It was also possible, they surmised, that this mutation might have been the result of the supposed spaceship's impact on landing, wherever that had been, causing burns all over the creature's body and changing its physical aspect.

During interviews with villagers in Pretare, the investigators spoke to a friend of Filiberto's who, for the first time, confessed to having had a sighting of the creature. 'In a trembling voice, he told us how he had been awakened one night by the screaming,' said Filiberto. 'When he plucked up courage to get up and look out of the window, he actually saw the outline of a small creature running screaming across the pastures, scattering the sheep and pursued by sheepdogs. My friend's father, being an experienced hunter, instinctively reached for his gun. He would have given chase had it not been for his dependence on a dialysis machine.'

Rivalry continued to play a part in the investigations into Filiberto's story, particularly when the UFO groups learned that an important French newspaper, *Le Figaro*, wanted to run an article and that Filiberto had been invited to appear on national television. Clearly, such exposure threatened to undermine the ufologists' hopes of securing a central role in managing the story.

I FATTI VOSTRI

In late October 1993, Filiberto, together with his father and grandmother, was invited by the state television channel RAI-2 to appear on a programme called *I Fatti Vostri* (Your

PLATE 21 This picture (Photo 3 – enlargement) was taken on the night of 10/11 August 1993 (prior to the two previous pictures). 'On its back was a brown lump,' Caponi reported. 'Short arms protruded from its sides. The legs were very long and still covered in bandages.'
(© *Filiberto Caponi*)

PLATE 22 The last picture in the series (Photo 6 – enlargement), taken on the night of 9/10 October 1993, in the presence of Caponi's grandmother. Reflections from the camera's flash on the creature's skin are due to rain.
(© *Filiberto Caponi*)

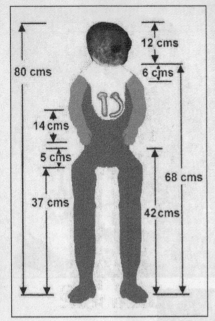

PLATE 23 Diagram by Professor Roger Green showing the creature's measurements, based on Photo 6 (Plate 22) and taking into account the dimensional information obtained from both standing and sitting images.

PLATE 24 (*Right*) The Polaroid camera used by Filiberto Caponi to take the photographs of the creature. (© *Timothy Good*)

PLATE 25 Diagram based on the image of the creature depicted in Photo 2 (Plate 18). Measurements are derived from the dimensions of the paving stones (20x20cms). (See Chapter 13 for details.)

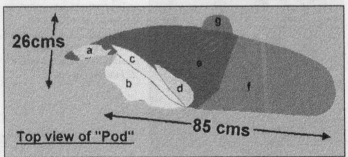

Top view of "Pod"

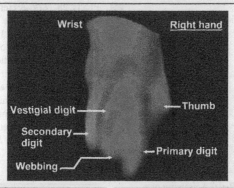

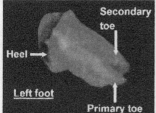

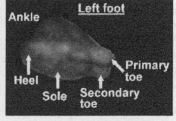

PLATE 26 (*Above*)
The creature's right
hand and left foot,
based on Photo 6
(Plate 22).

PLATE 27 (*Right*)
Bruce Renton, the
British reporter and
former intelligence
officer, who
introduced Filiberto
Caponi to the author
in Rome, February
1994. (© *Timothy
Good*)

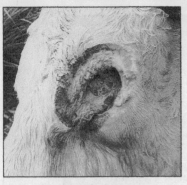

PLATE 28 (*Left*) A Hereford cow found mutilated in the Uinta Basin, Utah, October 1998. Note the immaculate excision of the eye, ruling out mutilation by predators or scavengers. In addition, the cow's heart had inexplicably been reduced to a pulp. Other bizarre findings included a missing foetus. (© *National Institute of Discovery Science*)

PLATE 29 (*Right*) A drawing of a 'chupacabras' encountered by José Miguel Agosto in Canovanas, Puerto Rico, August 1995. (*José Miguel Agosto*)

PLATE 30 (*Below left*) Agent José Collazo of the Canóvanas Police Department, who shot a 'chupacabras' at point-blank range in Campo Rico, Puerto Rico, September 1995. (© *Timothy Good*)

PLATE 31 (*Below right*) An artist's impression of one of the creatures captured by military personnel in Varginha, Brazil, January 1996. (*Carti* © *Vitório Pacaccini & Maxs Portes*)

PLATE 32 The Manzano Mountains, near Albuquerque, New Mexico. According to one of the author's sources, an alien base was sited in the vicinity of the US Air Force Manzano Weapons Storage Area. (© *Timothy Good*)

PLATE 33 (*Above*) A view from Rio Grande of 'El Yunque', the Caribbean National Forest, Puerto Rico. (© *Timothy Good*)

PLATE 34 'La Coca' waterfall in El Yunque. In August 1997 Dr Darby Williams, a dean of Bowling Green State University, Ohio, entered the forest at this tourist attraction and went missing for twelve days before re-emerging at the same spot. He has never revealed what happened to him. (© *Timothy Good*)

PLATE 35 A drawing (1) and photograph (2) by A. Hyatt Verrill of the ferocious 'Sun Dog', referred to in Chapter 16. (© *A. Hyatt Verrill/G.P. Putnam's Sons*)

PLATE 36 A photograph of the so-called 'serpent-bird', captured in Gurabo, Puerto Rico, in 1990. (*María Ortiz*)

PLATE 37 This skull was discovered in October 1990 in the region of Susamyr, Kirgizskaya, following numerous reports of UFOs and 'bigfoot'-type creatures. According to Dr S.B. Begaliev, the head physician at the Panfilovski Central Regional Hospital, the skull might have come from a creature with a highly developed intellect, but of no known species. The skull had a large cranium with a long nasal section, as well as a fixed joint attached to the skull where the neck vertebrae should join. (*Komsolomets Kirgizia, 7 April 1990*)

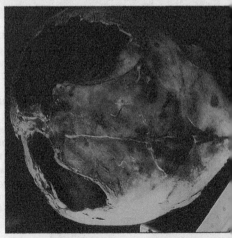

PLATE 38 An aerial view of the National Astronomy and Ionosphere Center, Arecibo Observatory, Puerto Rico – the largest radio telescope on Earth. (© *Timothy Good*)

PLATE 39 The control rooms at the Arecibo Observatory, January 1999. From right to left: Graham Sheppard, Dr José Alonso, Educational Officer and Director of the Visitor Center, and Edwin Vazquez, one of the Civil Defence employees assisting the author with his investigations. (© *Timothy Good*)

PLATES 40 & 41 One of the US Government's bases in the Republic of the Marshall Islands. These photos, taken prior to 1991, show Kwajalein Island, which features the world's largest lagoon and a 6700-foot runway. According to the author's sources, several alien bases exist in the Pacific Ocean, including one in the Kwajalein Atoll. (*Pan American World Airways/DynCorp.*)

Affairs), hosted by Giancarlo Magalli, to be transmitted live on the evening of 5 November at 20.30. A few days beforehand Filiberto went to Rome to discuss the format of the programme with one of its editors, Filomena, who emphasized that it was essential neither to frighten nor to disillusion the viewers. Filiberto took the advice of Renato Bianchi, his National Press Agency contact, to refrain from mentioning anything about the 'men in black' episode. All six Polaroid photographs would be shown, together with some of the sketches depicting the creature in motion. 'We were warned to expect the occasional joke to lighten such a "taboo" subject,' Filiberto explained. The studio layout included an informal setting of tables and chairs for the interviewees and audience.

Before approaching our table, the interviewer gave a short introduction, explaining that the public would see the photographs of the creature and connecting these events with those reported in Sulmona and Pescara, because the former air force officer, Zitella, had been a guest on the same programme. Then Signor Magalli put some pointed questions to all three of us.

Magalli asked Grandmother how she felt on first seeing the creature. He had wanted her to reply that she was convinced it was the devil. Partly for moral reasons, but perhaps mostly due to superstition, she refused to say as much, because it was a Friday and according to ancient superstitions in the village, one should never pronounce the name of the devil on a Friday! Innocently, she said that at first the creature had seemed to her to be a fairy or a spirit. The audience was plainly captivated by her. As to my father, he simply confirmed everything.

When the photos were shown, the studio audience reacted with a murmur of surprise and incredulity, followed by an immediate silence, which was interrupted by Magalli who made signs for applause. He commented on the photos with touches of humour; for example in comparing the creature's apparently burned skin to a roast piglet.

In a videotape recording of the programme, which I have reviewed many times, Filiberto, his father and grandmother come across as sincere witnesses, passionate in their conviction of having encountered something unearthly. The programme was an unprecedented success, drawing an estimated nine million viewers.

LE FIGARO

On 18 November 1993 a correspondent from *Le Figaro* arrived in Pretare to conduct an interview with Filiberto, his family and some of the villagers. 'We showed him the most attractive parts of the village which, until the arrival of that small creature, had been destined to remain unknown to the world, but which were now receiving the attention of the media,' Filiberto reported.

> No doubt this would help the village, which for years had been going through a financial crisis, like so many other Italian villages. Perhaps that little being would help us to promote its natural beauties and its regional crafts.
> We accompanied the correspondent to the next village, Arquata del Tronto, to make photocopies of my sketches of the creature. Many people now realized that a foreign newspaper was dealing with the event, and because of the ancient rivalry that my village had with Arquata, everybody looked at us with a certain hostility.

Following the television programme on RAI-2, Filiberto was filled with a disturbing presentiment: that the authorities, concerned about the widespread publicity and resulting public excitement, would finally intervene. He was right. Within hours of the interview with *Le Figaro* the Carabinieri of Arquata del Tronto arrived on his doorstep.

Chapter 12

Charges, Confessions and Denials

In Italy there are three branches of police: the Vigili Urbani, or municipal police, which handles traffic and other city police tasks; the Polizia di Stato, the national, or state police, subject to the Home Office; and the Carabinieri (often abbreviated to CC), the military police, subject to the Ministry of Defence, which deals with major theft, other serious crimes, demonstrations and military affairs.

Filiberto was not unduly surprised by the unannounced arrival of four carabinieri, having expected a visit ever since Gianfranco Lollino had warned him of the possibility. 'I told the carabinieri that I knew why they had come,' said Filiberto, 'and this statement made the officer in charge very suspicious. He asked if he could speak with me in private. I replied that this was my family, so they could discuss freely anything they wanted, but the commandant insisted on speaking solely with me. And at that moment, fear took hold of me.'

We went into my room where, with the doors closed, the commandant showed me a search warrant and an order to confiscate all the material in my possession concerning the affair of the alien creature. I was accused of having 'created panic and spreading false rumours liable to disturb the public peace'. This was ridiculous. Here I was in my own room with four carabinieri carrying out a search-and-seizure mandate. The commandant explained that there would be serious consequences if this alien story went any further. I had the right to continue with it, but this would mean a real penal case which would cost a great deal of money. I asked who had brought the charges against me. He replied that the story of the creature had not convinced the chief magistrate and that the charges were brought by the Carabinieri themselves, who had been investigating me for almost six months.

I was made aware of my responsibilities. On several occasions the CC had intervened to stop groups of excited people, sometimes fully armed, hunting the alien in the surrounding countryside with the intention of capturing it dead or alive. Had this continued, someone could have been seriously hurt. Moreover, the commandant went on, some elderly people and children had been so disturbed by the pictures that they were afraid of going out in the evening or sleeping alone. I had to admit this was not permissible, even though I believed that the villagers were rather more entertained than afraid.

The commandant suggested that the best way of resolving this problem was for me to confess that I had faked the Polaroid photographs, taking advantage of my knowledge of ceramics. I was only 23 years old and too young to compromise my life: I felt that it would be safer for me to co-operate. I handed over the Polaroids, as well as the lid of the box that had swollen, and explained that I really had seen a strange creature, but not being able to prove it, I had made a clay puppet reproducing the creature, using my professional skills.

The commandant seemed satisfied with this confession, but to close the case, he said, the magistrate would need a real puppet or at least a piece of one, so that they could explain the Polaroids more convincingly. No puppet was found in the house, so I went with the CC to the place where I usually throw away the material left over from my work. I picked up a piece of clay and pretended it was the piece belonging to the puppet – a leg or an arm.

The CC put the Polaroids together with the curved, burned lid of the box, and said they required a signed statement from me, which had to be taken down at the barracks. We then joined the rest of the family, who of course had no idea what I had told the police. At this point Giuseppe began to get angry with them because he thought they were abusing their authority. My mother was literally shocked, seeing her son surrounded by four carabinieri, without knowing the reason. She did not understand that they were fully within their rights and could turn the house upside down if they wanted, to look for further incriminating evidence, such as more photographs.

Before going with the CC to their headquarters at the barracks in Arquata del Tronto, I accompanied them to the places where I had encountered the creature, doing my best not to alert the whole village to what was going on. We then returned to the house, where the commandant explained that there was another problem to resolve – that of the article in *Le Figaro*. It was too late. The article had already gone to press and no official denial could alter the fact if it went ahead. The CC said that in this case their only course of action would be to send a helicopter to France that very evening. I still do not know if they managed to stop the French article in time because I never saw it, but I do know that the same article was sent by the same journalist to Germany, where it eventually appeared [as a brief piece, with one photo of the creature].[1] The officer added that the Japanese were also interested in the story, so my statement of denial had to be transmitted internationally and last several days. If the story reached foreign countries it would be difficult to prevent a flood of journalists and students of the subject from invading Pretare.

What would my friends think of me? What legal consequences would ensue from the official accusations? I had never even had a parking ticket, I pointed out. The commandant reassured me that my previous unblemished record would be taken into account. Regarding the official charge, he said I would be able to clear myself of it by paying a fine of not more than 600,000 lira. First of all, however, I would have to be questioned by the judge for preliminary investigations.

I became more and more convinced that I had done the right thing for my family and myself by denouncing the photographs. My mother, in particular, had recently been ill, and had this business continued she might have fallen ill again.

HEADQUARTERS

The commandant told Filiberto to follow him in his car to the Carabinieri headquarters in Arquata del Tronto. Although Filiberto's father wanted to go along, he was not allowed to do so. 'Before we went to the headquarters,' said Filiberto, 'I told the CC about the episode involving the "men in black" in Rome. They responded that this was yet another good reason to be rid of the story.'

At headquarters, the commandant typed out Filiberto's statement. About a quarter of an hour later, the deputy public prosecutor and a young man appointed as Filiberto's lawyer arrived.

It was explained to me that I should now repeat what I had already told the CC, taking care not to make any personal comment that might make my situation worse.

I had already decided on my defence, discounting the photographs but not the story. Before proceeding, the lawyer asked to speak in private with me. He explained that if I wanted to, I could stick to my story with the aid of a lawsuit, falling back on the proofs that had been taken away from me, but the real problem was the Polaroids. However, he warned, a lawsuit could mean waiting a long time and would be expensive. I thought it unusual that the deputy public prosecutor had been called out at that hour in the evening, considering the typical slowness of the judicial system in Italy. As far as I could gather, I was about to be subjected to a kind of trial at police headquarters.

The prosecutor began to ask me a lot of questions while the commandant typed it all down. The lawyer sat beside me with the book of the penal code in his hand, but he said little. At first I was rather afraid of the prosecutor because of his serious demeanour, but I soon realized that he was a very calm and sympathetic person. He reassured me that absolutely nothing would happen to me, even though the last word would rest with the judge. These formalities at the headquarters took about four hours.

When he left, the prosecutor explained that the following morning there would be a complete denial of everything in all the principal newspapers. Meanwhile, my lawyer would prepare a request for my acquittal on the basis of the investigations carried out by the CC, who supported both me and my story. Everything was arranged in the following way: the episode had really occurred, as was testified by reliable witnesses, but the real problem was the set of Polaroid photographs. In short, as long as one tells a story like mine, which cannot be proved, however absurd it may seem, nothing serious can happen. It can be explained away as an hallucination, for example, but if a story is supported with film or photographs, everything becomes more complicated because no longer can one talk of hallucination and one can end up trapped in a series of crimes which, though foreseen by the law, seemed absurd to me.

When I returned home and recounted to my worried family what had happened, father said that I should have simply hidden the Polaroids, as some others had advised. I pointed out that this would have been construed by the CC as an attempt to conceal evidence: they were the law and they knew how to apply it. So now I no longer had my precious Polaroids, and had to be satisfied with the excellent reproductions made by the newspapers and CUN.

SCANDAL

The following morning, a scandal hit the newspapers in Pretare and surrounding towns. THE UFO OF PRETARE ENDS UP IN COURT; FIRST HE SEES THE UFO THEN THE JUDGE were two of the headlines. Mostly, the whole affair was simply ridiculed; there were even comments that RAI-2 itself had fallen victim to the 'hoax'.

That same day, by chance, Filiberto encountered his defence lawyer. 'He was determined to sue the various newspapers for having published this before the final verdict,' said Filiberto. 'I appreciated his tenacity, but I had not escaped from one legal action in order to start another. The lawyer's name had appeared in the articles and it was clear that the case would certainly have helped his career. After all, it was not every day that a lawyer was called upon to defend a youth who met aliens by night!'

Fully expecting to have to endure mockery and insults, as well as further anonymous phone calls, Filiberto was pleasantly surprised when nothing happened, although he did have arguments in Pretare with some of the villagers. 'You see, I told you so,' they would tell him, 'it was all a fake.' The Caponi family also suffered from the changing relationship with their friends and neighbours. There were a few positive developments, however, such as when the mayor of Ascoli Piceno summoned Filiberto to his office to thank him for increasing tourism in the area! Paradoxically, all the denials had created more interest than the original story.

The Caponi case is not unique in leading to advice from the Carabinieri to 'forget all about it'. At the end of August 1977, seven witnesses at Sturno, Avellino, near Naples, encountered a humanoid being dressed in a silvery, one-piece suit, and a brightly illuminated cylindrical object. On the same day, news of the nocturnal encounter reached the CC barracks at Frigento and a team was sent out to examine traces at the landing site. All seven witnesses were interrogated separately, then together. Individual depositions were signed and the witnesses strongly advised by the police officers to remain silent about their experience. 'Better that you forget all about it – for the well-being of all,' they said. Asked why, the commandant said that they were acting on 'orders from superiors'.[2]

CLAIMS OF A HOAX

Filiberto was shocked by one newspaper headline stating that the National Ufology Centre no longer supported his claims. 'These people, who I thought supported me and should now have been at my side, now turned against me. I understood that they had to protect their reputation, but, astonishingly, this article implied that it was they who had discovered the "fraud".' It later transpired that CUN had visited Sergeant Tersigni, chief of the local Carabinieri, to share details of their investigation into the affair. Tersigni reportedly professed his conviction that the story was a hoax.

Although they were first to contact Filiberto following publicity about his initial claims, the Italian Centre for UFO Studies (CISU) remained the only main national organization that had yet to arrange a meeting with him. Following the scandal, they wrote him a letter accusing him of fraud. 'I wrote back, saying they had less right than anybody to accuse me, since they knew so little about the true facts,' said Filiberto. 'I also warned them that if they continued with these accusations I would resort to the law. They wrote me a letter of apology, blaming the superficial coverage by the press, and reiterating their intention to investigate the case properly, but the Rome Centre for UFO Studies, then investigating my case in depth, succeeded in steering them away from me.'

I wrote to Dr Edoardo Russo, an editor of the CISU's magazine, *UFO: Rivista di Informazione Ufologica*,[3] requesting clarification of CISU's current position on the Caponi case. In his reply, Russo enclosed a copy of a letter he had sent to a Brazilian researcher:

> In May 1993 a young artist in Pretare d'Arquata (province of Ascoli Piceno) allegedly saw and photographed on several different occasions a mysterious humanoid entity, seemingly wounded, which he heard crying. Some of the pictures mysteriously 'burned', some remained and he finally sold them to newspapers and TV. Ufologists and police were unimpressed and finally got him to confess he had falsified the story, by making a

plasticine puppet and photographing it. He was even accused of [spreading] false and alarming news. The case had been closed for three years when it was resurrected in December 1996 by the sensationalist magazine *Dossier Alieni*[4] (edited by Roberto Pinotti and Maurizio Baiata) who gave it the front-page story, omitting the conclusions of their own CUN investigator who had first demonstrated the hoax![5]

In his letter to me, Dr Russo makes it clear that he accepts the hoax verdict, although it is evident that CISU did not conduct a proper investigation.[6] As to the statement that Filiberto sold the photographs to 'newspapers and TV', that is only partially true, in that Filiberto received a relatively modest sum from *Visto* (200,000 lira). He and his family were given five-star hotel accommodation plus expenses for their appearance on the RAI-2 TV programme. Furthermore, Filiberto did not 'confess he had falsified the story': on the contrary, in his statement to the Carabinieri he 'confessed' that he had only fabricated the Polaroid photographs, not the story itself.

Dr Russo is correct in pointing out that CUN dismissed the story as a hoax. I have a copy of CUN's report, forwarded to me by Dr Russo, and their analysis of the case, particularly regarding the Polaroids, includes certain interesting observations:

The creature shown in [Photos 3–5] is completely different from the one [shown in Photo 6] . . . Probably the choice of the materials for fabricating the creature was different . . . The skin appears to have more reflective qualities. How is this possible? The skin does not appear to be monochromatic . . . we all remember playing with plasticine [as children] with different colours . . .

[We are] sceptical of the anatomical shapes, especially the hip and the calf; for example, on the other pictures, the calf is not as enhanced as the previous one . . . We were also very surprised by the static nature of the creature. Why so stationary if it was scared? The only thing that changes is the angle of the photographer. We think it's a puppet.

The most overwhelming factor that persuades us that this is a hoax is that the eighth picture – the previous seven pictures weren't available and he showed us an eighth – is completely identical to the third [i.e. sixth] one. It differs in one unique detail:

there is a white stone coming out of the groin area. The puppet has been put on a wall. We can prove this with a geometrical analysis of the shadows . . .[7]

Certainly, the creature depicted in Photo 6 differs from the one shown in Photos 3, 4 and 5, in that it appears thinner, seems more reddish in colour and is reflective. The reflection might be explained by the fact that, during that final encounter in the small hours of 10 October 1993, it was raining. It is also possible that the rain may have altered the apparent colour of the creature's skin. Study of Photos 4 and 5 reveals strata-type coloration, implying that Filiberto used multicoloured plasticine to fabricate the 'puppet', as claimed by CUN. But why would a faker go to the length of fabricating the bulbous 'sack' on the creature's back and encasing its legs in obviously terrestrial bandages (Photo 3), as well as fabricating that strange, whitish substance seen on its head, neck and chest, and those even more unusual white 'tubes' (Photos 4, 5 and 6)? Moreover, there is another case involving a strange substance and 'tubes' – a case that Filiberto could not have known.

One night, early in November 1989, two boys were confronted by a hideous creature that jumped out of some bushes in the Rabanal area of Puerto Rico, between Cidra and Aibonito. Described as about three feet tall with brown hairy fur, two large gaping eyes, a couple of holes for a nose and two sharp fangs, the creature remained for a while underneath a street lamp, trembling and writhing as if in pain, and emitting queer noises. It then began foaming at the mouth and from several 'fleshy tubes' in its chest emerged a foamy, green liquid.[8] Though dissimilar from the Caponi creature in most respects, this singular report in Puerto Rico provides a degree of corroboration for Filiberto's claims inasmuch as it was first published (in Spanish) in 1995.

Regarding the 'eighth photo', I wrote to Roberto Pinotti, Gianfranco Lollini and Maurizio Baiata requesting clarification, explaining that, as far as I was aware, there were only seven Polaroid photographs in all, the seventh (which I have) made at the request of the Carabinieri to identify one of the sites where the creature had been photographed.

'Really, we saw it,' Pinotti told me, 'but as far as we know, nobody else saw it, and it simply disappeared.'

Regarding the apparent contradiction with our earlier conclusions and our later article in *Dossier Alieni*, we decided to publish that old case because Caponi had problems with the Carabinieri and there was a lot of publicity about the charges, which from a legal point of view gave him a certain aura of rehabilitation. So it was this fact that obliged us to focus on the case again. We did not come to any conclusion because, as far as we know, there is no conclusion. To be honest, we cannot say that the case is a hoax, just as Caponi cannot demonstrate that it is true.

The problem is that Filiberto contradicted himself when we investigated the case, in that, regarding the sixth photograph, showing the creature standing, he said he had taken it on another occasion. And of course, we said no, this is not possible – to have another photograph of the same creature, in the same spot, on a different date. And he admitted that he had lied to me about this because he did not trust me. You must admit that all this is a bit suspicious. Frankly, this is a very difficult case. I cannot say anything positive, but we have no proofs to show that it is a fabrication.[9]

Gianfranco Lollino is unequivocal. 'According to our memory,' he explained to me, 'that picture with the puppet in a grass space was absolutely identical to the one that appeared in *Visto* [i.e. Photo 6] with the exception of a little detail: a small, white "something" in the area of the puppet's groin, probably a pebble used to support the puppet in its upright position. Not only that, the two pictures must have been shot in sequence and not with two days' interval as Caponi claimed: it would hardly be possible otherwise, with a creature running and hiding to-and-fro. Realising his naive mistake, Filiberto retained the picture . . .'[10]

Maurizio Baiata holds a different opinion. 'I never agreed with the way the Caponi case was handled by CUN,' he told me.

I'm convinced it was conducted not only with considerable prejudice towards the principal witness but also without paying

PRETURA CIRCONDARIALE DI ASCOLI PICENO
Ufficio del Giudice per le indagini preliminari

ORDINANZA DI RESTITUZIONE DI COSE SEQUESTRATE
- art. 262, 263, 549 c.p.p., 84 D.L.vo n. 271/89 -

Il Giudice dr. Nicola Mariani

Visti gli atti del procedimento penale n. _4.690/93 M_ nei confronti di

Caponi Filiberto nato 10/8/1970 in Ascoli Piceno

per il reato di cui all'art. _656 U_

Visto il decreto di sequestro in data _8/11/1993_

Letta l'istanza presentata da _ll' Av. Aniral Bellini_

in data _27/10/98_ con la quale si chiede la restituzione

di quanto in sequestro

Ritenuto che il procedimento è stato definito in data _____ con decreto di

archiviazione.

Visti gli artt. 262, 263, 549 c.p.p. e 84 D.L.vo 271/89

P.Q.M.

ordina la restituzione a _Caponi Filiberto n. 10/8/70 in AP e_

res. Agnete all' In. tras. bretoni Via del Gosforno 19 e

di N.7 foto; N.1 Pzzi di erpelle; un cartoncino; una tovolette;

Dispone che le spese di custodia e conservazione siano dovute dall'avente diritto per il periodo
successivo al trentesimo giorno decorrente dalla data in cui il medesimo ha ricevuto la
comunicazione del presente provvedimento di restituzione.
Delega per l'esecuzione _____

Manda alla Cancelleria per gli adempimenti di competenza.

Ascoli Piceno li **2 7 OTT. 1998**

IL CONSIGLIERE DIRIGENTE
Giudice Indagini Preliminari
Dott. Nicola Mariani

Depositato in Cancelleria il **2 7 OTT. 1998**

E' copia conforme all'originale
per uso _____
Ascoli Piceno, li _28/10/98_
IL COLLABORATORE di CANCELLERIA
Silvana Rosati

IL COLLABORATORE DI CANCELLERIA
Silvana Rosati

Figure 7. Papers from the Official Judiciary of Ascoli Piceno in 1998
declaring Filiberto Caponi's innocence of all the charges made against him
in 1993.

PRETURA CIRCONDARIALE DI ASCOLI PICENO

Ufficio del G.I.P.

N. 4690/93 PM

N. 1/94 GIP Mod. 27

Il Consigliere Pretore dirigente

Rilevato che dagli atti risulta che il Caponi ha tre difensori di fiducia (Avv. Mauro Gionni, Avv. Anna Balena e Avv. Giuseppe Fabio Fabiani);

che l'art. 4 della l. 30/7/1990 n. 217 stabilisce che l'ammissione al gratuito patrocinio non può essere concessa se il richiedente è assistito da più di un difensore e che, in ogni caso, gli effetti dell'ammissione cessano a partire dal momento in cui la persona alla quale il beneficio è stato concesso nomina un secondo difensore;

che sempre l'art. 4 stabilisce che nella stessa fase o grado del giudizio, il difensore può essere sostituito soltanto per giustificato motivo o previa autorizzazione del giudice che procede, pena la cessazione degli effetti dell'ammissione al beneficio;

Ritenuto, pertanto, che, poiché nel caso in esame, si sono verificate tutte e due le ipotesi previste dalla norma, l'istante deve essere dichiarato decaduto dal beneficio del gratuito patrocinio e l'istanza deve essere respinta

P.Q.M.

dichiara Caponi Filiberto nato il 10/8/70 in Ascoli Piceno, decaduto dal beneficio del gratuito patrocinio dal 22/10/98 (data della nomina dell'altro difensore) e conseguentemente, respinge la richiesta dell'Avv. Balena diretta ad ottenere la liquidazione dei diritti e degli onorari.

per uso.
Ascoli Piceno, li
IL COLLABORATORE di CANCELLERIA
Simona Rosati

Ascoli Piceno li 12/12/98

IL CONSIGLIERE PRETORE DIRIGENTE
(dott. Nicola Mariani)

PRETURA CIRCONDARIALE
di Ascoli Piceno
Ufficio G.I.P.
CANCELLERIA G.

12 DIC 1998

IL COLLABORATORE DI CANCELLERIA
SIMONA ROSATI

sufficient attention to *all* the witnesses' statements. Moreover, CUN never had the original Polaroid photos in their possession, and no proper, professional analysis was carried out; instead, Lollino's photographic experience was relied on and used to discredit the case. The matter regarding the alleged eighth picture still remains unclear, and Filiberto never mentioned the existence of such a picture in my presence. The Caponi case was closed too soon. I took the decision to reconsider the case, publishing the overall story in the December 1995 issue of *Dossier Alieni* . . .[11]

I asked Filiberto for his side of the story. He denies ever being in possession of more than six photographs of the creature, all of which were shown to Pinotti and his colleagues from CUN during their *first* visit. After that visit, Filiberto lent five of the photographs to Renato Bianchi of ANSA, but retained Photo 6 as a security precaution. Following rumours in Pretare that Filiberto might have even more photographs of the creature, CUN investigators returned to the Caponi household for a second visit and asked to see the other photographs. Filiberto explained that the complete set had been lent to 'a certain person' for a while. Pinotti, keen to gather this valuable evidence for exclusive analysis by CUN, began to criticize Filiberto for his blind trust in this (unnamed) person and tried to persuade Filiberto to part with the photos for 'safe keeping' with CUN. Partly to show that he had not been entirely trusting, Filiberto fetched the sixth photograph and showed it again to Pinotti. 'That's why Pinotti stated that this "additional" picture looked like the sixth one,' Filiberto told me, 'because it was simply the same one! The reference to the white pebble was due probably to faulty memory or an attempt to create difficulties for me. Incidentally, I should also point out that the Carabinieri numbered the Polaroids in the incorrect sequence, which created additional confusion.'

Gianfranco Lollino concludes that 'Filiberto's alien is a skilfully made puppet, meant to look like the best-known stereotype of an alien'.[12] In many respects, however, the creature is distinctly atypical, compared, for example, with Spielberg's 'ET', the most obvious stereotype that Filiberto would have chosen for his 'puppet' then, in that he was unfamiliar with UFO literature and with stereotypes depicted and described in best-selling books of the time, such as those by Whitley Strieber and Budd Hopkins. (An analysis of the creature's physiognomy, including allegations regarding its 'static' nature, appears in the following chapter.)

THE RETURN OF THE POLAROIDS

In March 1998 I asked Filiberto to try to recover the original Polaroid prints confiscated by the Carabinieri in November 1993. With the assistance of a politician and a lawyer, legal proceedings were initiated in October 1998. Filiberto was surprised to learn from his lawyer that the pictures should have been returned to him years ago because not only had he 'confessed' to having fabricated them, but the judge of the Court of Ascoli Piceno had acquitted him of all charges relating to his indictment under Article 656 of the Penal Code (see Figure 7).

Following an official summons to collect the photographs, Filiberto presented himself at the Court of Ascoli Piceno, together with his lawyer, on 12 December 1998. The photographs had been kept in an archive office, locked in a steel filing cabinet, from which a clerk of the court took out a large brown envelope, sealed with red wax. Witnessed by an official, Filiberto signed a document confirming that the photographs had been returned to him. Also contained in the envelope was the wooden box in which the first two pictures mysteriously transformed, a copy of the newspaper in which the story first appeared, Filiberto's sketches and the piece of clay used to make the 'puppet'. The court retained the newspaper.

Three weeks later I flew to Rome. Filiberto drove from Pretare to meet me, accompanied by his father and brother-in-law, and guarding the precious set of pictures. In addition to making copies, I thoroughly examined the prints and satisfied myself that these were indeed the original Polaroids. Having previously seen only copies, the rich detail in these images took me by surprise. But the question remained: Did they show an actual alien creature – or a skilful fabrication?

NOTES

1 *Berliner Zeitung*, 12 February 1994.

2 Verga, Maurizio, 'Seven Scared Witnesses and a Humanoid', *Flying Saucer Review*, vol. 25, no. 1, January–February 1979, pp. 17–19, 22.

3 *UFO: Rivista di Informazione Ufologica*, Italian Centre for UFO Studies (CISU), Casella postale 82, 10100 Torino, Italy.

4 *Dossier Alieni*, no. 3, December 1995, published by Futuro, Via Monte Penna 51, 00012 Guidonia Montecello, Italy.

5 E-mail from Dr Edoardo Russo to Philippe Piet van Putten, 7 February 1998.

6 Letter to the author, 23 April 1998.

7 *L'Ominide di Pretare: Il Caso di Filiberto Caponi*, Centro Ufologico Nazionale (CUN), Bologna, November 1993.

8 Martín, Jorge, '"Impossible Animals": What is going on in Puerto Rico?', *Evidencia OVNI*, no. 6, Puerto Rico, 1995, pp. 36–7.

9 Interview, 22 March 1999.

10 Letter to the author, 29 March 1999, translated by Alessandro Piccioni.

11 Letter to the author, 8 March 1999; interview, 14 June 1999.

12 Letter to the author, 29 March 1999.

Chapter 13

Analysis and Hypotheses

Filiberto Caponi's photographs were taken with a Polaroid AutoFocus 660 Land Camera, using 640ASA colour film in a ten-print pack. The shutter speed varies from 1/3 to 1/200 of a second. With a focal length of 106mm, the lens has a maximum aperture of f/12 and a minimum aperture of f/42, focusing automatically from a range of 60cm to infinity by the ultrasonic method. Effective flash range is from 0.6m to 3.5m. An individual photograph begins to develop once it is pulled out of the camera. Usually an image will begin to appear after two or three minutes, but full development can take up to 15 minutes or longer, depending on ambient temperature. (Data provided by Polaroid UK)

I commissioned Roger J. Green, Ph.D., an Expert Witness checked by the Law Society and Professor of Electronic Communication Systems at Warwick University, to conduct an analysis of my first-generation copies of the Polaroid photos. It is important to point out that the analysis is based exclusively on the images per se, not taking into account the information accompanying them, which would constitute 'hearsay evidence'.

'A series of six images purporting to be an unusual creature, seen several times in Italy, was examined,' Professor Green's report begins.

> With the exception of Photos 1 and 2, all images show the creature apparently seated in some position, showing predominantly the right side of its face.
>
> The skin texture is uneven. The face consists of a mouth, two apertures corresponding to human nostrils, and two eyes. The head is oval, with no ears apparent. In examination of Photos 4 and

5, several interesting features are seen. Firstly, the head is hairless, and appears layered towards the rear. A hole appears to exist in the rear outer layer, nearby which is a white area on the back of the head, which are both also seen in the other images.

The arms and legs of the body appear to be in the right places from the human point of view. The upper arms seem shorter than in the standard human case. The hands have an opposed thumb with maybe two other digits and appear webbed, the forefinger being longer than the other(s), which is seen clearly in Photo 6. The foot appears to have two toes.

The upper torso seems bulky in Photo 4, and slimmer in Photo 6. There is a bulbous region just below the knee and on the rear side of the leg in Photo 4, and a swelling on the upper part of the leg just above the knee seen in the same picture, on the right leg.

The upper body is deep, front to back, and, in all images except Photos 1, 2 and 3, two white tubes can be seen leaving the chest area and re-entering the body area near what would be the stomach in a human being. There is a white area, corresponding

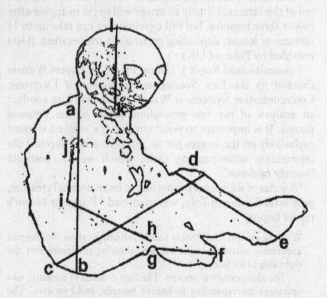

Figure 8. An edge–detected version of Photo 4.

to the white tubes, on the front of the throat area.

Photo 5 shows much the same – the creature is seated – but the white area at the back of the head is clearly visible. Certain bulbous regions are seen on the back. Photo 6 shows the creature sitting/standing against some vegetative background. A great deal of light from the camera flash is reflected from the throat area, under which area can also be seen the white tubes.

Photo 3 shows the creature's main upper body enclosed in a spherical black covering of some kind, with its legs folded under it, appearing quite white as though they are also covered. The structure of the eye regions is not apparent, and little if no light appears to be reflected from the eyes, as might be expected when a flash is used.

	Creature	1½-year-old child	Adult human
Height	80 cms = 100%	80 cms = 100%	180 cms = 100%
Head	<u>15%</u>	<u>25%</u>	<u>15%</u>
Torso	<u>32%</u>	<u>35%</u>	<u>35%</u>
Legs	<u>53%</u>	40%	<u>52%</u>
Foot length	<u>12%</u>	9%	<u>10–15%</u>
Forearm	<u>17%</u>	<u>17%</u>	25%
Upper arm	12%	18%	20%

Table 1

The underlined sections above represent comparable proportions. Data was extracted from *The British Medical Association Family Doctor Home Advisor*, ed. by Dr T. Smith, published by Guild Publishing, London, 1987.

Dimensional Observations

Figure 8 represents an edge-detected version of Photo 4 (Plate 19). Key dimensions of limbs are measurable using the lines indicated, and these may be compared with a human's limbs. The figure was reported as being 80 cms high, and this corresponds to that of an average 18-month-old child . . . All dimensions to be discussed (see Table 1) will be compared with the full height. In the photographs, there is no complete body image, so this will be composed of distances kl (the head), ab (the torso), cd (the thigh) and de (the lower leg). Certain proportions of the body correspond to that of an adult human, but one other, the forearm length, corresponds to that of an 18–month–old child. The upper arm is shorter than a child's or that of an adult human, in proportion to the length of the body. This is based on the visible length of the upper arm, and suggests modified development compared to a standard human.

Plate 23 represents a reconstruction of the creature as shown in Photo 6, taking into account the dimensional information obtained from images of the creature when standing (?) and sitting. In the case of the former, the exact same proportions of limb length were found as in the sitting figure images, strongly suggesting that all images were of the same creature. One curious observation that may be made firstly is that an external pelvis structure seems to exist, such that the legs are held apart. The hands and feet have interesting form in that there seem to be less digits compared to a human. The hands appear as in Plate 26.

The top image is of the creature's right hand, and the lower left image the left hand. There appears to be a thumb, primary digit, and webbing to a secondary digit, amongst which is a vestigial digit. This suggests a possible aquatic ancestry. The opposed thumb, as in a human hand, gives grasping flexibility and dexterity. The left- and right-hand images appear compatible, i.e. there does not appear to be asymmetry (as there is in some crabs' pincers, for example).

The foot has a different structure (lower right). Both images are of the left foot, from above and below. The foot appears to have only two main toes, again, as with the hand, with some possible webbing between them. There is a heel, as with a human foot. Looking at the lower right image, it may be seen that there is also a sole. The arches appear very substantial for the size of foot, suggesting a reasonable degree of muscle or equivalent.

Images of a 'Pod'

Photos 1 and 2 (Plates 17 and 18), showing a curious brown shape, henceforth referred to as a 'pod', were examined. These were compared with other features in the images of known size [i.e. the paving stones, which are 20 cm × 20 cm – T.G.], from which dimensional information was obtained. It may be seen that the size of the pod is compatible with the hypothesis that the creature could have been within it at some point. The object is shown in Plate 25.

The object is seen from the top. The depth in the vertical sense (into the picture) was measured as around 26 cms, so that the object is of approximately circular cross-section at its widest point. From one of the photographs, and indicated on the plate, several regions of interest may be seen. Region (a) appears to be some outside area which is a pale version of the outer skin (e), as also does (d). Regions (b) and (c) also appear to be light in colour, as a possible lining to the object. Region (f) is of a different brown to the main outer region (e).

There is a shape (g) seen protruding from the general area of the pod, and the colour of this, when compared mathematically with the colour of the 'alien', is a close match. This shape (g) may be seen in the colour photograph (Photo 2).

The pod seen in another image (Photo 1) shows a different shape. As the shape is symmetrical and about 85 cms long, it suggests that it is the undamaged form of the pod, and that the previous image (Photo 2) is the damaged form.

The alien images are consistent, and are indicative of the body of a creature around 80 to 85 cms in height, which is also compatible with the length of the pod. Therefore, the concept of the creature having been housed in the pod is clearly not unreasonable, especially as one of the images of the pod appears to show the creature emerging.

Comparison with Caponi's Paintings and Terracotta Work

The pictures of paintings by F. Caponi [as displayed in his brochure – T.G.] show a distinctive, neat artistic style. Also, there are photographs of terracotta work by him, using a clay which results in a similar colour to that of the creature. The contention may be that the creature is, in fact, a terracotta model.

An examination of the terracotta work reveals smooth surface textures whatever the colour of the finished object. The brown terracotta objects are constant in colour, unlike the coloration of the creature, which varies from brown to white. To create this colour variation would either require careful painting, or, even more difficult, dyeing of the clay when mixed and before sculpting. The only variation of colour of the terracotta objects when not painted is seen to be due to the illumination. To create the same colour variations on a creature model would require very skilful lighting effects to be set up, especially as the creature is seen from different views and still has the same coloration. The conclusion would be that, if a model, the creature has been painted.

The 'Static' Images

(The assumption is that Photograph 4 was taken before Photograph 5.)

The creature is seen to be in a similar sitting position in both pictures. The question arises as to whether or not the creature has moved in the interval between them being taken [a few moments, according to Filiberto – T.G.]. Various marks and features can be seen on the ground in the vicinity of the creature. In Photo 4, there seems to be a small object, possibly a piece of wood, not far from the creature's upper thigh, and this also appears in Photo 5. Another object, near the right foot in Photo 5, does not appear to be present in Photo 4. Similarly, marks elsewhere in Photo 4 do not appear in Photo 5. Therefore, this suggests that the two photographs had a time interval between them, although the photographic evidence cannot be used to determine what that was.

The position of the various limbs of the creature can be compared in the two photographs. As much as may be gained from these, it seems that the relative positions have not changed perceptibly. The right arm, positioned over the right leg, is in the same position. The inclination and direction of the head, relative to that of the body, also appear to be very similar, allowing for the different angle of view. The irregularities of the back also are identical. The position of the legs, relative to each other and to the body, is the same.

The inescapable conclusion which may be reached, in comparing these two pictures, is that, if they were taken at around the same time, then the creature has not moved much, if at all. There is just a slight suggestion from Photo 4 that the upper body is leaning further forward, relative to the remainder of it.

Further Hypotheses from the Images

1 If 'man-made', one viable hypothesis is that the 'alien' is in fact a child in costume, because all images seen have the creature sitting or standing against a supporting background, as would an 18-month-old child. Other than sketches made by the witness, no images of a walking or running creature are available. The bulbous regions on the back correspond to a costume which is bigger than the wearer, and which has folds in it that stick out. The same can be said for other regions on the limbs.

2 The so-called creature is, in fact, a corpse of a monkey mixed with other body parts, evidenced by the non-human proportions in some cases, the lack of very distinctive eyes, and the general air of fragility and decay in the rear of the head region. The texture of the skin, and the bulbous regions referred to earlier above, could be indicative of general tissue dissolution.

3 If at all genuine, the overall structure of the creature is human-like in terms of number of limbs, but the proportions appear non-standard. The white tubes from the chest region could be:

(a) Part of a circulation system for the white substance seen round the neck and head (coolant, nutrition, something equivalent to blood). It could be a medical device, in effect. The creature could have had modifications to its body for some purpose, perhaps to increase nutrition to the brain so as to enhance mental capability, or to give its brain (assuming it lies within the head) some degree of protection from excesses or fluctuations of temperature.

(b) Some kind of handle for a protective suit which the skin may actually be, and which adheres to the rear of the head. Therefore, the body covering could be a protective suit, which may explain why no separate digits are seen on the hands. The fact that the creature is seated much of the time suggests a preference for sitting rather than standing and moving about, perhaps due to weakness. If the outer layer is a skin, an impression is given of irregularity and deformity. This creature could be old and infirm.

'This is certainly an interesting case,' Professor Green told me after he had completed his report. 'It is not possible', he concludes, however, 'to determine the origination of such a creature from the images, whether "man-made" or otherwise[1] . . . Instinct suggests that the complexity of the evidence reinforces the idea that it is a genuine creature [which] does not really resemble a terracotta model by Caponi.'[2]

WHAT HAPPENED?

Assuming Filiberto Caponi's creature to be genuine, many questions remain. Is it possible, as some believe, that the creature was the survivor of a crash? In 1996 Massimo Fratini and Maurizio Baiata asked General Salvatore Marcelletti, a former pilot with the Italian Air Force and Aerolinee Itavia, (who is also well-known as a UFO researcher), to make some enquiries. 'We requested General Marcelletti to check with his contacts in the military to see if there was any possibility that a UFO crash had ever occurred in Italy,' Baiata told me. 'He was not only denied any answer, but was officially reprimanded.'[3]

'I really don't know if an unidentified flying object crashed in my area at the time,' Filiberto told me in 1999. 'I only remember that there was a report of a military aircraft having

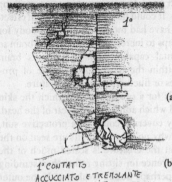

1°

1° CONTATTO
ACCUCCIATO E TREMOLANTE
COME INFREDDOLITO E METTENDO
UN LAMENTO

2°

(a) GARZE AVVOLTE

(b) DOPO AVERLO TOCCATO
COU IL PIEDE SALTA CON
LAMENTO CHE SI TRASFORMA
IN STRILLO ALTEZZA 1 METRO CIRC

Figure 9.[6] First contact. The creature squatting, shivering and whimpering.

Figure 10. (a) Bandaging. (b) After I touched it with my foot, it jumped about a metre into the air and the quiet whimper grew into a scream.

VELOCISSIMO

SENZA INVOLUCRO

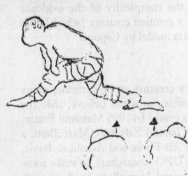

SALTO DEL MURO SENZA
L'AUSILIO DELLE BRACCIA
VELOCISSIMO ALZA LA SPALLA
DESTRA IN CORRISPONDENZA
DELLA GAMBA DESTRA E
VICEVERSA ALTERNANDO
QUESTO MOVIMENTO PER OGNI
PASSO

Figure 11 (above). Running very fast.

Figure 12 (right). Without its covering. It jumps over the wall without using its arms. Very quickly, for each step it takes, it raises the right shoulder at the same time as the right leg, and vice-versa.

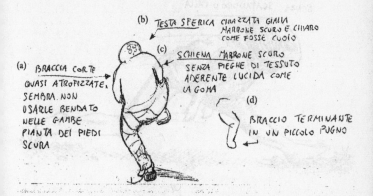

Figure 13. (a) Short arms, as though atrophied – it doesn't seem to use them at all. (b) Rounded head, tinted light and dark brown, like leather. (c) Dark-brown back. Skin taut, with no creases, shiny like rubber. (d) Arm ending in a little fist.

Figure 14. First contact position. Only the head appears bare and skin-coloured.

215

Figure 15. Running position, without covering or 'balloon'.

Figure 16. [Sitting position, with 'balloon' inflated.]

IN GRADO DI ASSUMERE
AUCHE
POSIZIONE
ERETTA

POSIZIONE-SFERICA

Figure 17. Standing up fully.

Figure 18. 'Spherical' position.

BALZO IN ARIA
RESTRINGIMENTO
DEL PALLONE O SFERA

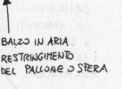

SALTO
DEL MURO

Figure 19 (left). As it jumps up, the 'balloon' reduces in size.

Figure 20 (above). Jumping over the wall.

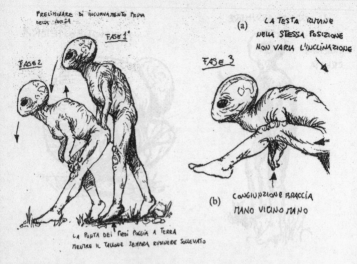

Figure 21 (left). (a) Phases 1 and 2: its preliminary position before running is bending down. (b) On tiptoe, the heel seems to remain raised.
Figure 22 (right). (a) Phase 3: the head maintains the same position, not changing its inclination. (b) Arms and hands remain together.

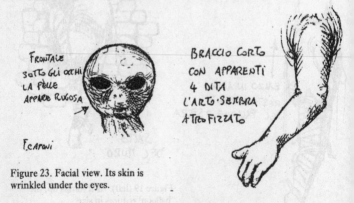

Figure 23. Facial view. Its skin is wrinkled under the eyes.

Figure 24. Short arms, ending in four digits. The arms appear atrophied.

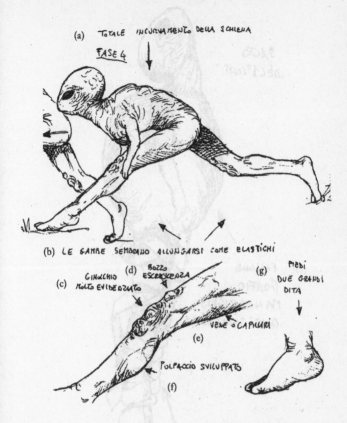

Figure 25. (a) Phase 4: back bent completely forward. (b) Legs extended like elastic. (c) Knee very prominent. (d) External protrusion. (e) Veins and capillaries. (f) Developed calf muscle. (g) Two big toes on each foot.

SALTO
DEL 1° CONT.

(a) PALLONE
GONFIO
MA NON RIGIDO
QUASI SEMIGONFIO

(b) STRANE
BENDE O GARZE MEDICHE

Figure 26. Jumping, at the first contact. (a) 'Balloon' half-deflated and quite soft. (b) Strange bandages or medical gauze.

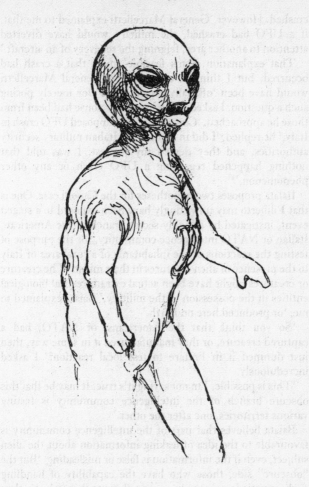

Figure 27. An uncaptioned sketch by Filiberto Caponi showing the creature in its fully extended standing position, with mouth open.

crashed. However, General Marcelletti explained to me that, if a UFO had crashed, the military would have diverted attention to another area, feigning the recovery of an aircraft.'

That explanation seems feasible, given that a crash had occurred, but I think it unlikely that General Marcelletti would have been 'officially reprimanded' for merely posing such a question. I asked him what the response had been from those he approached. 'Concerning the supposed UFO crash in Italy,' he replied, 'I did in fact ask the Italian military security authorities, and they denied my request. I was told that nothing happened regarding a UFO crash or any other phenomenon.'[4]

Baiata proposes two hypotheses for the Caponi case. One is that Filiberto may unwittingly have been exposed to a staged event, instigated by a highly secret branch of the American, Italian or NATO intelligence community, for the purpose of testing the reactions of the inhabitants of a rural area of Italy to the presence of alien creatures in their midst. 'The creature or creatures might have been actual extraterrestrial biological entities in the possession of the military,' Baiata explained to me, 'or produced here on Earth.'

'So you think that the Americans, or NATO, had a captured creature, or they manufactured it in some way, then just dumped it in Pretare to test local reaction?' I asked incredulously.

'This is possible. I'm not saying it's true. It may be that this obscure branch of the intelligence community is testing various territories, one after the other.'

Baiata believes that part of the intelligence community is favourable to the idea of leaking information about the alien subject, even if the information is false or misleading. 'But the "obscure" side, those who have the capability of handling such operations, want to keep everything to themselves – they don't even want the other side to know what's going on.'

Another possibility is that the creature seen by Filiberto might have been involved in a real UFO crash. Where is this creature now? The whereabouts of that creature is for me the most interesting aspect of this situation. In any event, the consequences for us researchers here in Italy have been serious. We know that some of us are being watched very closely. It is a situation very similar to that which later occurred in Varginha, Brazil . . .[5]

NOTES

1 Reports provided to the author by Professor Roger J. Green, Ph.D., C.Eng., FIEE, SMIEEE, MESEM, RPS, January–May 1999.

2 Letter to the author, 5 July 1999.

3 Interview, 15 April 1999.

4 Letter to the author, 7 September 1999.

5 Interview, 15 April 1999.

6 Figures 9 to 27 by Filiberto Caponi, © Filiberto Caponi.

Chapter 14

The Creatures of Varginha

The city of Varginha, located 3100 feet above sea level in the Brazilian state of Minas Gerais, about 200 miles north-north-west of Rio de Janeiro, became the centre of national attention in January 1996 when weird creatures were observed there on several occasions by numerous witnesses. Many claimed that an extraterrestrial craft had crashed and that several of the creatures had either been killed or captured by the authorities.

The encounter first reported occurred on the afternoon of 20 January at around 15.30. Two teenage sisters, Liliane da Silva (16) and Valquíria da Silva (14), together with a friend, Kátia Xavier (22), were walking past an open plot of land in Santana, just north of the Jardim Andere district of Varginha, when they encountered a strange creature. 'I thought it was a statue at first, but it wasn't,' said Liliane. 'Valquíria and I thought it was an animal, Kátia started to say it was a demon.'[1,2] Like the creature photographed by Filiberto Caponi, it had brown skin, but in most other respects it was dissimilar.

Squatting about 20 feet away, next to an abandoned cinder-block building, the hairless and apparently naked creature (without visible sex organs) looked to be about 80 centimetres in height. Its arms were thin, the left one between its short, thin legs, the right arm beside the building. The girls were unable to discern either hands or feet (the latter obscured by foliage). The creature had oily brown skin, a roughly triangular-shaped head,[3] with three large ridges running from front to back. The eyes were large, red, bulging, without pupils and slanted oval in shape.[4] It had a slit for a mouth, a barely discernible nose, no ears and huge veins, reminding

224

Valquíria of 'a big, soft bull's heart', which seemed to grow out of the neck and run down the shoulder, arms, chest and back. To Kátia, the creature was neither human nor animal. It looked repulsive, the huge red eyes particularly alarming the girls.[5] They screamed. 'The creature turned its head and looked at them, seemed almost frightened and crouched a bit lower, perhaps trying to hide from them,' reported Bob Pratt, an American journalist and author. 'The three immediately fled back to the street and didn't stop running until they reached the Silva home more than twenty blocks away.'[6]

Twenty minutes later, after the girls had calmed down, Kátia and the girls' mother, Luiza, arranged for a neighbour to drive them back to the site of the encounter. This time, there was no sign of the creature, apart from an area of matted grass where it had been, and a smell of sulphur or ammonia.[7] A young girl and an elderly woman, alerted originally by the girls' screams, remained near the location where the girls had seen the creature and said they witnessed firemen from the city fire department capture the creature and take it away, after the girls had departed.

The story attracted the attention of local investigator Ubirajara Franco Rodrigues, a lawyer and university professor. After interviewing the three girls, Rodrigues stated that he was impressed by their sincerity and noted that all three had been severely traumatized by the experience.

Rodrigues also interviewed Henrique José de Souza, a bricklayer who claimed to have seen a vehicle from the fire department at the location where the creature had been seen, on the same day, and who further claimed that a creature had been captured there between 10.30 and 11.00. Since this was considerably earlier than the encounter reported by the girls, Rodrigues concluded that two creatures may have been captured in Varginha on 20 January, a conjecture subsequently supported by others.[8]

At 01.14 on 20 January Oralina Augusta was awakened by the sound of bellowing cattle on a farm six miles to the east of Varginha. Opening the window, Oralina could see agitated cattle stampeding in the pasture 300 to 400 feet away, and a faintly illuminated submarine-shaped craft hovering above them. She awoke her common-law husband, Eurico de Freitas, and both observed the object.[9,10]

As investigators Bob Pratt and Cynthia Luce (who lives in Brazil) were told by Rodrigues, the couple could see grey smoke or vapour emanating from the back of the craft as it moved slowly in a rocking motion only about 15 to 20 feet above the ground. Neither Eurico nor Oralina ventured outside but stood at the window watching as the object slowly took 45 minutes to move out of sight beyond a ridge about 2000 feet away, heading in the direction of Varginha. The couple thought the craft was having difficulties because of the slow way it moved. 'If the UFO was making any sound, it was drowned out by the cows' bellowing. All this time the cattle remained panicky . . . but the couple's four dogs, although awake, showed no reaction. Eurico's and Oralina's four children, aged 12 to 20, slept through it all.'[11] The object was reported to be 'about the size of a small bus'.[12]

CAPTURE

At around 08.30 on 20 January four firemen from the Varginha City Fire Department answered a call about a strange creature seen near the woods in Jardim Andere. In Brazil the Fire Department is run by the Military Police, which act as state police under the aegis of the state's governor. Their duties include highway patrol, riot control, rescuing people in emergencies and firefighting. As national firefighters, one of their duties is capturing mad dogs, wild animals and dangerous reptiles.

By the time the firemen responded, it was reported that three boys had seen the creature in the Rua Suécia, a street which runs above the steep embankment that leads down to the wooded area near where the three girls reported their encounter seven hours later. A man and a woman also separately reported seeing the creature as it slowly made its way down the bank. The boys had been throwing stones at the creature until the woman told them to stop.[13] Under the command of Major Maciel, the firemen (including Sergeant Palhares, Corporal Rubens and Soldiers Nivaldo and Santos) arrived at Rua Suécia in a fire truck.[14] It was now about 10.00, by which time the creature had disappeared in the woods.

Wearing their regular uniforms with heavy gloves and carrying nets, the firemen searched for the creature, catching fleeting glimpses of it from time to time. Some reports state that it gave off a strong, unpleasant smell.[15] Two hours later the creature was confronted. Described as about one metre in height, with blood-red eyes, strange, oily, brown-coloured skin, three raised humps on top of its forehead and a very small opening for a mouth, it appeared to be injured.[16] The firemen threw a net over the creature, which offered no resistance, although it made a curious humming or buzzing sound.

During the search, one of the firemen returned to the fire truck and radioed his commander, requesting him to join the team. By the time the creature was carried to the Rua Suécia the commander had arrived, accompanied by an army truck plus two officers and a sergeant.[17] The army truck had been sent from the Escola de Sargentos das Armas (ESA), a high-security military academy training base in the city of Três Coraçoes, 25 kilometres from Varginha. Brigadier General Sérgio Lima Coelho, commandant at the base, immediately ordered troops to seal off and secure the area. Observed by Henrique José de Souza from the rooftop of a nearby building, the creature was placed in a wooden box,[18] about one metre square.[19] With a canvas cover over it, the box was put into the back of the truck, with two army men sitting beside it, and the truck returned hurriedly to the army base.[20] Lieutenant-Colonel Olímpio Vanderlei Santos, in charge, ordered all personnel involved not to discuss the matter with anyone: it was, he warned, 'a secret operation'.[21]

Another creature is believed to have been captured some hours later. Cynthia Luce and Bob Pratt learned about this incident from Ubirajara Rodrigues and Vitório Pacaccini, another experienced investigator who teamed up with Rodrigues and who has written a book on the Varginha incident.[22] 'Some time between 1:30 and 2 o'clock in the afternoon,' Cynthia and Bob relate, 'a jogger saw seven armed soldiers cross a small footbridge from Santana into the pasture next to the woods in the Jardim Andere ... Two of the soldiers were carrying automatic rifles and all were wearing side-arms. Two carried small rectangular aluminum-colored boxes or suitcases . . .'

> The soldiers grouped into a V formation and moved up the hill, searched a small grove of trees just below the [railroad] tracks, apparently found nothing, then turned and moved toward the big woods. The jogger . . . continued straight ahead for several blocks and then turned into the street leading to Santana. A minute or two later, three distinct shots were heard . . . the jogger returned to the street overlooking the woods and saw an army truck with soldiers in it parked there.
>
> At that moment, four of the soldiers who had gone into the woods came struggling up the steep embankment carrying two bags, two soldiers to each bag. One bag was squirming as if something live was in it, but the other had no movement. The bags were heaved into the truck, the soldiers climbed in, and the truck sped away.[23]

A lawyer living nearby also heard three shots and witnessed soldiers carrying something animate in a sack.[24]

Following a storm at around 18.00, as both military and police continued to search the area, two plain-clothes agents of the Military Police (P-2) saw another creature, similar to the one reported by the three girls at 15.30. 'The two men were able to capture it and force it into the back seat of their unmarked Military Police car,' Cynthia and Bob learned. 'It may have been ill, because the men reportedly took it to a small public health clinic, but the doctor there refused to go near the creature and told them to take it to a hospital.'

One of the police officers, Marco Chereze, is believed to have handled the creature with his bare hands when he captured it. A few days later he became ill and was admitted to hospital with a high fever. 'He rapidly lost use of his arms and legs, and was unable to feed himself,' report Cynthia and Bob.

> At the end, he turned blue and failed to respond to treatment. He died on Feb. 15. The only advice given his family was that the coffin should be sealed, the funeral should take place without delay, and burial should follow within a few hours . . . Chereze's family reportedly sued the Military Police because the cause of his death was never explained. The results of any autopsy were never

revealed – the only thing of note was a lab report saying 'a small quantity of toxic material' had been found in his body – and allegedly his official records were altered to state that he wasn't on duty that night.[25]

MEDICAL EXAMINATIONS

Following the captures, rumours proliferated that the second of the creatures had been examined medically, initially at the regional hospital of Varginha on the evening of 20 January, then at the more secluded and best-equipped hospital in the region, Hospital Humanitas, one and a half kilometres distant. Two days later the creature, by now dead, was transferred to the Escola Preparatorio de Cadetes (Army Cadet School), then to the University of Campinas, 230 kilometres away, in a military operation commanded by Lieutenant-Colonel Vanderlei Santos.[26]

A nurse told Ubirajara Rodrigues that for several hours during the night of 20 January a section of the regional hospital had been blocked off, with access denied to patients, visitors and employees. Soldiers and army vehicles had been parked outside, and physicians from other cities called in to examine the creature. Rodrigues informed Cynthia and Bob that on the following Monday, 22 January, all hospital employees were summoned to a meeting and told that everything that had happened that weekend was to be ignored because 'it was just a training exercise for doctors and military personnel' and that if anyone ('especially that lawyer Ubirajara') should ask questions about the incident, they were to deny everything.[27]

Interviewed by Graham Birdsall, editor of Britain's *UFO Magazine*, Vitório Pacaccini confirmed that the first creature captured on the morning of 20 January had been taken to the army academy (ESA) at Três Coraçoes. What happened after that is uncertain, but the second, injured creature had been taken initially to the regional hospital, then to the Hospital Humanitas. On Monday, 22 January, between 15.00 and 18.00, three military trucks were seen parked outside the Hospital Humanitas. By 18.00, reportedly, the creature was dead. A single truck entered the hospital grounds through a side entrance and backed up to a doorway. 'The scene on the other side of that doorway has been described by several witnesses who were present,' Birdsall learned. 'The second creature had been laid out in a small [0.60m × 1.70m][28] wooden casket: a lid was close by . . .'[29] In a recorded deposition with Pacaccini, an army officer disclosed the following:

There were a lot of doctors – over 15 of them – all wearing surgical suits: some had stethoscopes around their necks. There were military policemen, and firemen. One of the S-2 [military intelligence] lieutenants was filming everything with a portable camera, while the other one was taking notes. One of the doctors came over and opened that slit of a mouth, grabbed its tongue and rolled it out, using forceps. It was a long, black, flat tongue, about 12 centimetres long. When the doctor released it, it went straight back into that little slit.

There was an unbearable smell of ammonia. The creature was about 160 centimetres long, with big, V-shaped feet, and had dark brown skin, which looked oily. A big head – bigger than ours – with some kind of protuberances on the top of it – three of them. It didn't have a nose, just two holes, and it just had a slit of a mouth and big, round eyes with no pupils at all. Its legs were short and skinny, and long, thin arms.[30]

The creature had three fingers on each hand. No sexual organs, nipples, or navel were visible. There appeared to be joints in the knees, which were grazed and wrinkled.

Eventually, the lid to the box was screwed down and two military personnel, in face masks and gloves, wrapped it in black plastic sheeting before placing it in the back of a truck parked outside.

Among the Brazilian military personnel present at this examination were Lieutenant-Colonel Olímpio Vanderlei Santos; Lieutenant Tibério; Captain Ramírez; Sergeant Pedrosa, S-2 Military Intelligence (who filmed some scenes with a camcorder); Corporal Vassalo and Private De Mello (who drove the middle truck in the convoy taking the creature's body away from the hospital), and Private Cirillo. These personnel had come from the army academy (ESA): it is assumed that they returned there upon leaving the hospital. Later it was reported that a long convoy of trucks and private vehicles, led by a yellow Volkswagen van, headed out of Varginha at 04.00 the following morning, 23 January. Military and civilian witnesses confirm that the convoy drove to the Army Cadet School in Campinas. The creature then was transferred to the University of Campinas (UNICAMP).[31]

AUTOPSY

At UNICAMP the creature's body was autopsied by pathologists at the Department of Forensic Medicine, headed by Dr Fortunato Badan Palhares, a leading expert in the field. In 1985 Palhares had participated as a member of an international team in the post-mortem of the alleged remains of Dr Josef Mengele, the notorious Nazi 'Angel of Death', who died in Brazil in 1979. Although witnesses testified that Dr Palhares performed the creature's autopsy, officially he denies having done so. 'He doesn't talk to the press or anyone else about the creatures captured in Varginha,' Pacaccini explained to me. 'He just denies everything, and now he has threatened the press, saying that he'll sue anyone who tries to associate his name with the Varginha incident again. Of course, I know that he is involved up to his neck with the incident. I wouldn't be crazy enough to say such a thing like that to the whole press if I could not prove it.'[32]

Contacted in 1997 by Bruce Burgess, producer of a British TV documentary, *The Brazilian Roswell*, Dr Palhares declined to go on camera, although he did agree to make a statement over the telephone. 'I am not and have not actively and personally participated officially in the Varginha incident,' he stated. 'I have never been involved with any member of the national security service or the army in dealing with the issues relating to the ETs of the Varginha case.' Questioned by a student some weeks after the incident, Palhares reportedly responded differently. 'Well, young man,' he said, 'I'd really love to give you an answer, but please, ask this question in ten or fifteen years from now.'[33]

NORAD ALERT

The North American Aerospace Defense Command (NORAD) is responsible for protecting the North American continent from attack by enemy missiles and aircraft. As I have shown in my earlier works, there is a considerable body of evidence indicating that, accordingly, NORAD is and has been involved in monitoring UFO activity – or 'uncorrelated observations' – via its Unknown Track Reporting System (NUTR).[34] According to information supplied in late 1999 to Rubens Villela, the meteorologist, the Brazilian Air Force (FAB) detects an average of five UFOs a day. 'They know how to distinguish echoes by their speed, sometimes 40,000 kph and 600 metres or more in size,' Villela told me.[35] According to information leaked to Vitório Pacaccini by an FAB officer, on 13 January 1996 NORAD alerted CINDACTA, the combined military-civilian agency controlling airspace in Brazil, that it had tracked a number of unidentified objects over the western hemisphere that night and that one or more had penetrated Brazilian airspace. CINDACTA immediately alerted the ESA army command in Três Coraçoes.[36]

According to Pacaccini, advance warning by NORAD included co-ordinates of latitude and longitude, although the Americans were unable to say whether the object was about to land or crash. Pacaccini believes the potential of a crash – any sort – in a heavily populated area might explain why the Brazilian authorities were on the scene unusually promptly.[37]

CRACKDOWN

Pacaccini claims to have received many threats during his investigations, some made anonymously on the telephone. He told Graham Birdsall that on occasions he felt it necessary to wear a bullet-proof vest. 'It's now common knowledge', Birdsall reported in July 1996, 'that if anyone in the military so much as mentions [Pacaccini's] name, they are handed an immediate 10-day detention. Indeed, according to latest reports, the crackdown has begun in earnest. General Lima Coelho is reported to have issued an order banning anyone in the military from speaking or having contact with any Brazilian ufologist.'[38] I asked Pacaccini to confirm the foregoing. 'Absolutely!' he replied, in mid-1999. 'It hasn't changed, even at the present time. I know it sounds ridiculous, but it's true.'[39] Pacaccini, an export-import broker who owns three coffee plantations in Belo Horizonte, takes the threats so seriously that he regularly carries arms.[40]

Threats have not prevented researchers from gleaning new and significant information about the case. It has been learned, for instance, that an American civilian was present on the morning of 20 January when the first creature was loaded on to a military truck; that a large US Air Force transport aircraft (believed to be a C-5 Galaxy or a C-17 Globemaster) was seen at São Paulo International Airport on the morning of 20 January and that the same aircraft then appeared at Campinas Airport on 22 January.[41] Pacaccini and Rodrigues interviewed approximately 25 first-hand witnesses to the various incidents associated with the creatures in Varginha, including military policemen, army personnel, doctors and others, and learned the names of almost all the military personnel involved. A few witnesses stated that a crash and subsequent recovery of some type of aerial craft occurred in the vicinity of Varginha.

CRASH OR LANDING?

On the morning of 13 January 1996 Carlos da Souza was driving along the Fernão Dias highway that connects São Paulo and Belo Horizonte, at a point about three miles south of the intersection that leads to Varginha to the west and Três Coraçoes to the east, when he heard a muffled roaring sound. Da Souza claims that the noise came from a silvery, cigar-shaped craft about 400 feet in the air, travelling parallel to the highway at around 40 to 50 mph. It was estimated to be 30 to 40 feet long and 12 to 15 feet wide, Cynthia Luce and Bob Pratt were informed by the investigators, and had at least four windows along the side and what looked like a large, jagged hole in front, and a long dent or crack running from the hole to the centre of the craft, from which issued white smoke or vapour.

Da Souza gave chase in his pickup truck for about ten miles, at which point the craft disappeared in a dive behind some elevated terrain. He headed towards where he believed the craft might have descended and, about 25 minutes later, claims to have come across a field strewn with pieces of debris, some quite large, which were being collected by about 40 soldiers. Two army trucks, three cars, an ambulance, two male nurses and a helicopter were at the site, and a smell of ammonia or ether permeated the area. Da Souza picked up a piece of very light, aluminium-like material, which floated to the ground when he dropped it. Spotted by one of the men, armed soldiers shouted at him to leave at once. During a coffee stop going back to São Paulo, da Souza states that a car drew up and two apparent military men in civilian clothes approached, addressed him by name and warned him not to talk to anyone about what he had seen.

Da Souza's story remains unverified. He claims not to have known about the widely publicized report of the creatures seen in Varginha until September 1996, when he read a magazine article by Claudeir Covo, an investigator who had been working with Rodrigues and Pacaccini. Da Souza contacted Covo and eventually showed him and Rodrigues the site of the alleged crash, but no traces could be found and nobody in the area knew anything about it. Furthermore, as Bob and Cynthia point out, key elements in da Souza's story are suspiciously similar to those described in the famous story of the crash/retrieval operation near Roswell, New Mexico, in July 1947 and his description of the craft tallies rather too well with that provided by Oralina Augusta and Eurico de Freitas.[42]

I find it hard to credit that an army team could have been at the site within 25 minutes of the crash, even though the ESA base at Três Coraçoes is only seven miles away and even supposing precision guidance based on co-ordinates purportedly provided by NORAD. However, on a later visit to the supposed crash site, Rodrigues and members of his group discovered a 400-feet-square area of ground that appeared to have been replaced with fresh sod. Furthermore, several military witnesses are reported to have seen wreckage of a crashed craft being transported to the ESA base by two army trucks on 13 January. The witnesses also claim that the wreckage subsequently was taken by convoy to the National

Institute for Space Research (INPE) in São José dos Campos, near São Paulo.[43]

At a lecture in São Paulo on 11 December 1999 Juan José Benítez, the Spanish journalist and author, described finding unusual traces 30 metres from a fence at the site in Varginha where one of the creatures had been captured. These traces had apparently been overlooked by other investigators. Rubens Villela, who attended the lecture, gave me some details:

> On hard soil covered with grass and lying on a six to eight per cent slope, Benítez found three cylindrical holes about 20 centimetres deep and 20 to 40 centimetres wide, forming a right-angled triangle with an 11-metre hypotenuse. A tree very close to one of the holes had been felled and dehydrated. A stone in the middle of the pattern had been melted by a 1100 degrees C temperature, according to analysed samples he took to Spanish universities. Entomologists said there should be many more insects from the soil from the holes, which apparently had been sterilized.
>
> Benítez has decided to investigate Varginha further, because he thinks there are more things behind the events . . .[44]

MORE CREATURES

On 21 April 1996, 67-year-old Terezinha Gallo Clepf, together with her husband and some friends, had been at a restaurant in the Varginha Zoo Gardens. At around 21.00 Sra Clepf went outside on the veranda to smoke a cigarette. After a few minutes she began to feel uneasy, as though someone were looking at her. 'I turned to my left and saw a creature staring at me,' she stated. The creature was about four to five feet tall and around 15 feet away. 'I didn't know what it was . . . It was very ugly. It was brown and had a brightness or shininess to the skin. The eyes were big and red, and the mouth was just a stroke. He stayed there looking at me.' Terrified, Sra Clepf remained rooted to the spot for over five minutes, then slowly got up and went back inside the restaurant. She glanced back only once, to see the creature still staring at her.

About a week prior to this incident two deer, an anteater, a bobcat and a blue macaw at the zoo died suddenly in mysterious circumstances. According to the zoo's director, Dr Leila Cabral, no cause for the death of the bobcat or the macaw could be determined; the deer died of 'caustic intoxication without apparent cause', the anteater of an 'unidentified toxic substance'.

Another of several further creature sightings happened at about 19.30 on 15 May 1996. While driving from Três Coraçoes to Varginha, close to the farm where the submarine-shaped craft was reported on 20 January, Ildo Lucio Gordino, a 21-year-old biology student, encountered a bizarre animal which had started to cross the road about 40 metres in front of his car. 'The headlights shone on a dark brown thing with hair all over its body,' said the student. 'It had huge eyes that reflected red in the headlights. It covered its face with its hands and crouched down.'

Also in May a 20-year-old witness, Luciano Olímpio dos Reis, was walking home one night in Passos, about 40 miles north of Varginha, when he claims to have been attacked by a five-foot-five tall, hairy creature with a strange growl. The witness, who is six-foot-five tall and weighs 190 pounds, was knocked to the ground, his shirt and jacket ripped by sharp claws. 'He kicked out and knocked the creature off balance, jumped up, and ran, but was knocked down again,' report Bob and Cynthia. 'In the scuffle, Luciano kicked the creature in the groin, causing it to double over, and Luciano was finally able to escape to a nearby house.' Vitório Pacaccini, who examined Luciano's injuries and torn clothing, is convinced the incident (one of four in the area) really occurred, although he believes it was not related to the Varginha incidents.[45]

'MEN IN BLACK'

At about 22.00 on the night of 3 or 4 May 1996 Liliane and Valquíria da Silva, the first to report seeing a creature on 20 January, were asleep at home, as was their mother, Luiza, when there came a knock at the front door of their house in Santana. Opening the door, Luiza was confronted by four men dressed in dark suits. They gently pushed their way inside and insisted on talking to Liliane and Valquíria. 'Luiza got them up and everyone gathered in the small living room, the girls and mother on one sofa, the four men on another sofa opposite them,' report Bob and Cynthia.

One man was about 50, the others in their early 30s. They were polite but businesslike. Only the older man and one of the others talked. They never identified themselves, but spent more than an hour trying to get the girls to change their story, and even implied they would be paid a lot of money if they made their denials publicly on TV. Afraid to object, Luiza said they would think it over . . . The men finally left, but told them not to follow them to try to see what kind of car they were driving. The men were never seen again, and the girls did not withdraw their story.[46]

THE OFFICIAL VERSION

While pursuing his investigations in Varginha in 1997 Bruce Burgess managed to obtain two official explanations for the incidents relating to the capture of the creatures. Sub-Lieutenant Rubens of the Varginha Fire Department (under the aegis of the Military Police of Minas Gerais) was unequivocal. 'I think that the public should ask how it was possible that beings from another planet were expected to be captured by six lieutenant-firemen,' he declared. 'Everyone here, including the commander, doesn't believe it, because we never saw it.'

'To them, it was just another routine day,' reports Burgess. 'But when I asked them to tell us what they did on this routine day, they told me it was classified.'

At Três Coraçoes Burgess asked to interview the senior officer at the ESA high-security training base. 'After waiting for several hours, a major agreed to give us this exclusive interview, to set the record straight once and for all on the incident. If some of the descriptions by the witnesses of the incident seem a little outlandish, the official military version is bizarre in the extreme.'

'The appearance of an extraterrestrial did not take place,' Major Calza began, 'because it has never been officially proven.'

What happened was that, on 20th January 1996, there were violent storms in Varginha. Here in Três Coraçoes, we were having a ceremony, [and] we also had to send some trucks for maintenance while they were still under guarantee. So we sent two trucks into Varginha . . . To further complicate the story, there were more coincidences relating to the events. At the hospital in Varginha, there was an expectant dwarf couple, which coincided with ESA taking the creature to the hospital in Varginha. There must be a confusion between this and the dwarf couple who were expecting a baby . . .

What about the description of the creature, as given by the three girls in Santana, for example? 'In Varginha, there's a mentally handicapped man – a dwarf – who has a strange disfigured appearance,' explained Major Calza. 'As a consequence of these storms that we'd had, he had hurt himself whilst trying to take cover or get home. When this happened, he was near the area where these girls said they'd seen this strange creature, but, if we were to look at what they saw again, they could have confused this dwarf-man with something else, due to his disfigured physical appearance and dark skin.'[47]

A QUESTION OF PROOF

Much of this résumé of the Varginha incidents is based on information provided by Ubirajara Rodrigues and Vitório Pacaccini to Bob Pratt and Cynthia Luce, during their investigations in Varginha in March 1996 and in August 1997. A journalist for 48 years, Bob has visited Brazil on numerous occasions to investigate alien encounters, many of which are described in his important book, *UFO Danger Zone: Terror and Death in Brazil*. Cynthia holds a master's degree in anthropology and experimental psychology. She has lived for over 25 years in the mountain village of São José do Vale do Rio Prato, two hours from Rio de Janeiro, where I was a guest in her lovely home for several days in 1988. I know both Cynthia and Bob to be thoroughly professional in their research methodology. The fact that they have been impressed by the evidence presented to them is enough to convince me that the events occurred more or less as stated.

Regarding the capture of a creature (or creatures) in

Varginha on 20 January 1996, Pacaccini persuaded an active-duty military officer involved in the case to record a 42-minute deposition, during which it was confirmed that: (a) the sighting of the creature by the three young women is accurate, along with their descriptions; (b) the being produced a vocal buzzing sound, similar to that of a bee; (c) it was captured by personnel from the Varginha City Fire Department, then taken to the ESA base in Três Coraçoes and afterwards to the Hospital Humanitas, then transferred, as a corpse, to the Army Cadet School, thence to the University of Campinas; and (d) the overall military operation was commanded by Lieutenant-Colonel Olímpio Vanderlei Santos.[48]

There remains the question of proof. As Rodrigues explained to Bob and Cynthia, two months after the first incidents were reported:

> As an attorney, if I were in a court of law and had to prove that the firemen had captured an alien from another planet – with proof coming from an accredited place like the University of Campinas which would issue an official notice that said 'One dead alien . . . of this blood type' [et cetera] – we have not been able to get that. We believe such reports exist and that this actually happened. I can prove, with testimony and witnesses . . . that these things occurred, but we don't have any official reports. A creature was captured, but where it came from we can't prove . . .[49]

UNDER AMERICAN CONTROL

Another researcher involved in the Varginha investigations is Edison Boaventura, who told Michael Wysmierski, editor of *The Brazilian UFO Report*, that there were those in the military who wanted to release the information to the public but worried about possible repercussions from the government towards them and their families.[50]

Some Brazilian investigators are convinced that the creatures were taken to the United States, a conviction based partly on statements made, as Bob and Cynthia report, by Brazilian military personnel who 'resented the idea that Brazil would relinquish control and turn the aliens over to the US'.[51] As mentioned previously, an American civilian was present on 20 January 1996, when the first creature was loaded on to a military truck, and a heavy US Air Force transport aircraft was seen at São Paulo International Airport, and the same aircraft then appeared at Campinas Airport on 22 January.[52] Perhaps coincidental too was the visit to São Paulo and other parts of Brazil, early in March 1996, by Warren Christopher, then US Secretary of State, together with Daniel S. Goldin, Director of NASA, 'ostensibly to arrange for a Brazilian astronaut to join a future Space Shuttle flight'.[53]

That so many civilian, police and military witnesses have come forward with testimony, in most cases allowing their names to be used – particularly those present at the creature's medical examination at the Hospital Humanitas – is remarkable. The preponderance of evidence convinces me that several creatures were indeed captured by the Brazilian authorities, subsequently assisted by on-scene American advisers, in Varginha in 1996. The creatures may have been transported to the United States, a nation whose military and scientific intelligence community has, in my estimation, more experience than any other in handling such special operations. That other, similar creatures were seen at later dates begs important questions: Are they still here? Have they survived? And if so, what is their purpose?

NOTES

1 Wysmierski, Michael, 'The Mysterious ET(s) of Varginha, MG', *The Brazilian UFO Report*, vol. 1, no. 6, 1996, pp. 11–12.

2 Pratt, Bob and Luce, Cynthia, 'Varginha, Brazil, ET crash, capture?' *MUFON UFO Journal*, no. 364, August 1998, p. 3. Copyright 1998 by the Mutual UFO Network.

3 Pratt and Luce, op. cit., pp. 3–4.

4 Letter to the author from Cynthia Luce, 25 April 1999.

5 Pratt and Luce, op. cit., pp. 3–4.

6 Pratt, Bob, *UFO Danger Zone: Terror and Death in Brazil – Where Next?*, Horus House Press, PO Box 55185, Madison, Wisconsin 53705-8985, 1996, p. 326.

7 Pratt and Luce, op. cit., pp. 3–4.

8 Wysmierski, op. cit., p. 11.

9 Pratt, Bob and Luce, Cynthia, 'The Varginha ET Case', *MUFON UFO Journal*, no. 365, September 1998, pp. 10–11. Copyright 1998 by the Mutual UFO Network.

10 Birdsall, Graham W., 'Incident at Varginha: Brazilian UFO Crash Retrieval?' *UFO Magazine* (UK), September–October 1996, p. 10.

11 Pratt and Luce, *MUFON UFO Journal*, no. 365, pp. 10–11.

12 Wysmierski, op. cit., p. 12.

13 Pratt and Luce, *MUFON UFO Journal*, no. 365, p. 11.

14 Pacaccini, Vitório, 'Varginha Incident', *Beyond Boundaries*, PO Box 250, Rainbow, Texas 76077, no. 12, July–August 1998, p. 12.

15 Pratt and Luce, *MUFON UFO Journal*, no. 365, p.11.

16 Birdsall, op. cit., p. 10.

17 Pratt and Luce, *MUFON UFO Journal*, no. 365, p. 11.

18 Birdsall, op. cit., p. 10.

19 Pacaccini, op. cit., p. 12.

20 Pratt and Luce, *MUFON UFO Journal*, no. 365, p. 11.

21 Pacaccini, op. cit., p.12.

22 Pacaccini, Vitório and Portes, Maxs, *Incidente em Varginha*, Ediçoes Cuatiara, Belo Horizonte, Brazil, 1996.

23 Pratt and Luce, *MUFON UFO Journal*, no. 365, pp. 11-12.

24 *The Brazilian Roswell*, directed by Bruce Burgess and produced by Jackie Stableforth, Transmedia Productions, London, 1998.

25 Pratt and Luce, *MUFON UFO Journal*, no. 365, p. 12.

26 Wysmierski, op. cit., p. 12.

27 Pratt and Luce, *MUFON UFO Journal*, no. 364, p. 5.

28 Pacaccini, op. cit., p. 13.

29 Birdsall, op. cit., pp. 11-12.

30 *The Brazilian Roswell*.

31 Birdsall, op. cit., pp. 11–12.
32 Letter to the author, 5 July 1999.
33 *The Brazilian Roswell*.
34 Good, Timothy, *Beyond Top Secret*, pp. 373–4.
35 Letter to the author, 24 October 1999.
36 Pratt and Luce, *MUFON UFO Journal*, no. 364, p. 3; no. 365, p. 8.
37 Birdsall, op. cit., p. 57.
38 Ibid., p. 58.
39 Letter to the author, 8 June 1999.
40 Pacaccini, op. cit., p. 13.
41 Birdsall, op. cit., p. 58.
42 Pratt and Luce, *MUFON UFO Journal*, no. 365, pp. 8–10.
43 Ibid., p. 10.
44 Letter to the author, 8 January 2000.
45 Pratt and Luce, *MUFON UFO Journal*, no. 365, pp. 12–13.
46 Ibid., p. 13.
47 *The Brazilian Roswell*.
48 Wysmierski, op. cit., pp. 11–12.
49 Pratt and Luce, *MUFON UFO Journal*, no. 364, p. 6.
50 Wysmierski, op. cit., p. 11.
51 Pratt and Luce, *MUFON UFO Journal*, no. 365, p. 13.
52 Birdsall, op. cit., p. 58.
53 Pratt and Luce, *MUFON UFO Journal*, no. 365, p. 13.

Chapter 15

A Predatory Threat

The National Institute of Discovery Science (NIDS), a Las Vegas-based organization founded by real-estate businessman Robert Bigelow, employs a staff of multi-disciplinary scientists who, since 1995, have been conducting scientific research into unconventional areas, including unidentified aerial craft and animal mutilations, phenomena which frequently appear to be linked. One such case is the unexplained death of a cow in north-east Utah late in 1998.

At 16.00 on 16 October 1998 the owner (who requested anonymity) of a property located in the Uinta Basin called the Institute to report that his best cow, an expensive three-year-old Hereford, was lying dead, apparently mutilated, in a waterlogged area of his pasture about 20 feet from a paved road used by local residents. Nobody reported anything unusual in the previous or subsequent days. The owner had seen the pregnant animal in perfect health the previous day. Immediately, two investigators from the Institute were dispatched to the scene. They arrived as it was beginning to get dark, less than two hours after receiving the initial call. The Institute's official report, by Drs Colm Kelleher, George Onet and Eric Davis, kindly provided to me by Dr Kelleher, is cited throughout this summary. It states:

> . . . the animal was lying on its front (sternal recumbency) with front legs tucked in under and rear legs splayed behind. Within feet of the head and sides of the animal the ground was waterlogged. There were no signs of a struggle and no visible tracks . . . the animal was lying in a north-south axis with its head pointing north. This north-south pattern conformed to all 16 cases of mutilations that one of the investigators had investigated

in the previous several years in the Uinta Basin. The meaning of this non-random placement of mutilated animals in the Uinta Basin is unknown . . .

The cow's left ear had been cut off and its left eye was missing, together with a half-inch diameter piece of tissue around the top of the eye. An unusual, bluish-coloured, gelatinous substance was observed around the eye of the animal, as well as on its anus and vagina area, and a small amount on its ear. One of the investigators took some of the bluish gel from the anus area and put it into a test tube and, within an hour, placed the tube in a freezer (–10 degrees C). 'He also took a sample of the bluish gel from the eye together with a tissue sample. Finally, he removed a part of the ear which contained the cuts for subsequent histological analysis.'[1] (Histology is the study of the minute structure of tissues.)

On 17 October a local veterinarian, Dr Blaine L. Whiting, was contracted by the Institute to conduct a necropsy. His report follows:

SPECIES: BOVINE
BREED: HEREFORD
DATE: OCTOBER 17, 1998
11:00 AM NECROPSY ON COW FOUND DEAD YESTERDAY ABOUT 3:00 PM. COW WAS IN STERNAL RECUMBENCY WITH REAR LEGS STRADDLED OUT. TIP OF LEFT EAR REPORTEDLY WAS CUT OFF AND THE INVESTIGATOR HAD REMOVED END OF EAR LAST NIGHT. THE LEFT EYE WAS MISSING WITH ABOUT 2–3 CM OF ENTIRE UPPER EYELID. NO SIGNS OF STRUGGLE IN WET GROUND COW WAS IN. APPEARED TO HAVE DIED INSTANTLY AT THAT LOCATION. SUBCUTANEOUS HEMORRHAGES WERE FOUND IN NECK AND INGUINAL AREAS, EXTENDING DOWN LEGS WITH ASSOCIATED EMPHYSEMA. ABDOMEN WAS OPENED AND STOMACH WAS NOT VERY DISTENDED WITH GAS, ALTHOUGH FULL OF NORMAL FEED CONTENTS. SMALL INTESTINES WERE SEVERELY DISTENDED WITH GAS. ALSO FOUND A BLOOD CLOT AMONG SMALL INTESTINES ABOUT 4 CM DIAMETER AND ABOUT 40 CM LONG. INTESTINES WERE VERY FRIABLE AND TORE WITH

SLIGHTEST TENSION ON THEM. SPLEEN WAS DARK AND SOMEWHAT HEMORRHAGIC. LIVER WAS VERY FRIABLE. VENTRAL DIAPHRAGM WAS ALSO HEMORRHAGIC. THORACIC CAVITY SHOWED GREENISH/BLUE TINGE COLOR ON SEROSAL SURFACE AS DID SURFACE OF THE SKIN AT CUT EDGES AS WELL AS LIPS OF VULVA AND RECTUM. LUNGS SHOWED EVIDENCE OF EMPHYSEMA AND PALER THAN NORMAL. HEART WAS EMPTY OF BLOOD AND VERY FRIABLE. WHEN TOUCHED HEART, IT FELL APART AND WAS ALMOST UNIDENTIFIABLE AS CARDIAC TISSUE. SOME BLOOD WAS COLLECTED FROM BRACHIAL ARTERY, AND SOME THAT POOLED ON THE SKIN FROM THE SUB-CUTANEOUS HEMORRHAGE IN THE NECK. SAMPLES WERE ALSO TAKEN FROM THE CUT EDGES OF THE SKIN NEAR THE EYE, LIVER, SPLEEN, LUNGS AND HEART. THE HIGH TEMPERATURE YESTERDAY WAS ABOUT 45 DEGREES AND ABOUT 50 DEGREES TODAY. THE AMOUNT OF DECOMPOSITION SEEMED MORE ADVANCED THAN EXPECTED WITH THE CLIMATIC CONDITIONS, ALTHOUGH OTHER TISSUES SUCH AS STOMACH AND SKELETAL MUSCLES SHOWED DECOMPOSITION ABOUT AS EXPECTED. NO DEFINITIVE CAUSE OF DEATH WAS DETERMINED BASED ON RESULTS OF GROSS NECROPSY.

UTERUS WAS ENLARGED ABOUT 10–12 CM. ON PALPATION NO EMBRYO OR FETUS WAS PALPATED IN UTERUS. THERE WAS ALSO NO FLUID EVIDENT IN UTERUS. UTERUS WAS COLLAPSED AND FLACCID. I DIDN'T OPEN THE UTERUS SINCE THERE WAS NO FETUS PRESENT.

PER THE OTHER VETERINARIAN'S REQUEST. ADDENDUM ON NECROPSY PERFORMED 10–17–98. THE SKIN SHOWED A GREENISH-BLUE TINT ON ALL CUT EDGES, I.E. AROUND THE EYE AS WELL AS NECROPSY INCISIONS. ALSO SHOWED THE SAME DISCOLORATION IN THE VULVA/RECTUM AREA. WHEN THE THORAX WAS EXAMINED, THE SAME TINT WAS FOUND IN A SPOT ABOUT 6 CM BY 10 CM ON THE SEROSAL SURFACE OF THE RIBS ON LEFT DORSAL THORAX. THIS AREA WAS THE ONLY PLACE THE COLOR WAS OBSERVED INTERNALLY . . . AS I

LIFTED THE HEART FROM THE THORAX MY THUMB PENETRATED THE MUSCULATURE. AS I COLLECTED THE TISSUE SAMPLES, THE CARDIAC TISSUE DETERIORATED TO THE POINT WHERE THE CONSISTENCY WAS SIMILAR TO PUDDING. IT SEEMED AS IF THE FASCIA COVERING THE CARDIAC MUSCLE WAS ALL THAT WAS HOLDING THE TISSUE TOGETHER, I.E. THE MUSCLE FIBERS HAD LOST THEIR INTERNAL STRUCTURE. THE SKELETAL MUSCLES ON THE OTHER HAND SHOWED NONE OF THIS DETERIORATION UPON MANIPULATION.[2]

THE CUTS

The cut around the eye (see Plate 28) appeared to have been made with a sharp instrument, as confirmed by a veterinary pathologist from Purdue University and by the Institute veterinarian, using a Wesco dissecting microscope equipped with an Olympus digital camera.

> The photographs indicate that under low microscopic power, the hair around the eye appears to have been cut, rather than torn by a scavenger's teeth. It was further established histologically that there was *no* high heat or cautery used in making the cuts, according to veterinary pathologists from Purdue State University and Colorado State University. These two opinions were confirmed by the NIDS staff veterinarian. In summary it was established by three independent experts that the cuts were made with a sharp instrument and not by a predator/scavenger . . .[3]

Regarding the cut found on the cow's ear, veterinarians agreed that the ear had been removed with a non-surgically sharp instrument, i.e. not a scalpel, but not by a scavenger or predator. 'However,' the report stresses, 'in comparing sharpness of instruments, a caveat needs to be inserted. It is not appropriate to compare a "sharp instrument" used on a freshly dead animal with a sharp instrument used on tissue that has been soaked in formalin. Formalin makes the tissue much easier to cut and therefore these cuts will look sharper, with clearer edges, than a cut with the same instrument made in the field before the sample is put into formalin.'[4]

Typically, official explanations for animal mutilations, such as the one put forward by the FBI following their investigations in the late 1970s, blame predators or scavengers,[5] although many ranchers disagree. 'We don't know who's doing it or why they're doing it,' said John Wortman, executive director of the New Mexico Livestock Board, in 1994, 'but we know for sure it's not predators.'[6]

In 1997 I visited Les Roberts, manager of the 2300-acre Double D ranch, near Taos, New Mexico, where, arguably, a majority of animal mutilation cases are reported, particularly in north-central New Mexico, which includes Taos. He concedes that conventional explanations apply in some cases. 'Our trouble here is usually dogs,' he explained. 'Though they deny it, the Game Department has introduced wolves to this country from Mexico. There are people in Taos who raise half wolf and half German Shepherd dogs. These run in packs and chase our cattle, then usually rip the back of the cow's leg muscle and sometimes kill for entertainment; they don't eat them. As for coyotes, I don't worry about them so much, though they will injure cattle occasionally. I've raised animals all my life: as far as predators are concerned, I rule that out.'

'So what about the genuine mutilations?' I asked.

'All the vets can tell you, they have no answers. Last year I lost a cow. I've no idea what happened. She was pregnant . . .'[7]

PREGNANCY TESTS

In the Utah case an enlarged uterus, which can mean pregnancy, was found by the veterinarian who performed the necropsy. Two different blood tests confirmed that the animal was pregnant very close to the time of death, as the report reveals:

> The blood progesterone levels were high, but by themselves were not conclusive of pregnancy, since progesterone levels are known to cycle during estrus. Therefore, a second confirmatory blood test was ordered – Pregnancy Specific Protein B (PSPB). The blood PSPB test was also positive. Since PSPB is only made by the placenta, which itself is only present during pregnancy, the combination of the two tests shows that the animal was pregnant at or close to the time of death. Yet, there was no fetus present.

The half life (clearance from blood) of progesterone following spontaneous abortion is relatively rapid (approx. 24 hours). This indicates that if the animal did spontaneously abort, it did so very close to the time of death. The NIDS investigators examined the rear of the animal for traces of bodily fluids that might indicate a recent abortion (according to the owner, the animal should have been approx. 90 days pregnant) but found no traces of blood/bodily fluids that might indicate this. An ectopic pregnancy was ruled out since (a) the veterinarian did not find any sign of enlarged fallopian tubes and (b) the enlarged uterus indicated a quasi-normal pregnancy. As the necropsy report indicated, the veterinarian was sure there was no fetus present . . . Another possibility is that the fetus was removed by unknown means at or close to the time of death.[8]

THE HEART

According to the necropsy report, the cow's heart was 'almost unidentifiable as cardiac tissue': the Institute investigator remarked that 'it looked like it had been blown apart'. Two veterinarian diagnostic laboratories stated that the heart was so badly decomposed that it was beyond obtaining useful information. Nonetheless, unusual discoveries were made.

One diagnostic laboratory reported large numbers of bacterial organisms throughout the tissue. Numerous large round spaces indicative of gas accumulation were present. Sarcosporidia parasites and cysts were also present in expected numbers. Examination by the NIDS veterinarian pathologist under the microscope at various magnifications ($10\times$ – $60\times$) revealed multiple white-yellowish amorphic structures in the heart muscles. These structures appeared unevenly sized and irregularly shaped. Cysts usually appear regularly shaped and sized and do not have amorphic structure. Rather, they usually appear translucent. In the opinion of the NIDS veterinarian, there is little probability that the structures found in the dead animal's heart were calcified parasitic cysts. If they were, they still should have been uniformly shaped and sized. One of the diagnostic labs also reported that the structures were possibly bacterial conglomerations.

As stated before, the heart contained multiple bacteria and gas pockets. In the opinion of the NIDS veterinarian, neither of these findings explain the extreme friability [crumbling] of the heart.

248

Based on the available laboratory findings it is difficult to explain the profound myocardial changes which resulted in the severe damage described by the investigators when they first opened the animal.[9]

BLOOD ANALYSIS

The report notes that the original intention was to obtain as much blood as possible from the heart of the animal, but because the heart was shredded and fell apart when the syringe needle was inserted into the tissue, blood samples were taken from the nearby artery and from the abdominal cavity. Both samples were hemolyzed. 'Hemolysis is usually caused by either too little salt or too much salt in the red cell's environment,' Dr Kelleher explained to me. 'It is not unusual for blood from a dead animal to be hemolyzed since upon death the finely balanced ratios of salt inside and outside the cells are disrupted.' The report continues:

The blood from the abdominal cavity showed 10 times the expected potassium (K) levels (50 versus 4–5 milliequiv/liter). Although a large increase in K is not unexpected in a post-mortem sample since the intracellular stores of K are released back across the concentration gradient into the extracellular space after death, it was decided to test the ratios of Na (sodium), K and Cl (chloride) in the animal's arterial blood. NIDS is cognizant of the difficulty in examining and interpreting post-mortem ion levels. Arterial blood from the dead cow was added to an inert matrix and a SEM/EDX [Scanning Electron Microscopy/Electron Dispersive X-ray analysis] was run on both the matrix and the matrix plus blood.

[There was] a large increase in the K (potassium) and Cl (chlorine) levels in the blood when compared to Na (sodium), the other dominant electrolyte in the plasma. It may be inferred from this analysis that there was a higher than usual concentration of potassium and chloride in the arterial blood of the animal; the ratios were much more marked than those in the abdominal blood. This discrepancy leads to the possibility that potassium chloride might have been used to kill the animal. Further tests are underway to test this hypothesis. It is noteworthy that potassium chloride is a favored method for killing since (a) it is relatively easy to obtain, (b) its presence is extremely difficult to detect in post-mortem samples, and (c) it kills the animal rapidly – if sufficient *KCl* is injected into a vein, the animal dies in seconds.[10]

TOXICOLOGY

A summary of the NIDS toxicology report states that

The animal was negative for heavy metals and all standard toxicology assays were negative. Liver copper was extremely low (4.8 ppm) and liver Vitamin A was low (3.18 µg/g versus normal Vitamin A liver levels of 30–80 µg/g). Without delineating liver Vitamin A levels from other dead livestock we cannot determine if this finding is significant. For example in another previous animal mutilation that we investigated, the animal had a *large excess* of liver Vitamin A. Such an extremely low liver copper value can be considered unusual since according to the veterinarian, the owner and both NIDS investigators, the animal looked in excellent nutritional condition. An extremely copper deficient animal would be expected to suffer pronounced weight loss [and] have a rough patchy coat. The dead animal did not display any of these symptoms. The Uinta Basin area is not noted for high molybdenum (*Mo*) levels, which is a common cause of dietary copper deficiency. Indeed the animal's tissue *Mo* levels were normal. It is well known that an animal's liver copper reserves need to be extremely depleted before the blood copper levels begin to be affected. The extremely low liver level of 4.8 ppm in the dead animal should have been reflected in the abnormally low blood levels in the animal and in other animals in the pasture if the deficiency was caused by dietary imbalances. The SEM/EDX analysis of the arterial blood . . . did not show any copper level in the animal's blood. Two random blood samples were taken from other animals in the same herd to determine if the entire herd was suffering from copper or other mineral deficiency. An ICP scan of all minerals showed that neither animal was mineral deficient . . . Finally, we have previously found low liver copper levels (5–6 ppm) in another mutilated animal from a different area. The significance, if any, of low liver copper levels in these animals, remains to be seen.[11]

THE BLUE GEL

In the experience of both veterinarians, the blue gel-like substance found on the animal's eye socket, anus, vagina and ear appeared to be unusual and had no precedence of being found on a dead animal in the Uinta Basin. Accordingly, a multilevel analysis was conducted, including SEM/EDX, Gas Chromatography Mass Spectrometry analysis (GCMS), Infrared spectroscopy, Formaldehyde test, Inductive Coupled Plasma Mass Spectrometry (ICPMS), Liquid Chromatography Mass Spectrometry (LCMS) Electrospray analysis, and Head-space Gas Chromatography Mass Spectrometry (GCMS).[12]

Analytical conclusions from those tests are summarized as follows:

> The sample can be characterized as a complex mixture of organic substances of biological origin and an aqueous solution containing formaldehyde. Since there is no biological process that produces formaldehyde and it is not a common environmental contaminant, the source of formaldehyde is unknown . . .[13] Because of the low levels of formaldehyde present in the blue gel-like substance and under advice from the NIDS science advisory board, it was decided to investigate whether the blue gel was comparable to any known embalming gels currently in use in the United States . . . It was determined that only three blue embalming gels made by different companies existed on the market in the United States [and] it was found that no mortuaries in either Vernal or Roosevelt, Utah, admitted to using blue embalming gels. In order to compare the blue gel found on the dead animal with the three available blue embalming gels [another] analysis was conducted . . . The conclusion from this part of the work was that the blue gel-like substance found on the cow in Utah *did not* conform to any of the blue embalming gels currently in use in mortuaries in the United States . . . It was determined that the gel-like substance was a complex mixture containing decomposed biological tissue (it had been scraped from the cow's anal region) as well as formaldehyde and significant levels of a synthetic phenol containing compound (2, 6-bis-dimethylethyl-4-methyl phenol).[14]

GENERAL CONCLUSIONS

'The totality of the evidence that is described in this report,' concludes the National Institute of Discovery Science, 'suggests that this animal did not die a natural death. In addition, the blue gel-like substance was probably added to the animal shortly prior to, during or shortly after the time of death, and before the arrival of the rancher . . .'

The animal mutilation field has been plagued by a severe lack of reproducible results. It is the opinion of the NIDS scientific staff that investigation of animal mutilations is tantamount to being useless unless a full necropsy is performed . . . After about 48 hours, post-mortem in the summer (or 96–120 hours in the winter or at high altitudes), the value of in-depth investigation becomes progressively and rapidly diminished. Hence, claims of 'surgery' involving 'high heat' or 'laser surgery' being found on animals found several days after death are dubious at best. Even the highest quality forensic analysis cannot interpret severely decomposed tissue.[15]

Dr John Altshuler, a haematologist and pathologist, was the first to conduct a post-mortem of a mutilated animal, the horse Lady, on a ranch in Alamosa, Colorado, in 1967. Since then, he has analysed hundreds of tissue samples, some of which he has given me, together with control samples, taken from mutilated animals. His conclusion is that high heat has been used to cut the animals. In effect, the Institute disputes his findings, so I asked him for a comment. He stated as follows:

The authors of the NIDS report failed to read and examine the photomicrographs published in Linda Moulton Howe's book, *An Alien Harvest*.[16] In that book, I showed photomicrographs of skin that had pallisading of nuclei and the string-bean effect which only may be caused by high heat. Decomposition of tissue cannot cause or change this microscopic finding. I am enclosing a copy of a photograph from the text of *Histologic Diagnosis of Inflammatory Skin Diseases* by A. Bernard Ackerman, MD. If one compares the photomicrographs from Howe's book and the text, the findings will be seen to be identical. Please note that the legend in the text [of Ackerman's work] states, 'Blister secondary to electrodessication . . .' Any physician knows that electrodessication is high heat. The data are irrefutable.[17]

I asked Dr Kelleher if there was any evidence that the cow had been 'dropped'. 'The rancher insisted that the animal had been dropped,' he replied. 'He said there was an impact crater under the animal. Neither of our two investigators were convinced. The animal was found in soft, very wet ground and was heavy. Our investigators ascribed whatever crater was under the animal to these features, not to being dropped.'[18]

MILITARY INVOLVEMENT

On many occasions helicopters have been observed in the areas where livestock mutilations occur, typically before or after, but apparently never during, the event. For two years, starting in August 1991, Ted Oliphant III, a documentary reporter, former patrolman and criminal investigator with the police department of Fyffe, Alabama, assisted in investigating 35 cases of cattle mutilation in northern Alabama, a state which has seen large numbers of mutilations. 'Among those law enforcement agents who have thoroughly investigated these bovine excision sites, there is a consensus that some kind of medical testing is going on,' says Oliphant. 'The additional presence of helicopters on scene, before and after cattle are found dead and missing specific organs, leads both victimized farmers and investigating officers to conclude that there is a connection.'

On 9 January 1993 Chief Detective Tommy Cole of the Albertville police department lost a Black Angus steer to mutilators. The previous day his wife had seen an 'unmarked' helicopter over their pasture. (Military helicopters are often painted very dark, with subdued, low-contrast markings, impossible to see unless one is close.) A Federal Aviation Administration investigator was called in by Cole to investigate this and other helicopter sightings, and Cole took him for a ride in his police car, reports Oliphant.

> The FAA investigator was skeptical until an unmarked helicopter flew near them. [He] couldn't believe his own eyes and pulled out a hand-held radio and hailed the helicopter. The helicopter pilot didn't respond and ignored demands that he identify himself. This infuriated the FAA investigator, who had now reversed his skepticism. He was able to trace the helicopter to Maxwell Air Force Base in southern Alabama. When he launched an inquiry at the base, he was immediately told to drop it and never talk about it again.

A week later the FAA investigator called Cole to tell him that while out on nearby Lake Guntersville in a boat, he and his family had seen a large, triangular-shaped craft manoeuvring above them.

Through a confidential source, identified as 'Phil', Oliphant claims to have been given inside information about military involvement in the cattle mutilations. There is a connection, Phil learned, with Bovine Spongiform Encephalopathy (BSE), or 'Mad Cow Disease', and the related Creutzfeldt-Jakob Disease (CJD), which affects humans. 'It was Phil's idea that I research Transmissible Spongiform Encephalopathies and their connection to the investigations I carried out as a police officer in 1992 and 1993,' writes Oliphant.

> When I checked out his statements, I found they fit in with several leftover pieces from the official investigations carried out by the Alabama State Troopers, the Albertville Police Department and myself.
>
> In 1993, Phil told me that some of the helicopters we were seeing were equipped with thermographic infrared scanners [which] allow pilots to see in the dark and fog. Every living or moving thing produces a heat signature . . . When a cow is in trouble, sick or dying, the first thing it experiences is peripheral circulatory shutdown. This causes an immediate temperature reduction of the animal's outside skin. When a helicopter flies low and slow over area pastures and has the infrared scanner operating, it will notice a cow with a lower thermographic reading than the others in the herd. Find the cold cow, and you've identified a cow in trouble . . .

Phil claimed that, in addition to a public- and a private-funded group studying Transmissible Spongiform Encephalopathies, there was a government group funded by the 'black budget'. This group supposedly is behind most of the animal mutilations. 'I don't pretend to explain every bovine excision case that's occurred across the country,' says Ted Oliphant. 'I can only speak of those cases where I was directly involved in on-site investigations, working as a police officer. In 90% of the cases we investigated, helicopters were reported seen over the affected pastures the day before or after suspicious livestock deaths occurred. Because of the foreign substances found at the scene and in the bloodstreams of the animals, we (farmers and cops alike) suspected at the time that there was some kind of medical testing being performed.'[19]

That military (and sometimes apparently civilian) helicopters often appear at the sites of livestock mutilations is beyond contention. Clandestine investigations into BSE and CJD is a possibility, as is sampling of livestock tissue to test for levels of nuclear contamination. David Perkins, who has been researching the phenomenon for 25 years, discovered a high correlation between where the cows were being mutilated and the proximity of those mutilations to nuclear waste or reactor sites, for instance, but he is not persuaded that all the mutilations can be explained this way.[20] As Oliphant and others point out, helicopters are seen only before, or after, but never during the mutilations. How could personnel perform the rapid draining of the animal's blood (exsanguination), immaculate excisions and removal of organs without leaving some trace? Furthermore, if the military is targeting sick cows, why are most of those mutilated found in previous good health?

Assuming, as I do, that aliens are responsible for genuine mutilations, what role is played by the helicopters? 'Jim Evans', a former US Air Force security officer whose ranch, close to a US Air Force base in Colorado, had been plagued by livestock mutilations in the mid-1970s, believes he has the answer. 'I figured out early in the game', he said, 'that the government is sending in helicopters in large numbers from several sources, but they are doing it to cover what is really happening.'[21]

ASSOCIATED PHENOMENA

At about 17.30 on 13 September 1994, during a wave of livestock mutilations in New Mexico, Colorado and Nevada, Larry Gardea was checking a herd of cattle belonging to Estevan Sanchez, in Luna Canyon, near Las Vegas, north-east New Mexico, when he heard a loud, dull hum, 'like a transformer, or the sound an arc welder makes'. The cows began running away from the noise, but Gardea noticed that three appeared to be pulled by an invisible 'beam' towards the sound. 'They were struggling and bawling and were pulled through the trees,' said Gardea. 'I shot at the beam with a 30.06 rifle and the hum stopped and the cows stopped bawling.'

One cow was found dead and mutilated, another injured and another missing. Frightened, Gardea returned to the ranch house and reported the incident to the sheriff's department. Greg Laumbach, Mora County Sheriff's Deputy, accompanied Gardea to the area where the incident occurred and examined the dead cow. Its jaw appeared to be skinned on the right side, and its tongue, anus and reproductive organs had been removed. 'The wounds looked like they were done with a really sharp instrument,' said Laumbach. 'There was no blood or anything [and] they weren't jagged.' There were no tracks around the animal or any sign that the animal had been dragged anywhere.[22] And no helicopters either.

Canada has seen large numbers of livestock mutilations, particularly in Alberta and Saskatchewan. Fernand Belzil, a farmer from St Paul, Alberta, has investigated dozens of cases. Like most investigators, he rules out predation as a cause, not only because of the type of excisions but also because predators (and scavengers, I may add) typically will not eat mutilated carcasses; perhaps, he surmises, owing to the high levels of radon (a naturally occurring radioactive gas) found in the soil around the mutilated animals.

There is another curious aspect to the phenomenon. 'Often,' reports Belzil, 'whoever does this will come back and cut up the same animal two or three times.' In September 1995 a farmer in northern Saskatchewan called Belzil to report a dead cow 500 yards from his house. Although the animal had not been mutilated, the farmer suspected that it soon would be. Belzil and an assistant installed a light on top of a pole and an outdoor video camera that fed a wireless signal to a video camera recorder, loaded with a ten-hour videotape, in the farmhouse. After watching the monitor for a few hours, Belzil and his colleague headed home. Over the ensuing few days the camera worked perfectly, with the exception of two night-time incidents when, inexplicably, the screen 'whited out' for about 12 minutes at a time. On both occasions the cow was mutilated; the cow's tongue and half her face sliced away the first time, her anus excised the second time. 'Everything would be going along fine and – bang!' Belzil explained. 'The tape would be totally overexposed. There were no fluctuations; it was like someone was shining a 1000-watt light into the camera. I slowed the tape right down and the change [in the light] is still instant, bang! It's unexplainable . . .'[23]

ALIEN INVOLVEMENT

'Jim Evans', mentioned earlier, is adamant that aliens were responsible for the livestock mutilations on his ranch. 'They are being lifted into the air, they are being drained of blood, they are being mutilated, and they are being lowered,' he declared.[24] They are not always lowered. David Perkins reports that, judging from bone fractures, some cattle appear to have been dropped from as high as 1000 feet.[25]

In *Alien Base* I reveal an extraordinary mutilation case that occurred in Puerto Rico, the initial stages of which were witnessed by a security guard and former police officer, 'Piedro Viera', who recounted to Jorge Martín and me that while driving in the small hours of 12 January 1997 he had seen a large circular object coming from the direction of the El Yunque Rain Forest, then hovering above some cows in a pasture. A blue-green conical beam of light came down from the craft and engulfed two of the cows, one of which was 'levitated' towards the craft. 'The cow vanished suddenly when it was about five feet from the underside,' Viera told us. 'Then the craft began to move away slowly.' Viera was about to follow the disc in his truck when a black 4 × 4 pickup came along and two men, dressed in black 'military-style' clothes (more commonly worn by law enforcement personnel), ordered him to stay where he was for at least ten minutes. The men returned to their pickup and followed the craft. After 15 minutes Viera set off. He soon came across a cow lying on the side of the road, identical to the one levitated aboard the craft. 'It had apparently been dropped from above,' he explained, 'because two of its legs were badly broken.' The cow had also been mutilated.[26] If Viera is correct in his assumption that the two men were American federal agents, it suggests, at least, that they were monitoring the situation.

THE ABDUCTION OF ELK

Another case involving a witnessed animal abduction occurred in 1999, in the Mount St Helens area of Washington State. This time, however, the incident was reported by three witnesses, in broad daylight. The case was investigated by Peter Davenport (Director, National UFO Reporting Center), and Robert Fairfax, Ruben Uriarte and Kathleen Anderson (all of the Mutual UFO Network).

On 25 February 1999, shortly before noon, fourteen Hispanic forestry workers were heading for their crew vehicle for the lunch break. 'Francisco and Augustine were nearly at the turnout (1900 ft elevation), Manuel and two others were walking up the slope (about 1600 ft elevation) from an old overgrown access road, while the rest of the crew was scattered, most midway between the two groups on the north-facing hillside,' begins the MUFON incident report. Stopping to rest, Francisco watched a herd of elk on a nearby slope to the north-east. Suddenly, from the north-east, came an unusual, moving object.

> The UFO, presumably, had already dropped some 70 feet down the height of the Douglas fir trees bordering the dirt road and was now drifting over a hilltop. Skimming . . . at brush top level and hugging the contour of the hill, the UFO appeared to be heading slowly toward the herd of elk. The object's initial location was approximately 800 yards distant and 200 feet lower in elevation than Francisco's location.

Initially, Francisco took the object for a bi-coloured paraglider drifting in for a landing: it had a red patch on the right half and a white one on the left. It moved with a strange, slow wobble. Hugging the ground, the object advanced towards the herd of elk, which bolted. 'Most tried running up the slope to the east, but the going was slow. A lone elk separated from the herd and headed north. The craft targeted the loner and moved in. Surprised and astounded, Francisco shouted to Augustine, "Look at that!"'

The terrain, strewn with numerous small deciduous trees that had been cut about 18 inches off the ground, their trunks lying all over the place, prevented the animals from escaping quickly. Still wobbling, and moving no more than an estimated seven mph, the craft easily overtook the lone elk.

Augustine had missed the pursuit but caught sight of the UFO as it took the elk. Down-slope, Manuel (crew supervisor) also witnessed the capture – 500 yards distant. Nearly every other person's attention had been diverted toward the main group of fleeing animals.

The craft moved directly above the female elk and somehow lifted it into the air without any visible means of support ... At this point, the animal ceased discernible movement - no kicking legs, no struggling body, and no indication of consciousness. The witnesses were amazed that the craft could lift the 500-pound animal. The 'wing span' of the object measured not much longer than the length of the elk... The captured elk, its head apparently against the ventral surface of the craft, and body standing stiffly upright, was lifted off the ground – just enough to clear the underbrush. The craft continued its slow, wobbling oscillation. The suspended elk moved likewise as if she were a solid metal sculpture welded to the craft. After the craft acquired (without pause) the animal, it moved away at the same slow pace, to the north, following the contour of the land. The elk's feet were observed sweeping circles, in conjunction with the craft's movement, just above the brush and treetops.

Soon, the craft approached the end of the clear-cut area, apparently hitting some low branches.

After hitting the branches, the witnesses saw it dip sharply and reverse direction before ascending vertically in front of the tree line. All three had the impression that the object had almost dropped the animal. Once above the tree top level, it moved over the forest margin and continued northward, dipped out of sight momentarily ... then ascended at roughly a 45-degree angle into the distance until it was obscured by clouds. Meanwhile, the rest of the herd had gathered into a tight huddle near the tree line, a normal behavior when a predatory threat is perceived.

The craft was estimated to be seven to eight feet in span, five to six feet in 'length' and 14–18 inches in thickness. In general, the colour of the craft was grey. One witness thought the dull red and reflective white patches were lights. All three witnesses indicated that the craft's oscillations were 'similar to that of a spinning coin as it is winding down and closely approaching a flat surface [and with] an oscillatory period of about 2 to 2.5 seconds'.[27]

There are other interesting parallels with this case. Piedro Viera also told me that, like the elk, the cow he saw suddenly became motionless while being levitated.[28] However, whereas Viera later encountered the mutilated cow beside the road, there is no indication of what happened to the elk. Was it mutilated, then left in the area, or taken away?

On 25 October 1974, Carl Higdon, a 40-year-old oil rigger, was hunting elk in Medicine Bow National Forest, Wyoming, when he noticed a group of five elk huddled together a few hundred feet away. Raising his Magnum rifle, he aimed at one of the animals and squeezed the trigger. 'Instead of hitting one of the elk,' said Higdon, 'the bullet left my rifle very slowly [and] dropped into the snow only 50 feet away.' Amazed, he went to recover the 7mm bullet. (He found only the mangled copper jacket, but not the lead bullet.)[29] 'Immediately, I sensed a peculiar tingle in the air, like you feel in an electrical storm.'[30] Suddenly, a tall, bow-legged humanoid, dressed in a black jump-suit, appeared and (as in the Cahill case) 'glided' towards Higdon.

'There were no hands at the ends of his arms, just empty sleeves,' said Higdon. 'The right sleeve had a [pointed] bar coming out of it and every time he waved the bar, something moved or disappeared. His face was Oriental – a yellowish brown, with slanted eyes. He had no lower jaw. His hair was like straw – about the same color. It looked like he had antennae on his head, but it could have been his hair.'[31]

The humanoid asked Higdon if he was hungry and, without waiting for a reply, threw him a transparent envelope containing four pills, which he felt compelled to take. Next, Higdon suddenly found himself inside a small, transparent, cube-shaped contraption. 'All I know', said Higdon, 'is that he pointed his "arm" at me and before I knew what had hit me, we were inside this strange contraption, with the five elk – all paralyzed and off in a separate compartment.'

As in many other cases, spacial distortion characterized this event, for though only seven by seven feet on the outside, the contraption inside contained five elk, a second humanoid, seats and control panel. It was as though everything had been 'shrunk'. Not only that. 'My conception of time was thrown off entirely,' said Higdon. The humanoids placed a 'helmet' on him with a strap under the chin and wires sticking out and said they were going to their 'home planet'.

Higdon's conscious recollections became vague at this point. He found himself 'back' on Earth, confused and hysterical. Eventually he located his truck, three miles from where he had parked it. After summoning help via his radio, he was rescued at 23.40, eight hours after his initial encounter, by a sheriff's party. Higdon's wife, Margery, later joined the team.[32] While waiting two or three miles from the area where Higdon was located, Margery and two others observed an odd flashing light, changing colours in a pulsing pattern and moving in an arc.[33]

'When I first saw Carl,' said Margery, 'he was obviously in a state of panic and unable to say a word. Only after I asked him if he got any elk, did he come alive and start looking out the windshield up at the sky [and] began shouting: "They took my elk! They took my elk! Where are the pills? The lights – they hurt!" '[34]

Higdon spent two days undergoing a variety of tests at Carbon County Memorial Hospital in Rawlins, Wyoming. In addition to suffering from headache and backache, he could not endure exposure to bright light and his eyes became bloodshot and watered profusely. No traces of drugs or alcohol were found in his blood. Curiously, X-rays taken of his chest indicated a lack of scar tissue on his lungs, which had been there before, according to Dr Tongca, the attending physician.[35]

Higdon's displaced truck brings to mind Graham Sheppard's displaced aircraft (Chapter 2) and another, little-known case, also from Wyoming. In October 1973 rancher Pat McGuire had been hunting elk in snow near Jackson, then resting while a cloud or fog passed through the area. Suddenly he found himself in another location, nine miles away from his initial position. During the 1970s McGuire reported that mutilations were common on his ranch in Bosler, Wyoming; moreover, he and other witnesses encountered numerous unknown objects, with flashing coloured lights, apparently under intelligent control, some estimated to be as large as 500 feet long.[36]

A BREEDING PROGRAMME

Placed under hypnotic regression by Dr Leo Sprinkle, Associate Professor of Psychology at the University of Wyoming, Higdon revealed that on arrival at the aliens' 'home planet', following his transcendental transportation, he encountered other human abductees: two men (aged around 19 and 40–50) and three girls (around 11, 14 and 18), although they did not communicate with him and appeared expressionless. After being scanned by a device, Higdon was told that he was 'not what they needed', which brings to mind the 1974 case involving the Australian, 'Ben', and the 1983 case of the British abductee, Alfred Burtoo (described in *Alien Base* and *Beyond Top Secret*, respectively). Ben felt he was of no use to the aliens, while Higdon attributed his rejection to the fact that he had had a vasectomy.[37] Burtoo was told simply that he was 'too old and infirm'.

In the case of Ben, there are two other important parallels with Higdon's case. Once on board the craft, Ben found to his amazement that the craft appeared much larger inside than outside; furthermore, two young Caucasian girls, aged around 8 or 9 and 12 or 13, were on board, motionless, appearing to be 'in some type of trance'.[38] Ben's encounter, which took place in the same year as that of Higdon, was first published in 1998.

Assuming at least a modicum of truth to these accounts, it may be inferred that a breeding programme is on the alien agenda. Higdon did not learn the reason for the presumed hybridization of humans, but was told that, to supplement their diet of concentrated food, the aliens needed to breed Earth animals and, because their seas were lacking in the requisite elements, they also required our fish![39,40]

262

MAMMALIAN MUTILATIONS

In the latter context it should be mentioned that, apart from land animals, there have been a number of unexplained mutilations of marine mammals, for example those reported along the French Mediterranean coast in February 1998. The scale of deaths was described by one official as 'unprecedented and stunning'. Twenty-two striped dolphins were washed up at the rate of one a day on the beaches of Languedoc-Roussillon between Agde and the Spanish border. Most of these protected mammals were found with gaping wounds, some six inches in diameter, in the area of the throat or lower jaw. Researchers at the Mediterranean Dolphin Study Group stated that the circular wounds found on more than 70 per cent of the dolphins were unlikely to be man-made, inasmuch as they were 'on the underside and not on the top part of its body, which is clearly more accessible to man'.

Hypotheses for the mystery mutilations included aggression by a 'killer dolphin', accidents caused by trawler nets, a virus similar to one that killed 65 Mediterranean dolphins in 1995, and a claim that the dolphins had been trained by the US Navy at one of its Mediterranean bases, had escaped and were then killed by a 'radio-controlled explosion of their signal collars so that no one could find out their missions'. Although these hypotheses were ruled out, it does not mean that aliens were responsible, particularly since there was but one similarity with the mutilation of livestock – the precise excision of jaw tissue. 'All the wounds are located in almost exactly the same place,' said Guy Olivet, president of the study group. 'The extreme precision suggests that we can rule out accidental causes.'[41]

Although we have palpable evidence linking the mutilation of animals with the activity of alien intelligences, proof remains elusive. However, the preponderance of evidence suggests that some species on Earth do indeed face a predatory threat – from species of undetermined origin.

NOTES

1 Kelleher, Colm A., Ph.D.; Onet, George E., Ph.D. and Davis, Eric W., Ph.D., *Investigation of the Unexplained Death of a Cow in N.E. Utah, October 16, 1998*, The National Institute of Discovery Science, 1515 E. Tropicana, Suite 400, Las Vegas, Nevada 89119. Email: nids@anv.net. Web site: http://www.accessnv.com/nids, June 1999, pp. 1-3.

2 Ibid., pp. 23–4.

3 Ibid., p. 5.

4 Ibid., p. 6.

5 Good, Timothy, *Alien Liaison*.

6 'N.M. cattle mutilations probed', *Denver Post*, 4 September 1994.

7 Interview, Taos, New Mexico, 12 March 1997.

8 Kelleher, Onet and Davis, op. cit. pp. 5–6.

9 Ibid., pp. 6–8.

10 Ibid., pp. 8–9.

11 Ibid., pp.9–10.

12 Ibid., p. 11.

13 Ibid., p. 14.

14 Ibid., p. 22.

15 Ibid., p. 22.

16 Howe, Linda Moulton, *An Alien Harvest: Further Evidence Linking Animal Mutilations And Human Abductions To Alien Life Forms*, Linda Moulton Howe Productions, PO Box 3130, Littleton, Colorado 80161, 1989.

17 Letter to the author, 20 October 1999.

18 Letter to the author, 12 August 1999.

19 *UFOCUS*, vol.2, no. 1, 1997, pp. 7–11, ed. Dr Leo Sprinkle, The Institute for UFO Research, 1304 South College Avenue, Fort Collins, Colorado 80524, originally published in *CNI News*, ed. Michael Lindemann.

20 Carpenter, Rick, 'Using "out of this world" research to try to solve mutilation mystery', *Signature*, La Veta, Colorado, 10 November 1994.

21 Good, op. cit., pp. 52–4; *Alien Base*, p. 400.

22 Buchanan, Andrea L., 'Bizarre cow mutilation in Luna Canyon', *Daily Optic*, Las Vegas, New Mexico, 15 September 1994.

23 Sheremata, Davis, 'Dead cows tell no tales', *British Columbia Report*, Vancouver, 2 March 1998.

24 Good, op. cit., pp. 52–4; *Alien Base*, p. 400.

25 Carpenter, op. cit.

26 Good, *Alien Base*, p. 397.

27 Fairfax, Robert; Uriarte, Ruben; Davenport, Peter and Anderson, Kathleen, 'Daylight abduction of elk updated', *MUFON UFO Journal*, no. 375, July 1999, pp. 3–6. Copyright 1999 by the Mutual UFO Network.

28 Interview, 28 November 1997.

29 *The APRO Bulletin*, vol. 23, no. 5, March 1975, p. 3.

30 Bourke, Frank, 'I was kidnapped by a UFO bubble', *National Star*, Lafayette, Indiana, 22 March 1975.

31 Burt, Bill, 'I was kidnapped by a UFO', *National Enquirer*, 24 October 1978. (NB In the 1970s, unlike later, this newspaper's coverage of UFO reports was generally accurate.)

32 Bourke, op. cit.

33 Sprinkle, Dr R. Leo, 'Rawlins, Wyoming Case: The Investigation', *Skylook*, MUFON, no. 85, December 1974, pp. 10–11.

34 Bourke, op. cit.

35 Weber, Scott T., 'The Higdon Abduction', *Official UFO*, vol. 1, no. 12, pp. 36, 53–4.

36 Lorenzen, Jim, *Cattle Mutilations – The UFO Connection*, Aerial Phenomena Research Organization (APRO) Symposium, San Diego, California, 16–18 November 1979.

37 Weber, op. cit.

38 Good, *Alien Base*, pp. 344–6.

39 *The APRO Bulletin*, March 1975, p. 3.

40 Sprinkle, op. cit.

41 Macintyre, Ben, 'French baffled by mystery of dolphin deaths', *The Times*, 25 February 1998.

Chapter 16

Creatures Galore

The mutilation phenomenon is not restricted to large animals. Over the years, probably thousands of cases involving small farm animals, sometimes domestic pets, have been reported worldwide, particularly in Puerto Rico, the so-called 'Island of Enchantment'.

In the second week of January 1999 ten hens and four Canada geese were killed in mysterious circumstances in the village of La Laguna, Guánica, south-west Puerto Rico. Graham Sheppard and I happened to be staying in the area shortly after these events occurred, so we were able to visit the site and talk with witnesses. Dorina Garcia Lugo, whose family owned the hens, told us that such incidents happened periodically. 'It always happens in this type of terrain, near to mountains, and it always attacks at night,' she told us, through our interpreter. She had no doubt that the notorious *chupacabras* ('goat-sucker') was responsible for the attacks. 'Every time it kills the animals it usually makes a whistling sound,' she explained. 'It happened some time between 01.00 and 02.00 on Tuesday, and the hens were killed inside a new cage we had just built. We don't know how it got inside. It put the dead hens in a circle, the heads facing the back part of each one. The injuries were on the back of the neck. There was no blood left.' The following day, neighbours alerted the police, who spent a couple of hours studying the cage. The mayor of Guánica also visited the site.[1]

The hens had been buried by the time we arrived, so we were unable to examine them, but we did examine the remains of one of the geese which had been killed the same night, in the garden of a neighbouring house. Unfortunately, the bird had decomposed to the extent that we were unable to ascertain anything. 'On the Sunday, we found a goose with holes in the neck,' the owner, who asked for anonymity, told us. 'He was still alive, though he looked unsteady. Two days later we found a dead goose and noticed that two others had disappeared, close to the chicken cage. Something took it out of the cage and killed it. Geese are normally very noisy when strangers are around, but we heard nothing. On Wednesday, we heard a noise like a lot of bees around, on top of the house, and the dogs were barking furiously.'[2]

THE VAMPIRE OF MOCA
During a wave of sightings of unknown aerial craft and bizarre beings in north-west Puerto Rico beginning early in 1975, innumerable strange killings of animals occurred in and around the town of Moca. Investigations were carried out by the authorities, including veterinarian Mariano Santiago of the Federal Department of Agriculture, who confessed bewilderment at the manner of the deaths. 'The situation is preoccupying, and occupying all the time of my department,' admitted the Assistant Secretary of Agriculture, Felipe N. Rodriguez.

Sebastián Robiou Lamarche, a leading investigator, noted that the wounds on animals appeared as though caused by a sort of 'punch' or sharp instrument which cuts through organs and bones. 'The wounds seem to vary according to the size of the animal,' noted Robiou. 'In the case of birds, the diameter of wounds is about one quarter of an inch; in cases of goats, the diameter is over an inch . . . there is never a drop of blood anywhere around the wound. Furthermore, the wound remains open . . . as though the instrument producing the wound has simultaneously extracted any flesh or organs which it encountered. In the majority of cases they occur near the neck of the animal or in its thorax.'

Robiou's findings include a list of animals killed by the 'Vampire of Moca' during this period, and their percentages:

Domestic fowls	182 (58%)
Ducks	40 (12.70%)
Goats	33 (10.50%)
Rabbits	20 (6.38%)
Geese	8 (5.70%)
Cows	8 (2.55%)
Sheep	5 (1.59%
Pigs	3 (0.96%)
Dogs	3 (0.96%)
Cats	1 (0.32%)

Robiou found that the preponderance of killings at that time involved animals kept in pens and hutches. Descriptions of the creatures responsible for the deaths varied: 'hairy creatures' (similar to the yeti), a 'gigantic bird' and a 'terrible greyish creature with lots of feathers and a long thick neck' were typical.[3]

THE SERPENT-BIRD

One night in April 1989, during a spate of mutilations in Ceiba Norte, near Gurabo, east-central Puerto Rico, Señor Ortíz and others, fishing in the River Jaguas, heard a strange howl. Shining their electric torch in the direction of the sound, they saw a strange-looking bird with two large fangs. As soon as the beam of light struck the bird, it fell to the ground, motionless. The creature was captured and taken home, where it was kept in a cage for several days. Señora María Ortíz exhibited the 'serpent-bird', as it was called, to many people, including officials of the local government administration office, the Department of the Environment, the Department of Natural Resources, Civil Defence and the Police. The fierce creature, which 'howled like a dog', had large, white fangs – unknown in birds but common to certain snakes – and ate only raw meat. It looked like a small fowl, but had rough, toad-like skin and no feathers on its head.

Some days later María Ortíz was asked by the mayor's office to bring in the creature for examination. 'But when she got there, she found a police van and two policemen waiting for her,' reports investigator Magdalena Del Amo-Freixedo.

'One of them asked her if she had got the bird in that cage, and, as he was asking her, the other policeman snatched the cage from her and made off in the van at top speed.'[4] Fortunately, photographs of the creature exist and two of these have been published by Puerto Rico's leading investigator, Jorge Martín, in his book on the chupacabras phenomenon,[5] one of which has been reproduced in this book (Plate 36).

Similar creatures were reported by others at the time. According to a source from the Department of Natural Resources, the 'serpent-bird' had been confiscated by members of a 'task force', which included American federal personnel, and taken to a secret laboratory where specimens of other strange, apparently mutated creatures were kept. Martín's source stressed that Puerto Rican personnel were not allowed to participate in investigations at the laboratory.[6]

There have been other instances when strange creatures, including the chupacabras, have been captured by federal and military personnel in Puerto Rico. In one case a preserved specimen of a very small hominid creature was confiscated by federal personnel who reportedly stated that they worked for NASA. As in the case of the 'serpent-bird', photographs of the creature exist, two of which I published in *Alien Base*.[7]

THE 1995 WAVE

On 2 April 1995, at 18.00, in the midst of a spate of animal mutilations and sightings of strange creatures in the areas of Orocovis, Morovis and Naranjito, north-central Puerto Rico, fifteen witnesses encountered a dark grey, humanoid-shaped being about three feet high, with luminous, white eyes, making a hissing sound. One of the witnesses, Román Colón, told Jorge Martín that the creature made rapid side-to-side movements, almost as though it were 'floating' just above the ground (as reported in the Cahill case). Colón eventually went to the local police station and reported the incident. At 21.00 police officers returned to the site with Colón. The creature was still there, hiding among bushes and trees, and occasionally making strange 'whispering' noises. Colón asked if he could borrow a revolver from the police, but they explained that their mandate was to capture it alive; they were forbidden to shoot it. On attempting to approach the creature, one of the officers, Agent Cruz, was overcome by a terrible headache and a peculiar 'ill' feeling.[8] Martín reports that a similar creature, seen a week earlier in Orocovis, also made the witness feel ill, although he did not get a headache.

In *Alien Base* I describe a few sightings in 1995 of the chupacabras in Canóvanas, to the north of the El Yunque Rain Forest, reported by witnesses I interviewed in 1997 who had been introduced to me by Jorge Martín. Two of these witnesses were Madelyn Tolentino and her mother. Another witness I met briefly, but whose account I did not publish, was Madelyn's husband, José Miguel Agosto, who saw the creature a few hours earlier, in August 1995. 'There was a terrible noise, a loud thumping, and then I saw this creature land on the ground near me,' he told Linda Moulton Howe, the American investigator. 'It was about three to four feet high and it moved in a crawling way. But then it just stood next to the cyclone fence about eight feet away and jumped straight over into the tall grass.'[9] Chad Deetken, a Canadian investigator, relates further details of the creature, as given him by Madelyn Tolentino:

She described it as three to four feet tall, covered in a coarse dark brown/black hair . . . She did not notice any genitalia. Its arms, which it kept pulled up close to its body, were long and thin, ending with three long claws. It had what appeared to be a long 'comb' of feathers down its back. It also had several bare circular patches on its skin which were purple in colour and looked as if they were burn marks. Its jaw was prominent, it had a slit for a mouth and two holes for a nose, small ears and large slanted eyes which were grey in colour, lacking the whites. She described the eyes as being moist or gelatin-like. When it moved its head, it seemed to be in slow jerky mechanical motions.

Her mother, Isabel Maldonado, followed the creature and was joined by [a] mechanic. At this point, her mother and the mechanic saw that the 'comb' on its back was in fact spikes which it was able to raise, like those of a prehistoric lizard. And when it opened its mouth, they could see four fangs.[10]

In October 1998 I returned to Canóvanas, together with my girlfriend and Graham Sheppard, to investigate additional cases. On this and subsequent occasions we were offered a great deal of assistance by the mayor of Canóvanas, Hon. José 'Chemo' Soto Rivera and his staff, as well as by Civil Defence officials, all of whom take the chupacabras reports seriously. One of the witnesses we were taken to interview was 'Milly' Eufemia Rivas, who encountered the chupacabras on several occasions in February–March 1995. As she explained through our interpreter from the Civil Defence, Ismael Aguayo, Milly first saw the creature walking on a neighbour's roof.

> It was not so high, about four feet, with membranes under its arms and what looked like coloured spines coming down its back. It had big red eyes, like ovals. It started to lift the neighbour's roof cover then it came down through the roof, forcing the neighbours out of the house. They called the Civil Defence. The creature was in the house for two hours, keeping people away. Then it flew to the house over there, and then it flew towards our house and stood on my roof! It was greenish-grey, with an oval, skinny face, small lips, a proboscis and long teeth.
>
> At its closest it was only seven to ten feet away from me. I saw it three separate times, very close. It sucked rabbits . . . I was very frightened. This animal is not from Puerto Rico, but maybe from another planet, because it has certain supernatural powers. It's got a remarkable way of gazing . . . The spines on its back change colours, not because they *are* different colours but because they can change them somehow. It has very long claws on its hands and feet, and a membrane between the claws. On both elbows was something like a spike. The creature walked with heavy steps. My sister saw it, too. On another occasion, I saw something like a baby chupacabras. It made a different noise, like a whistle.[11]

A CHUPACABRAS SHOT

In mid-September 1995, at the height of the chupacabras scare, Agent Juan Collazo Vazquez of the Canóvanas Police Department was asleep in his house in the Community of Campo Rico. He had retired early, as he had to be up at 04.00 the following day. At 23.10 the sound of his car's burglar alarm awoke him. 'I put on a T-shirt, grabbed my bullet-proof vest and my .357 Smith and Wesson Magnum, and went downstairs,' he told Graham and me, through Civil Defence interpreter Edwin Vazquez, at Canóvanas police station.

> When I got to the garage, I saw my chow dog struggling to get away from something. As a precaution, I didn't turn on the light, so there was only some ambient light from the Moon. I got to within about nine feet away, and saw this animal. It held the dog by its short arms and was trying to spike it in the neck with something. My chow is an aggressive dog and quite large. I assumed at first that it was another dog, but then I noticed that it looked something like a kangaroo, with an oval-shaped snout. It was about three feet in height. I tried to approach, but I never saw anything like it; it had oval-shaped eyes, from side views at first. And then, I went into shock.

At this point in the interview, the hairs on Agent Collazo's arms stood on end. Clearly, he was still affected by the incident, three years on. After a pause, he continued:

> I pulled back, then pulled out my gun to aim at the creature and fired one shot. I can never forget it. The creature kind of squealed, and reacted. It became like a ball of hair, to protect itself. I used a hollow-point, split-end [dumdum] bullet. I realized the bullet went into it, but did not exit it. That's amazing! My car was on the other side of the creature and there was no impact point. The creature was sort of catapulted on to the wall, and then he springs back up again.
>
> I was so shocked. I scraped my knees running away and up the outside stairs. My wife started to come downstairs – she thought I'd been shot. I grabbed her by the hair and ran back with her into the house. I was shaking all over. I couldn't believe what I saw. My wife started slapping me and asking what had happened. On coming out of my shock, we returned downstairs. We found blood and hair – very thick hair, which the forensic section of the police examined. It smelled terrible, like rotted blood.
>
> The next day, the blood on the garage floor was still liquified; it should have coagulated by then. It rinsed away real quick, but it had this terrible smell. Jorge Martín brought some people and took samples of blood and hair for analysis. That dog was traumatized! The chupacabras had sort of shaved off the area it

wanted to pierce, but it didn't actually do that. Afterwards, the dog began to shake and seemed ill. When he bit my son in the back, we decided to take him to the animal refuge.

We asked Collazo how the chupacabras left. 'I didn't stay to see that!' he replied. 'But it left tracks in the mud – three big toes – outside my house. It must have been pretty heavy.'[12]

NO KNOWN SPECIES

Blood samples from the Collazo chupacabras incident were taken away by police forensic specialists. I do not know the results, but samples of blood (and other associated materials) from a chupacabras which had been injured in the area two nights later were collected by Jorge Martín and analysed by doctors specializing in genetics. Fearing professional repercussions, the doctors insisted on anonymity. Although the original analysis indicated that the sample showed similar characteristics to the blood of human Type A Rh. Positive, later analyses ruled this out. In his definitive book on the chupacabras phenomenon, Martín cites the doctors' report, part of which states that the ratios of traces of magnesium, phosphorus, calcium and potassium, as well as the proportion of albumin to globulin, were not compatible with either human or known terrestrial animal species.

> From the results of the analysis it can be inferred that, since the characteristics found in the sample could not be classified as those of any known organism, the organism from which this one originates might be the product of highly sophisticated genetic manipulation, an organism foreign to our environment, or perhaps an animal species totally unknown to present human science.[13]

New species of terrestrial and aquatic creatures are discovered occasionally. Could the chupacabras be indigenous to Earth? I do not believe this to be the case. In addition to the remarkable results from the blood sample, the creature's speed and method of flying and of killing its victims is phenomenal. Its description matches no known species. In cases where new terrestrial species are discovered (such as the 'Sun Dog', described shortly), their genetic heritage is traceable. What descriptions of the chupacabras *do* match, in certain critical features (such as the eyes), however, is that of the most widely reported alien hominid creature in Puerto Rico. A logical hypothesis, then, is that the chupacabras is an alien creature, perhaps a hybrid, created by an alien species for a purpose we can only guess at for the time being.

GOAT-SUCKER FEVER

'It has the fangs of a vampire, the wings of a bat and the personality of an extraterrestrial,' reported the *Washington Post* in May 1996. 'And now there are sightings everywhere, all across Mexico . . . even on the ranch of Guanajuato state Gov. [later President] Vicente Fox.'

Accounts of close encounters with the goat-sucker, which began with reports of farm animal slaughters and have spread to fantastic tales of human confrontations, are filling Mexico's newspapers, headlining the nightly television news . . . the government became so concerned about quelling the mania that the state of Sinaloa ordered a zoological task force into the field to find the mystery animal.

On 8 May the government task force issued its report. 'We have ruled out the theory that the attack on sheep and goats was carried out by a supernatural being or a blood-sucking bat,' declared Javier Delgadillo, a scientist. Instead, he said, pollution had now reached such high levels in the country that animals had been driven mad, giving them the appearance of 'crazed alien creatures'. Another theory was offered by Ernesto Enkerlin, a wildlife biologist at the Technological Institute of Monterrey, who attributed the frenzy to 'collective psychosis'.

Undoubtedly, collective psychosis played a large part in the proliferation of bizarre tales from Mexico (and elsewhere) that year, following as they did from the chupacabras epidemic reported in Puerto Rico the previous year. But not all reports can be dismissed, and there were some disturbing accounts of human victims, such as Abigael Pavon, a nurse who claimed her arm had been severed by a 'giant bird that swooped into her house' in Mexico State.[14] Another victim was José Angel

Pulido of Tlajomulco, Jalisco State. While walking home at 23.30 during the first week of May 1996, he was attacked by a creature that felt like 'a plastic bag filled with soft jelly; no bones, no muscles', and with a large round head. The creature left two puncture holes just above Pulido's right elbow and a triangle-shaped puncture on his right wrist. He suffered from nausea for about three days afterwards.[15]

According to Marco Reynoso, results of necropsies performed on mutilated animals in Mexico indicated that

> . . . the perforations in the thoracic cavity go straight down, converging on the heart, which is destroyed, along with the other vital organs, liver and lungs etc.; the blood is totally extracted – at times together with some organ or other, via the perforations, the diameter of which runs from 1cm to 1.5cm.
>
> In 70% of the cases, there are sightings of UFOs in the same night or the preceding night, but we still have not been able to find a direct relationship between the two phenomena.[16]

In 1997 hundreds of animal mutilations were reported in south-central Brazil. A few cases involved attacks on humans. On 4 July Rogério Roche Grance, a 22-year-old forester, was attacked while walking along an unlit stretch of road in the municipality of Jardim by a large, foul-smelling creature 'with big hairs scattered all over its body'. Grance was treated at hospital for wounds to his left arm caused by the creature's claws. Reportedly, the Brazilian Army asked that anybody who had been attacked should first present themselves at army barracks before giving any interviews to the media.[17]

'SUN DOGS'

Is it possible that the chupacabras and similar creatures are an unknown but terrestrial species? Consider the case of the mysterious 'Sun Dogs', or 'Wari-Wilkas' as they were called by the ancient Peruvians. Numerous representations of these fierce creatures were made by the Inca, the Maya, the Aztecs and the Toltecs, who used them to guard the 'Sun God', depicting a quadruped with 'large, sharp claws and offset thumb-like toes, a long narrow tongue, out-jutting lower jaw, retracted lips showing long, sharp fang-like teeth . . . and a long tail with slightly prehensible tip', as author A. Hyatt Verrill writes in his book, *America's Ancient Civilizations*. 'The Indians [of South and Central America] declare that it is absolutely fearless, will unhesitatingly attack any creature it meets including man, and that it moves, springs, strikes with its hooked claws, and slashes with the terrible teeth with incredible speed and agility, and they all firmly believe that it is a more or less supernatural creature inhabited by a devil.'

The actual existence of such a creature was disputed for many years until Hyatt Verrill was brought a live specimen in the late 1940s by a Lacandon Indian from Chiapas State in southern Mexico. 'To be sure, it was a young animal, barely two feet in length,' he reported (fully grown, they reached at least five feet), 'but it had all of the characteristics shown in the immeasurably old sculptures and paintings . . . the only known specimen of a supposedly long extinct semi-mythical animal . . . He was the most ferocious and dangerous animal for his size that I have ever seen . . . his paroxyms of fury [made] the more terrifying by fearsome deep throated snarls and loud hisses.'[18]

A photograph of the creature is included in Hyatt Verrill's book and is reproduced in Plate 35. There are few similarities with descriptions of the chupacabras and other 'related' species, neither is there any evidence that the Sun Dog sucked blood from those animals or humans it attacked. The point here is that creatures thought to be extinct or mythical do come to light occasionally.

'CHICKCHARNIES'

While holidaying in the Bahamas in 1999 I learned about the legendary and elusive 'chickcharnies', creatures said to nest in the forests of Andros, the largest but least developed island in the Bahamas. Seminole Indians are credited with originating the myth of the chickcharnies, which supposedly wreak havoc on those who fail to respect them. In light of stories about the chupacabras, the Mexican goat-sucker and other creatures, the description of chickcharnies made me wonder if some truth is contained in the myth. Described as a cross between a man and a bird, with owl-like features, beards, green feathers, red eyes, three fingers and three toes, they are said to hang upside down by their tails from pine trees.[19, 20]

'To you or I, the cheeky chickcharnie is a product of local imagination,' comments Christopher Baker, a travel and natural sciences writer. 'But to the Androsians, the devil-in-disguise is as real as the nose on your face.'[21] Of coincidental interest, a couple of miles off the east coast of North Andros lies the Tongue of the Ocean, a canyon more than five miles deep, and the joint US–UK Navies Atlantic Undersea Test and Evaluation Center (AUTEC) anti-submarine warfare testing facility is based one mile south of Andros Town.

THE HYBRID PUNKS

Close to the El Yunque Rain Forest in Puerto Rico lies the pleasant housing settlement of Colinas del Yunque. On a very hot day in August 1992, at about 17.00, two extraordinary humanoid creatures were seen strolling calmly down the street outside the house of Soraya Collazo and her family. In November 1997 Jorge Martín took me to meet Señora Collazo and her sons, Didier and Gabriel Rosado, and daughters, Naomi Collazo and Ava Saudí Rosado.

'They walked slowly,' Señora Collazo told us. 'But I didn't see them from a very close distance.'

> It was very hot, and they were wearing no shoes – that's what caught my attention. I called the kids. The creatures were of a greenish-greyish colour, about four to five feet tall, and had long, skinny arms. The hair was sort of in lumps and their eyes were oval; I could see no white or colour in them. I thought they were crazy – it was too hot. They wore only short pants. I couldn't see their feet clearly, but they were possibly elongated.

'We saw these creatures with straw-like, beige-coloured hair sticking up, walking down the street,' recounted Didier Rosado, nine years old at the time of the encounter. 'We went after them on our bikes, with another kid – there were five of us altogether. We followed them about six to eight feet away, but they wouldn't let us come closer. They walked at an even pace. They had black eyes, greenish, long arms, almost down to their knees, and oval-shaped heads with a pronounced chin, hardly any nose and small, pointed ears.'

'The colour of their skin was a mixture of brown and green,' recalled Ava Saudí Rosado, who is one year older than Didier. 'I was a little bit scared, but I laughed at them as we followed them because I just couldn't believe it.' She pointed down the road. 'Then they turned off down there and disappeared into the brush.'

The children described the creatures' hair as swept up in a sort of 'punk' style. Naturally, it will be suggested that the odd couple actually *were* punks, wearing masks, but the witnesses insist that the creatures were not only far too thin, there was also something about them that was 'different'. None of the children could explain why, for the most part, they all felt so calm in the face of such bizarre beings.[22]

There was another occasion when alien creatures were seen strolling down a road in El Yunque, witnessed at night by Luis Torres and two other police officers and their wives in 1991,[23] but the Colinas del Yunque case is unique in that it took place in broad daylight and the creatures appeared to have hair, a rarity in cases involving this species. Jorge Martín and I wondered if this development heralded the emergence of an alien/human hybrid – a hybridized species which many abductees claim to have been shown by their abductors. Whatever the case, it certainly seems as though the creatures wanted to be seen, perhaps to test local reactions.

'I know that something strange is happening over there,' Soraya Collazo told us, looking at the mountains of the rain forest. 'Many neighbours have seen things . . .'

NOTES

1 Interview, Guánica, 17 January 1999.
2 Interview, Guánica, 20 January 1999.
3 Robiou Lamarche, Sebastián, 'UFOs and Mysterious Deaths of Animals: Part I', *Flying Saucer Review*, vol. 22, no. 5, 1976, pp. 15–18.

4 Del Amo-Freixedo, Magdalena, 'Current Happenings on Puerto Rico', *Flying Saucer Review*, vol. 36, no. 4, Winter 1991, pp. 19–20, translated by Gordon Creighton.

5 Martín, Jorge, *La Conspiración Chupacabras*, CEDICOP, PO Box 29516, San Juan, Puerto Rico 00929–0516, 1997.

6 Martín, Jorge, '"Impossible Animals!" What is going on in Puerto Rico?', *Evidencia OVNI*, no. 6, 1995, p. 37.

7 Good, Timothy, *Alien Base*, pp. 393–4.

8 Martín, Jorge, 'What are the creatures seen in Orocovis, Morovis, and Naranjito?', *Evidencia OVNI*, no. 6, 1995, pp. 19–20.

9 Howe, Linda Moulton, 'Chupacabras: The Mysterious Bloodsuckers', *Nexus*, June–July 1997, p. 58.

10 Deetken, Chad, 'Chupacabras: Mystery or Hysteria?', *UFO*BC Quarterly*, vol. 2, no. 1, January 1997, 1810 Hamilton Street, New Westminster, British Columbia, V3M 2P4, Canada.

11 Interview, Canóvanas, 23 October 1998.

12 Ibid.

13 Martín, Jorge, *La Conspiración Chupacabras*, pp. 116-17, translated by Margaret Barling.

14 Moore, Molly, 'Mexico Hears a Sucking Sound', *Washington Post*, 11 May 1996.

15 Howe, op. cit., pp. 59–60.

16 Del Amo-Freixedo, 'Chupacabras Galore!', *Flying Saucer Review*, vol. 42, no. 2, Summer 1997, p. 3, translated by Gordon Creighton from *Enigmas* (Madrid), vol. 2, no. XI, 1996.

17 Stieven, Mauren Andrea, 'Chupacabras rampant in South-Central Brazil (1997)', *Flying Saucer Review*, vol. 44, no. 4, Winter 1999, pp. 13–16, translated by Gordon Creighton from the Brazilian magazine *UFO*, no. 53, September 1997.

18 Verrill, A. Hyatt and Verrill, Ruth, *America's Ancient Civilizations*, G. P. Putnam's Sons, New York, 1953, pp. 120–4.

19 *Fodor's 98: The Bahamas*, ed. Stephen Wolf, Fodor's Travel Publications, 1997, p. 134.

20 Baker, Christopher P., *Bahamas, Turks & Caicos*, Lonely Planet, 1991, p. 313.

21 Ibid.

22 Interviews, Colinas del Yunque, 26 November 1997.

23 Good, op. cit., pp. 389–90.

Chapter 17

Island of Enchantment

'Up at El Yunque a year ago,' Soraya Collazo told Jorge Martín and me, 'some armed men, dressed in black, ordered us to leave the area.'

It was a story I had heard from many local people. 'I don't know what's going on up there,' Juan Antonio Skerret, of Río Grande, told us in 1998. 'Before, you could go up to any place there and have a good time. American military people often stop us. Someone is hiding something up there.'[1]

I do not doubt that, at certain times and in certain areas of the Caribbean National Forest, visitors are harassed by military personnel, but in many cases the reasons are not related to the alien phenomenon. I have yet to be harassed by anybody, or anything else in El Yunque for that matter, apart from mosquitoes. Possibly this is owing to my being 'in the wrong place at the wrong time' or to not being a local inhabitant. True, there are restricted areas, but these are usually marked. For example, a typed notice from the US Department of Agriculture Forest Service, dated 26 August 1997 and signed by the Forest Supervisor, Caribbean National Forest, states in part:

> . . . it is hereby ordered that the following prohibition hereinafter set forth apply to the following described area . . . entering, or being upon the Molindero Road . . . Except for: (1) Any Federal, State, or Local officer, or member of an organized rescue or fire fighting force in the performance of an official duty. (2) Any authorized person engaged in official administrative duties regarding National Forest Administration. Violation of this order is prohibited by provisions of the regulations cited . . . any such violation is subject to punishment by a fine of not more

than $5000.00 or imprisonment for not more than six months, or both.

The 28,000-acre rain forest, popularly named after its second-highest mountain, El Yunque (1065 metres), has numerous nature trails, some of which, like the roads, are periodically (some say conveniently) closed due to flooding, landslides or hurricane damage. Both the US Navy and the Federal Aviation Administration (FAA) have radar and communication facilities in El Yunque, such as on Mount Britton (941 metres), access to which sites is restricted. Sometimes forestry repairs are carried out by a partnership of the US Department of Agriculture Forest Service, the US Navy and the FAA.

In my view there is another reason why, periodically, military personnel seem to appear out of nowhere, ordering visitors to move away from certain areas. Roosevelt Roads Naval Air Station is relatively close and I have been told that the US Navy stores nuclear weapons, as well as conventional ordnance, in El Yunque. Ordnance is also stored on Vieques, an island some ten miles south-east of Roosevelt Roads. Currently there is a dispute about the Navy's 60-year hegemony over this island, which 9300 residents share with the Atlantic Fleet Weapons Training Facility, a huge bombing range. Crews on all ships (including flight crews) carry out exercises with live bombs and sometimes civilians get hurt. What worries many Puerto Ricans, understandably, is that napalm and munitions containing depleted ('spent') uranium have been used by US forces training in Vieques: it is claimed that the cancer rate there, by far the highest of any of Puerto Rico's 78 municipalities, is linked to these exercises.[2]

Carlos Pérez Figueroa, an editor for Channel 11 News in Puerto Rico, lives in the Canóvanas area which borders El Yunque. One night in November–December 1997, Jorge Martín told me, Pérez was with some friends in Palmasola when all of them saw a brilliant light approaching the house, accompanied by a loud roaring sound which shook the house. As it came closer, the light could be seen to be at the front of a huge, dark, triangular- or boomerang-shaped craft with what looked like engines underneath, towards the back.[3] No tailplane, fin nor control surfaces were discerned. With heat emanating from it, the craft moved at no more than 30 to 40 mph. Pérez described the engines as like two broad, flexible tubes, curving out towards the base and with two large openings or exhausts. The craft appeared to be much wider than, but not as long as, a Boeing 747 jumbo jet. It flew just above trees, following the contour of the terrain, before disappearing between El Yunque and El Toro (at 1074 metres, the highest mountain in the forest). Afterwards, Pérez told Martín, loud explosions could be heard coming from that direction.[4]

On the night of 22 November 1997 Carlos Pérez took three friends to visit El Yunque. Having spent an hour on Mount Britton in the rain and mist, they decided to walk back down to their van, parked some considerable distance away, each carrying electric torches. Suddenly, Martín told me, the shrubbery began to move around them and a camouflaged, armed soldier emerged, then others, wearing nets over their camouflaged faces. Pointing rifles and automatic pistols, and shining torches into the faces of the witnesses, they demanded, in English, to know what Pérez and his friends were doing there and asked if the van parked further down the road was theirs. Pérez, who speaks little English, asked to talk to a Spanish-speaking soldier and began remonstrating with him, pointing out that they were not in a restricted area. As the situation became tense, one of Pérez's friends pleaded with him to comply with the soldiers' orders to leave the area, which they did.[5]

Had Pérez and his friends innocently stumbled on a military exercise? Exercises are carried out periodically by US armed forces in El Yunque, and such exercises routinely and legally encroach on public land, sometimes to the consternation of local inhabitants. Owing to sightings of strange craft in El Yunque at that time, such as the one seen by Pérez (which he assumed to be of American origin), one has to wonder if the military was involved in an actual operation of some sort, particularly because, on a number of occasions, strange, apparently military craft have been accompanied by even stranger, more sophisticated craft.

Jorge Martín reports that, in the small hours of 21 January 1997, Juan Hernández, a security guard, was driving in north-west Puerto Rico when he claims to have encountered a huge, triangular-shaped craft. The craft, covered with lights that changed colour, seemed to be piloted by a typically described 'grey' alien. Suddenly, a beam of light from the craft engulfed Hernández, who by this time had stopped to watch. He became imbued with a sensation of peace such as he had never experienced.

Underneath the craft 'fan blades' rotated slowly and silently. Deciding to follow it, Hernández got back into his car, but found his way blocked by an official-looking vehicle, occupied by several men. As with 'Piedro Viera' (Chapter 15), Hernández was warned by the driver not to follow the craft, but in this case the warning was followed by a threat that something would happen to him if he tried to do so. He then overheard one of the men announcing to the others that two more craft were coming.

According to Hernández, two more craft then appeared, identical to the previous one but with twin engines, emitting exhaust and making an extremely loud jet-like noise. These followed the first craft, which surrounded itself in a turquoise-coloured light that changed to violet, then shot off vertically, leaving the others behind. Finally, the men left in their vehicle, apparently following the two craft, which headed in the direction of where Ramey Air Force Base used to be located.[6]

Hernández speculated that the second and third craft were of terrestrial origin, perhaps incorporating extraterrestrial technology, and that the men in the vehicle were monitoring a test flight. In that case, I wonder, was the first craft also monitoring the flight?

The similarity in descriptions of the 'military' craft seen by Carlos Pérez and Juan Hernández is remarkable. Furthermore, Jorge Martín discovered that in the early hours of 21 January 1997, two similar craft with equally noisy engines were reportedly seen landing by several witnesses at the former Ramey Air Force Base (now Rafael Hernández Airport), in an area still controlled by the US Air Force.[7]

DISAPPEARANCES

It is not difficult to become lost in El Yunque. In most cases, people find their way back to one of the trails or roads, but in a few cases some have never returned. Jorge Martín reports that one night in 1967, while a group of biology students and teachers were camping in a densely forested area of El Yunque, a strange humming sound pervaded the area for several minutes – then silence. Shortly afterwards, the group observed a luminous figure walking some distance away. One of the teachers, Professor González, decided to investigate, taking a boy, Ramón Quiñones, with him.

Later, the teacher returned, without Ramón, who had disappeared after taking a different path. González searched for him in vain. Then a slim, tall man, dressed in a tight-fitting silvery suit, with a large head, long arms and hands, appeared before the group, and held them immobilized for 15 minutes. After the entity had walked away slowly, the students and teachers recovered their mobility and once again searched unsuccessfully for Ramón. The following day, police and forest rangers searched the area to no avail. Members of the group were forbidden by police and federal authorities from discussing the matter publicly, and for five months, allegedly, were watched by government agents.[8]

Jorge Martín has told me about some disturbing disappearances of children, and others involving military personnel. In 1976, two US Navy officers stationed at Roosevelt Roads vanished without trace. According to one of Martín's sources, some soldiers who disappeared on El Yunque in the 1960s and 1970s were officially declared to have gone missing in the Vietnam War.[9]

On 2 August 1997 Dr Darby Williams, a dean of Bowling Green State University, Huron, Ohio, left his rented car beside the well-known 'La Coca' waterfall in El Yunque and, according to some reports, went looking for Puerto Rico's unique-sounding tiny tree frogs, the *coquí*. When Williams's return was long overdue, his family alerted authorities. 'The federal police kept it to themselves for a long time,' Martín told me.

That's unusual. They took his car back to the rental place, but didn't notify the Puerto Rico police until later. After starting the search, they suddenly suspended it.

The Dean was very well connected, even at the White House, I'm told, so another search was ordered. Though federal authorities made up stories that he had been seen in various towns, after 12 days he reappeared at the Coca Falls. When people get lost, they rarely come out of the forest at the same place they entered. He was very nervous, and he had a strong sunburn. Why? He also had marks on his legs, and possibly his wrists, which looked like shackle marks.

The 'feds' wouldn't let him talk to the media. One journalist who tried to interview him had her cellular phone taken away. He was taken first to a hospital in San Juan, given emergency treatment, then to the main Puerto Rico police headquarters, where the superintendent is an FBI agent. Williams seemed afraid, and he was always escorted forcibly. Then he was sent back to the mainland United States.

'So what happened?' I asked Martín in San Juan, less than a month after the incident.

'I don't know. *Something* happened to him. Either he had an encounter with alien beings or he accidentally came across a secret US facility and was arrested for security reasons. Everyone here will tell you it was illogical. He seemed to be hiding something. And he went into the forest with a camcorder but did not come out with it.'[10]

It is possible, of course, that there is another explanation. I contacted Dr Williams. 'I am most interested in learning what actually happened to you while you went missing in El Yunque in August 1997,' I wrote. 'As a reporter dedicated to getting the facts and avoiding sensationalism, I would be delighted to have the story from you.'[11] Although Dr Williams received my letter and subsequent copies, he chose not to reply.

While many strange things undoubtedly have occurred in

El Yunque, there are those who live there who say they have yet to see anything unusual. In October 1998, for instance, Graham Sheppard and I introduced ourselves to Professor José T. Quiñones III, a retired US Navy lieutenant commander, as he was repairing damage to his house caused by Hurricane Georges. We casually mentioned our research. He seemed interested but regretted that he himself had never seen anything.[12] Conspiracy theorists might suggest that his US Navy background made him an official collaborator with the 'cover-up'. That was not our impression. Regarding the US military presence, on at least one occasion Graham and I have tailed US Navy vehicles as they made their way up El Yunque. Personnel inside the vehicles seemed uninterested, although as previously explained, we have learned that there are indeed sensitive areas, such as weapons storage sites, to which access is understandably denied.

THE OFFICIAL VIEW

On the morning of 30 April 1997 Dr Pedro Rosselló, Governor of Puerto Rico, held an official meeting with General Wesley Clark, US Army Commander-in-Chief, Southern Command, to discuss the siting of US Army South at Fort Buchanan in Guaynabo. According to two of Jorge Martín's highly placed sources, another unofficial and secret meeting supposedly took place on 1 May between Governor Rosselló and a number of US military officials on board a US Navy ship anchored between Fajardo and the island of Vieques off the east coast of Puerto Rico. Shortly before 02.00, Martín told me, a huge, disc-shaped craft appeared in the sky, made a pass above the ship, then plunged into the sea. 'Was this by pure chance, or perhaps a "demonstration" put on for the benefit of the Governor?' Martín speculated.[13]

Governor Rosselló is a Yale- and Harvard-educated surgeon who has been a popular leader of his people since 1992. Despite the extraordinary number of alien encounters reported in Puerto Rico, the subject seldom receives attention by the serious media and relatively few officials have spoken out publicly. In 1999 I wrote to Dr Rosselló, mentioning that

I had visited the Commonwealth on seven occasions since 1990, investigating the claims of men and women from all walks of life. 'While I remain sceptical about many of the stories regarding an alleged alien presence in Puerto Rico,' I pointed out, 'it would be dishonest of me not to admit that I find a number of these stories highly convincing.

'From normally reliable sources,' I continued, 'I have been informed that there is indeed an alien presence based in your country and around its waters, and that certain US military/intelligence authorities are well aware of this . . . I have often wondered if you might have been briefed by the Americans on these matters.' I went on to ask the Governor if he had discussed the 'forbidden subject' with General Clark, for example, because a lot of 'activity' had been reported around that time, and if there was any truth to the rumour that during the alleged unpublicized meeting on board a US Navy ship, some 'activity' had occurred.[14] I received the following reply:

> I commend you for having invested so much time and energy to investigating a topic which – though fascinating – inevitably provokes scorn and even ridicule in many quarters.
>
> Accepting your inquiry in the best of good faith, I can assure you that *nothing I have heard, read or experienced has given me any reason to believe that extraterrestrial creatures have ever visited Earth*. Please accept this as a categorical affirmation of total ignorance on the subject, because the preceding sentence is emphatically *not* a 'craftily-worded' disclaimer designed to withhold any item or items of information. That said, I appreciate your interest in the United States' Island of Enchantment in the Caribbean Sea, and hope you will contact me at once if your research eventually yields tangible evidence that Puerto Rico has been visited by beings from other worlds . . .[15]

Responding to my request for further clarification, Governor Rosselló wrote to me as follows.

Never has any government official or institution directly or indirectly briefed me, or otherwise provided me with information, either on the topic of unidentified flying objects or with respect to evidence that the Earth may at some time have been visited by extraterrestrial creatures.

On one or more occasions during my incumbency, I have been aboard United States Navy vessels. On no such occasion, however, has anything transpired that could even remotely be deemed pertinent to your studies.[16]

My scheduling staff has exhaustively searched our files and determined to my complete satisfaction that on May 1, 1997: I visited no U.S. Navy vessel; I met with no person or persons serving in or employed by the U.S. Navy. Once more, let me stress that this and my previous responses to your inquiries have been as candid, accurate and comprehensive as I could possibly make them. I have concealed no relevant information. I have in no way endeavoured to mislead you.[17]

It is unlikely that either Governor Pedro Rosselló or Jorge Martín are dissimulating. My conclusion, therefore, is that Martín was fed disinformation by his sources.

'I confess that the extensive material about mysterious happenings hereabouts struck me as ironic,' wrote Dr Rosselló, responding to extracts from this book which I had sent him for review. 'Critics (both local and external) regularly accuse us of societal self-absorption ("an island surrounded by mirrors" is one phrase that's been utilized in this context) – that is, a tendency to behave as if the universe revolved around Puerto Rico; yet your writing might almost lead a reader to suspect that we indeed *are* situated at the center of the universe!'[18]

FEDERAL INVOLVEMENT

In 1990, following a lecture he had given at a symposium of the Mutual UFO Network (MUFON) in Pensacola, Florida, Jorge Martín was approached by a man named César Remus Ramírez, a US citizen with a Venezuelan father and Puerto Rican mother. Remus expressed much interest in the UFO situation in Puerto Rico. Two years later he moved to the island for reasons connected with his work as a mechanical engineer, he said, and contacted Martín.

'Every time we talked about his alleged work, he would become very nervous,' said Martín. Eventually, Remus confessed to being an FBI agent, but stressed that his work had nothing to do with his interest in the UFO subject. He claimed to be a member of a special 'task force' investigating bank robberies and international drugs traffic. Shortly afterwards, however, Remus contacted several of Martín's friends and co-investigators, also disclosing that he was an FBI agent, and falsely claiming to be working with Martín. 'At the same time, he began asking everyone what I knew about the UFO/alien situation in El Yunque. He insisted on asking us and our friends repeatedly to camp at night in El Yunque. Upon our refusal to do this, he, very annoyed, discarded the whole idea. If he wanted to go to El Yunque, why was our presence so indispensable?'

In July 1993 Martín participated at a MUFON symposium in Richmond, Virginia. Prior to boarding the flight at San Juan's Luís Muñoz Marín international airport, he and his wife were surprised to meet Remus, who said he was also attending the conference in a strictly unofficial capacity. 'He assured us he had financed his air tickets with his own money, but we noticed that he did not travel with regular air tickets,' said Martín. 'At each stop on the trip, the agent filled in a series of "vouchers", a lot of papers, together with the airline employees, showing them his federal agency ID, but did everything possible to prevent us from seeing the ID. Was it perhaps to conceal the fact that he worked for someone other than the FBI? . . . He explained that he had to fill those papers because he was travelling with his official gun. But if that was the case, why did he not have any regular air tickets?' A member of MUFON, a police officer who joined the flight later, confirmed to Martín that this was indeed a puzzling irregularity.

At the symposium, Martín's lecture focused on the UFO situation in El Yunque, voicing his suspicion that 'the US Government kept certain flying saucer-type crafts there' and that there might be 'official US/alien contact in a site close to the rain forest: Roosevelt Roads Naval Air Station'. It seems Martín had touched a sensitive nerve. Prior to departure for Puerto Rico, he learned that Walter Andrus Jr, Director of MUFON, had held a lengthy meeting with César Remus on the previous evening. Andrus asked Martín if he knew Remus. 'We told him we knew the man, but it was a real surprise to us to know that Andrus had been talking in his room with the agent for "a good part of the previous night", as he had said.

'At that point Andrus ordered us to appoint the agent as MUFON's assistant state director for Puerto Rico, which would have made him my direct assistant. I asked Mr Andrus if he knew about the man's job back in Puerto Rico, and he answered: "Yes, he is an FBI agent. So what? Is there any problem with that?" ' Back in Puerto Rico, Martín telephoned Andrus to voice his objections.

> We told him that, clearly, the mere fact of being an active federal agent did not exclude or disqualify anyone from being a MUFON member . . . but we also explained that there had been harassment and threats to witnesses in Puerto Rico, allegedly made by U.S. federal agents. Due to this, there was some fear pertaining to the presence of federal agents in the presence of UFO situations . . . We also explained that our confidential military and police sources, and our collaborators in different fields, would not trust us any more and would distance themselves from us, thus stopping the flow of data.

Andrus insisted on the appointment, prompting Martín's resignation. A few days later Remus phoned Martín, claiming that Andrus's idea of appointing him assistant state director was 'absurd'. He nonetheless took over Martín's position as state director.

Remus continued to spread the word that Martín and he were collaborating, effectively sowing seeds of suspicion. 'But what really alarmed us', said Martín, 'was that we started receiving reports from our friends and associates that the agent visited them and asked them to go outside their homes and to his car.'

> He opened the car's trunk and showed them several guns, asking them to hold them in their hands and examine them (carbines and automatic rifles), which unfortunately they did . . . some days later, the agent visited our office and asked us to go outside with him [and] once at his car he opened its trunk and showed us the guns, asking us to handle and examine them. We refused . . . To the best of our knowledge, this behaviour by an active federal or

FBI agent violates that agency's regulations, unless [there was] an official directive from the agency.

During this period Martín's office was broken into. 'The robbers only took our computer, the secretary's computer and the fax machine – nothing else,' he reported. 'This was rather strange, as our computers were small, old and cheap models, and there were several other newer and more expensive ones there, as well as an expensive laser printer. Were the robbers common criminals, or was it that "someone special" wanted to know what type of data was in our computer?'

Even if an official operation had been underway, Remus's conduct strikes me as highly unprofessional, by FBI standards. 'Due to his strange behaviour,' said Martín, 'we consulted with several police specialists, as well as lawyers, including the well-known US lawyer Daniel Sheehan. They all expressed the same opinion: we had to be careful, because such actions seemed to imply that an operation was underway, maybe to fabricate a case around us.'[19]

In March 1996 Chad Deetken, the Canadian investigator, spent a week in Puerto Rico assessing evidence for the chupacabras, interviewing eyewitnesses, journalists, and several scientists and veterinarians. Through a scientist he was introduced to César Remus, who asked if he could accompany Deetken to act as interpreter at an interview with Madelyn Tolentino and her husband (Chapter 16). On the return to San Juan Remus revealed that he was an FBI agent and showed the astonished Deetken his photo ID and badge. A black bag in Remus's car contained a bullet-proof vest, gun and holster. 'I swear,' said Remus, 'this is just a coincidence. I'm really interested in this stuff and just happen to be working for the FBI.' Remus left Deetken at his hotel and the two arranged to meet the following evening. The meeting did not take place, Deetken opting instead to investigate the mutilation of three sheep earlier that day.

At the mutilation site Deetken, accompanied by a reporter, Eddie Deese, members of the local Civil Defence and others, including the mayor of Canóvanas, took photographs and collected blood and hair samples for analysis in Canada.

Returning from the site, everyone was overcome by something noxious. 'The irritant was rather debilitating, making it difficult to breathe,' Deetken explained. 'We scrambled out of the area as fast as we could. Our throats were burning for some time after. The area was searched by the Civil Defence a second time next morning and again, severe throat irritation was experienced . . . Experiences similar to this are frequently reported in cases of chupacabras attacks.' What happened later was equally disturbing.

> I got back to the hotel from the sheep case at 3 a.m. that night and went to bed exhausted. I had to fly home that morning and needed some sleep. At 5.30 a.m., I was awoken by a terrible commotion next door [of] several men pounding on the door of the suite next to me. I picked out the words 'goddamned Canadian' in the midst of their cursing. They were also yelling 'Police, police! Open up!' and kicking at the door. I managed a quick glimpse through the blinds and saw they were plainclothes officers. At that point I realised I felt terribly ill, possibly from the noxious smell . . .[20]

Fortunately, Deetken had switched rooms days before, because the room next door was too noisy. 'I thought I was going to die,' he told me. 'I was sweating and I had throbbing headaches. There were at least three agents involved. The owner of the hotel later claimed he didn't know anything about it, although it would have been impossible for him not to have heard the commotion in such a small hotel.'[21]

In the morning Remus phoned Deetken and asked if they could meet.

> I said that wasn't possible since I had to get to the airport right away. I made no mention of the night's events. He made some small talk and then started asking which airline I was flying with, what time my plane departed, was I flying direct or did I have a stopover in the US, was I carrying any agricultural products with me? I lied about everything.
>
> I began to worry. I divided samples I took at the farm between my carry-on and check-in luggage then proceeded to the airport, still not feeling well.
>
> The plane made its way to the end of the runway [and] was there a few minutes when the pilot announced that there was an

electronic problem and we would have to wait until it was repaired. A van pulled up and several men entered the cargo hold . . . You could hear things being knocked around and I was sure someone was about to pounce out of the hold, apprehend me and drag me off the plane. But after an hour, the van left and the plane departed.

Upon arriving in Vancouver, I anxiously opened my suitcase. The contents had definitely been rearranged, but to my surprise, the plastic ziplock containing the samples was still in my dirty laundry bag where I had put it.[22]

'Remus had given me a phone number to get hold of him on my return to Canada,' Deetken told me. 'That number was the FBI training headquarters in Florida.'[23]

On 30 December 1997 the Puerto Rico Police arrested César Remus at a shooting range he had set up in a wooded field in the municipality of Gurabo. 'Hoist with his own petard', he was accused of owning and handling non-registered automatic rifles and carbines which he had introduced illegally to the island. At the preliminary court hearing, Remus faced seven charges, with a bail of $1000 per charge, which was reduced to only 10 per cent of the total. Neither Remus nor his legal adviser, also employed by the FBI, made any comments to the media. The judgement, in the Judicial Court Center in Caguas, took place on 2 March 1998. The FBI admitted that Remus worked for the agency but disavowed responsibility for the weapons and recommended that the Puerto Rican Justice Department should continue to press charges.[24]

THE AEROSTAT

There is another area in Puerto Rico where the existence of an alien liaison with US military forces is rumoured: the US Air Force Tethered Aerostat (balloon) Radar Site at Lajas, on the south-west coast. I have spoken to a number of witnesses who claim to have seen all manner of strange flying objects in the vicinity. While some reports seem credible, others do not. In the early 1990s rumours about an alien base proliferated when a diagram was supplied to Jorge Martín and to another reporter depicting a subterranean base, complete with flying saucers and little aliens, beneath the radar site. The diagram was made by a man who claimed to have been taken to the 'top-secret US/alien facility' by a tall, human-type alien, during an 'astral projection'.[25]

Fascinating as they may be, observations obtained during an astral projection can hardly be considered reliable evidence. Nonetheless, rumours persisted about the aerostat site, including claims that 'NASA personnel' periodically visited the site in the middle of the night. Graham Sheppard and I decided to investigate. In October 1998 we obtained permission from the site manager, Joseph Bohunko, to overfly the site. This we did, at low altitude, obtaining good photographs and video film. But more information was needed. In January 1999 we asked Bohunko if we could visit the site. He unhesitatingly agreed and a visit was arranged for 18 January.

We spent three hours at the site. Because originally we were preparing an article about the aerostat operation for *Aerospace International* magazine, at no time did either Graham or I mention our interest in UFOs. Only two areas were out of bounds: the operations centre (a modest-sized room) and the aerostat winch pad, although we were assured that a visit to both might be possible in the future, subject to permission from Air Combat Command (ACC).

Jorge Martín claims to have learned from a confidential source that whenever an unknown flying object registers on the aerostat's radar system, Puerto Rican technicians are ordered to leave the control room. This is unlikely. Although administered by the US Air Force's ACC Contract Programs Squadron, we learned that the site is staffed and managed almost exclusively by Puerto Ricans.

'Construction of the site began in 1989,' Bohunko told us.

We are not allowed to say how many people work here, but they're all civilian contractors, and 99 per cent of them are Puerto Rican. Most employees have been here for five years, and some have been here longer. All we do is manage and maintain the equipment. Our command centre is Lockheed Martin Corporation (Systems Support and Training Services) in Chesapeake, Virginia, and they liaise with our client, the US Air Force, who provide the training.

Launching and recovering the aerostat is a complex and demanding procedure. The pre-flight checks, for example, take twice as long as that for a Boeing 747. 'There's a lot that can go wrong,' explained Bohunko. 'The crew is kept very busy: the aerostat, the winches, the tower, tether and cables can all be damaged. We've lost a couple of aerostats on the launch tower. Currently, we're using the 420K, manufactured by ILC. The fabric for the balloon alone costs around a million dollars.'

Although previous aerostats used at the site went up to 15,000 feet, the 420K currently in use is typically winched no higher than 9300 feet. 'The aerostat provides radar coverage for air traffic control and for drug smuggling – we don't do weather returns,' Bohunko continued. 'We provide an output for San Juan [airport] only. At altitude, the radar gives a 360-degree view of all aircraft. We tape for security reasons – archival purposes – we don't do any analysis here. Our bandwidth is classified.'

We asked about possible disturbances from the aerostat radar picked up by the Arecibo radio telescope. 'Our radar is a "jammer" for their very sensitive equipment,' conceded Bohunko. 'They see our "spikes" because we're in a narrow frequency band. We take care not to interfere with them.'

Graham and I mentioned local rumours about a military presence on site and periodic visits by military and NASA personnel. 'No armed or uniformed personnel are on site,' Bohunko assured us, and neither were any in evidence during our several excursions to the site perimeter, nor during our visit. In fact, we were impressed by the very informal atmosphere. 'However,' Bohunko continued, 'the US Air Force can turn up at any time, unannounced. They usually fly down from Chesapeake.' Presumably the Air Force collects the tapes for a variety of reasons. As to NASA personnel visiting the site, Bohunko told us there was simply no reason for them to do so. 'We're just local on the information we provide here,' he said.

'There have been stories that we do all sorts of strange stuff here,' Bohunko added. 'Some guy even produced a diagram showing an alien base underneath the site! There's nothing underneath here at all.'[26] Having detected not the slightest evidence to the contrary, we could only agree. Which is not to discount the possibility that an alien base exists in the vicinity.

ALIEN BASE

In *Alien Base*, I recount the story of Carlos Mañuel Mercado, who claims to have been taken in an alien craft to a base in the Sierra Bermeja, adjoining the Laguna Cartagena, south-west Puerto Rico, in 1988. 'As the craft approached the El Cajúl mountain,' Mercado told me, 'I saw this brilliant light, something opened up, and the craft went in there, through a sort of tunnel and into a large cavern . . .'[27]

Another case involving a trip to an alleged alien base is recounted by Jorge Martín. In 1980 Iván Rivera Morales, a Puerto Rican police officer, lay bed-ridden with rheumatic fever. Racked with pain and unable to move, he prayed for a cure. Some nights later, the room filled with golden spheres of light. A voice in his head told him not to be afraid, and the spheres materialized into two four-foot-high beings – the typical 'greys'. Suddenly, as in the case of Carl Higdon (Chapter 15), Morales found himself inside a bizarre, transparent contraption, standing up beside the beings, who placed a helmet on his head, supposedly to facilitate communication. With a gentle hum, the craft took off and Morales was transported at a fantastic speed to a point high above Earth, then back to Puerto Rico – off the south-west coast. In a manner similarly described by Enrique Castillo (Chapter 6), the craft dived rapidly toward the sea; 'the waters separated and a sort of tube formed in it, a void around the craft through which it went on descending to the depths'. Morales describes being taken to an underwater mountain, to which the craft was admitted via a large sluice door that closed behind them, allowing the sea-water to drain slowly away.

Inside the dimly lit and freezing-cold base were other, similar beings. Morales was given a bitter-tasting drink and placed on a metallic bed. The next thing he knew, the beings had returned him to his house in Ponce. Three hours had elapsed. Remarkably, though not completely cured, he no longer suffered from the pain and deformity caused by his illness. Later, according to Martín's report, Morales recalled further details typical of the abduction procedure, supposedly including the taking of samples such as semen, and a bizarre mental 'bonding' with one of the beings, imbuing him with a great sense of peace.[28]

Martín told me that although Morales later elaborated on his story when fêted by ufologists, he believes the trip to an alien base essentially happened. One reason for this belief stems perhaps from information provided to Martín by a high-ranking US Navy officer, in the presence of witnesses. 'We know that in the subsoil of the south-west of Puerto Rico there is an enormous subterranean facility, which extends under the sea as far as the Isle of Mona,' Martín was told. (Mona Island, which is uninhabited, lies in the Mona Passage, 45 miles to the west of Cabo Rojo.) 'It is a base of "something" or "someone" that is not from here, that appears to be something "extraterrestrial". We have been following and watching the situation for many years and we know that they are down there . . .'[29]

THE ARECIBO CONNECTION

Yet another site in Puerto Rico which has given rise to rumours of a top-secret US–alien alliance is the Arecibo Observatory, now part of the National Astronomy and Ionosphere Center, operated by Cornell University (Ithaca, New York) under a co-operative agreement with the National Science Foundation. Set amid the limestone hills of north-west Puerto Rico, the world's largest and most sensitive radar and radio telescope has been used since 1963 by thousands of scientists. About three-quarters of the observing time is assigned to radio astronomy: receiving, detecting, amplifying and recording electromagnetic radio signals produced by distant astronomical objects, e.g. pulsars (rapidly rotating neutron stars which emit strong, pulsed radio waves); different types of stars; interstellar clouds in which new stars are born; and galaxies and quasars (quasi-stellar radio sources, apparently the central regions of young galaxies within which a tiny volume of matter releases an enormous amount of energy).[30]

297

During my second visit to the observatory, in January 1999 together with Graham Sheppard, I interviewed Dr José Alonso, the observatory's educational officer. 'Around 200 to 300 projects are carried out here each year,' Dr Alonso began. 'At the moment, most of the research time is allocated to atmospheric research. SETI [the Search for Extra-Terrestrial Intelligence] gets only about five per cent of research time. This includes Project Phoenix, conducted by the SETI Institute, and SERENDIP III, a SETI programme run by the University of Berkeley, California.'

Currently, Project Phoenix searches are in a bank of frequencies between one and three GHz, divided into 2000 million independent channels. Telescopes involved are aimed at the nearest sun-like stars. By the end of the year 2000, one thousand such star systems will have been covered.

'Are any classified projects conducted here?' I asked.

'No classified studies go on here,' Dr Alonso assured us. 'This is a civilian institute. Data belongs to the scientists; we cannot control that. It is available to all and is supposed to be shared for the advancement of science. Twenty scientists work here on a permanent basis, as well as another twenty high-level technical staff. The rest are maintenance staff. The US Navy also comes here periodically.'

'Regarding the SETI projects, what about interference from local sources which could give rise to confusion?' I enquired.

'If it's localized, it usually tends to be periodic, or a periodicity of a typical radar, such as AWACS [Airborne Warning and Control System],' Dr Alonso replied. 'The US Navy has combined military exercises which sometimes cause radio emission problems. The aerostat is a very fixed frequency: we can filter it out or block it out. When we have our radar on, we become the most powerful transmitter on Earth. We use different frequencies, depending on the application; for example, when doing radar astronomy involving planets in the solar system.'

'As you may be aware,' I remarked, 'many people in Puerto Rico claim to have had actual encounters with alien beings. They wonder if anything strange is going on here. It does seem somewhat paradoxical that SETI projects search for signs of extraterrestrial intelligence sometimes thousands of light years away, when, if these local reports are to be believed, that intelligence is already operating on your own doorstep.'

'A lot of people think we deal with the alien phenomenon,' Dr Alonso responded frankly.

This is a complicated issue. Sometimes I think it's military experiments. There are people who say this is a US Government cover-up. Listen, the US Government can't prevent, let's say, a Chinese scientist from stealing secrets![31]

As to aliens, it's a question of belief. People like to believe we're not alone, but we scientists have a way of doing things. Statistically though, there *has* to be something. Data tell me they exist. There are between 200 to 400 billion stars in our galaxy, and ten per cent of them are of the same type as our sun. If they exist, it's only a matter of time and technology. I think we're going to be intercepting their communications *with each other* – they're not going to send us some message! And it could take years to understand those communications.[32]

As the late Carl Sagan put it, 'a civilization very much more advanced than we will be engaged in a busy communications traffic with its peers; but not with us, and not via technologies accessible to us'.[33]

Ironically, sightings of unusual craft and beings have been reported in the vicinity of the radio observatory itself. Jorge Martín describes reports by several independent witnesses in Hato Viejo, in 1991–2, who claim to have seen a huge disc, and later on the same night, not far from the radio observatory, three triangular-shaped objects. Others have reported craft directly above the observatory, including a large boomerang-shaped object 'hanging' above the radio telescope, and a large, dazzling object which hovered above a security officer checking one of the three support towers.

Another case reported by Martín provides further evidence of a liaison between different types of alien beings. One night in 1981, Gertrudis Mendoza of Dominguito and her daughters encountered a large, brilliant, circular object, 20 feet away on the side of a road, 'suspended' about three feet in the air. Three beings on the ground appeared to be examining the craft. One was about three feet high, with a large, bald head, while the other two were taller and quite different. 'They were of human type,' Señora Mendoza stressed.

Many local residents believe that scientists at the observatory have established communications with aliens.[34]

AN ALIEN ALLIANCE?

Early one evening in the beginning of March 1997, 'Carmina' (as I shall call her), an insurance broker qualified in clinical psychology and specializing in medical malpractice cases, was working alone late in her office just below the top floor of a well-known building in the Hato Rey district of San Juan. 'Everybody who enters after 6.30 p.m. has to sign in and out,' Carmina told Jorge Martín and me. 'We had the office door locked. The cleaner was working in a different office. I usually always leave between 6.30 and 7.30 p.m. Suddenly, at about that time, this guy knocked on the door.'

'The office is closed,' Carmina told the stranger. 'Please come back tomorrow.' In English, the man explained that he just wanted to talk with her. He also spoke Spanish well, although with a strong, guttural accent, possibly German or Czech. 'I just came here to tell you to tell your daughter that there is a military operation in El Yunque,' he insisted. 'There is a big base there.' (Carmina's daughter, a television reporter, had made some investigations into the alien phenomenon in El Yunque, about which she had spoken on Channel 4 a few days earlier.)

'I asked him why he was telling me that,' said Carmina, 'and he replied that he couldn't talk with her directly.'

I asked him whether he worked for a government agency, but he said he couldn't tell me anything about that. 'I just want you to tell your daughter that she should keep investigating what is going on and get it out to the public,' he said. He also mentioned that Jorge Martín, who knew my daughter, was being watched by American intelligence people and that I was to get that message to him; he couldn't visit him in person because he himself was being watched. He said my daughter would be all right. When he came into the office, he saw that I was having a problem with my lap-top computer. I told him I couldn't fix it because I was tired out.

'What you need is more practice,' he said. All of a sudden, he went close to it – he didn't touch it – and it began blinking. Was it something he was wearing? Then he touched it, went to Windows 95 in seconds and showed me what to do. I don't know what he did to it.

He didn't have a card but he gave me his name and said he was part of a team and that he worked at the Arecibo Observatory. At least, that's what he implied; he had to be someone who knows all about that place. He said that although allegedly just astronomical work was done there, they were investigating other things that the public didn't know about that had nothing to do with astronomy. He also said there was an investigation into aliens going on at El Yunque. He said there was a big base there, that they were investigating people from another planet who live there. Once someone finds them, he said, they'll never come out – 'they' have taken people away.

I flew as a flight attendant with Pan Am for nearly 20 years, and I had the feeling that he was German or Czech and asked him if he came from one of those countries. 'No, no,' he replied. He spoke very calmly. He was very smartly dressed, with beige, European pants, a light-beige, short-sleeved, open-neck shirt and sandals. He was over six feet tall and slim, with suntanned skin and light-brown hair. He looked no more than 38 years old and was quite normal apart from his very long fingers, lack of facial stubble or hair on his arms and chest, and especially his eyes. They were larger than normal, and I've never seen such a colour before, a sort of lilac colour. I'm sure he wasn't wearing contact lenses. I shall never forget his beautiful eyes, which I can compare to those of Carmina Domenicci [a reporter for Channel 4]. There was nothing effeminate about him: his manners and voice were very masculine.

'You must have studied to become a doctor,' I said, 'you have such long fingers.' He just laughed. 'I'm not here to answer any questions, I'm just here to give you some information,' he said. I think he was sincere and concerned. It seemed to me he wasn't human, and he *implied* that he himself was an alien, collaborating with the US Government. He knew everything about me and about my ex-husband, where I lived, and so on.

When he left, I didn't see which way he went. I'm on the 15th floor and he didn't take one of the six elevators – I would have heard the bell sound – and the cleaner was cleaning the floor by the elevators and she didn't see him either. My door is right by the exit to the stairs, but there's no way he could have got out there without the security guards opening it. After 6.30 p.m. security is tight here: everyone has to sign in and sign out, and we have guards on each floor. In the main entrance lobby the guard there did not see him arrive or leave. On my floor the female guard saw him go into my office, but not out.

After that, I came home. I was scared to death and my daughter said I looked very pale. I told her what had happened, but she thought it was just some crazy person. It took me about two days to recover. I couldn't sleep, going over it all in my mind, and I was kind of confused . . .[35]

Carmina seemed sincere, down-to-earth and matter-of-fact. The latter quality struck me particularly while we chatted about her career as a flight attendant with Pan Am. She casually mentioned that she had been one of the few to survive the world's worst air disaster, which occurred on 27 March 1977, when a Boeing 747 of KLM collided on take-off with a Pan Am 747 taxiing on the runway at Tenerife in the Canary Islands. Five hundred and eighty three people were killed.

Carmina had no interest in the alien phenomenon prior to this incident, thus her description of the visitor intrigued me, not least because she corroborates certain details that are mentioned in some other cases of contact with human-type aliens, such as the long fingers and large, strange-coloured eyes. In *Alien Liaison*, for example, I cite the case of Dr Leopoldo Díaz, a pediatrics and anaesthesia specialist from Guadalajara, Mexico, who medically examined a man claiming to be of extraterrestrial origin. Dr Díaz noted that the colour of the man's eyes was difficult to describe, 'like violet', and that the iris was wider than normal. Like Carmina's visitor, the man disappeared mysteriously on leaving the doctor's office.[36] Carmina had not read my book.

Whatever his origin and nature, Carmina's office visitor seems to have been of benefit to her. At the time of the encounter she had a large cyst on her left breast. Later, X-rays showed no sign of it.[37]

Aliens who communicate with us personally in our own homes or offices, rather than via radio messages transmitted from light years away, remain scientifically unacceptable. Yet personal contact appears to be a favoured *modus operandi*.

Reports of a positive nature involving encounters with human-type aliens have decreased in recent years. But if true, what Carmina was told implies a continuing, if limited, alliance with a selected few in the military and scientific intelligence community.

NOTES

1 Interview, Río Grande, 11 April 1998.
2 Ross, Karl, 'Death at Navy Bombing Range Resonates Through Puerto Rico', *Washington Post*, 19 August 1999.
3 Interview, El Yunque, 11 April 1998.
4 Martín, Jorge, 'El Yunque and its Enigmas', *Evidencia OVNI*, no. 16, 1998, pp. 21–2, translated by Margaret Barling.
5 Interview, El Yunque, 11 April 1998.
6 Martín, Jorge, 'UFOs Escorted by Mysterious "Military" Men in Black', *Evidencia OVNI*, no. 13, 1997, pp. 3–6.
7 Martín, Jorge, 'El Yunque and its Enigmas', p. 24.
8 Martín, Jorge, 'Disappearances of People on El Yunque Mountain', *Evidencia OVNI*, no. 7, 1996, pp. 33–4.
9 Interview, San Juan, 5 September 1997.
10 Ibid.
11 Letter, 29 September 1999.
12 Interview, El Yunque, 19 October 1998.
13 Interview, San Juan, 5 September 1997.
14 Letter, 24 September 1999.
15 Letter to the author, 7 October 1999.
16 Letter to the author, 29 November 1999.
17 Letter to the author, 20 December 1999.
18 Letter to the author, 24 January 2000.
19 Open letter from Jorge Martín, 1998.
20 Deetken, Chad, 'Chupacabras: Mystery or Hysteria?', supplied to the author.
21 Interview, 10 February 2000.
22 Deetken, op. cit.
23 Interview, 10 February 2000.
24 Open letter from Jorge Martín, 1998.
25 Copy of diagram and accompanying details supplied to the author by Jorge Martín.
26 Interview, US Air Force Tethered Aerostat Radar Site, Lajas, 18 January 1999.
27 Good, Timothy, *Alien Base*, pp. 398–9.
28 Martín, Jorge, 'Healed by "ETs" in Puerto Rico', *Flying Saucer Review*, vol. 42, no. 3, 1997, pp. 18–22, translated by Gordon Creighton from *Evidencia OVNI*, no. 3.
29 Martín, Jorge, 'Strange UFO events in Lajas', *Evidencia OVNI*, no. 11, 1996, p. 46.
30 *Arecibo Observatory: National Astronomy and Ionosphere Center*, Office of Communication Strategies and Office of Publication Services, Cornell University, Ithaca, New York, 1998.

31 Dr Alonso was referring to the case of Wen Ho Lee, a Chinese physicist who in the late 1990s was accused of stealing top-secret design data for a nuclear warhead from Los Alamos National Laboratories.

32 Interview, Arecibo Observatory, 13 January 1999.

33 Sagan, Carl (ed.), *Communication with Extraterrestrial Intelligence (CETI)*, The MIT Press, Cambridge, Massachusetts, and London, 1973, p. 366.

34 Martín, Jorge, 'Are UFOs watching the U.S. Radio Astronomical Observatory at Arecibo?', *Flying Saucer Review*, vol. 44, no. 4, Winter 1999, pp. 23–5, translated by Gordon Creighton from *Evidencia OVNI*, no. 17, 1998.

35 Interview, San Juan, 28 November 1997.

36 Good, Timothy, *Alien Liaison*, pp. 74–6.

37 Interview, 28 November 1997.

Chapter 18

Resident Aliens

In 1995 I was introduced to a senior reporter in Washington, DC, who has provided me with information pertaining to the alien presence, which he in turn obtained from a senior US Air Force officer. My source, whom I shall call 'John', is a US Army Intelligence veteran, a highly respected author, magazine editor and correspondent, a career reporter currently specializing in aerospace journalism. John's name is known to Lord Hill-Norton, who can also vouch for his impeccable credentials.

Although he has a long-standing interest in the UFO subject, dating back to his army days in the 1950s, John is not a 'believer' as such. 'I'm receptive and open-minded, and approach all this as a reporter,' he emphasizes. Over the years, John has protected the identity of his source, incorporating some false details about his background. What seems certain is that he worked at the Pentagon in the USAF Air Staff and Joint Staff. In 1986 he approached John. 'I knew my source *before* he began telling me all this,' stressed John. 'It certainly sounded pretty far out to me, and of course, I was sceptical.'

Acutely aware, as a reporter, that he might be the target of Pentagon disinformation, John concedes nonetheless that the officer seemed serious about the alien presence. 'He told me that others in the media and entertainment industry had been approached too, including Steven Spielberg, though he himself was not dealing with that side of it. He didn't meet anyone else in the news business.' Meetings took place over a two-year period.

DOWN TO EARTH

According to the officer, aliens have been coming to Earth for a very long time. Following the Second World War, they began to establish permanent bases here, in Australia, the Caribbean, the Pacific Ocean, the Soviet Union and in the United States. By that time, the officer explained, a number of alien craft had crashed and had been recovered, together with bodies, by the military. Initially, these were taken to Wright-Patterson Air Force Base in Dayton, Ohio, then later to Homestead AFB in Florida.

It is worth mentioning here that, in 1958, Dr Olavo Fontes, a respected and credible investigator, learned from Brazilian Navy intelligence officers that, up to that date, 'six flying disks already crashed on this earth and were captured and taken apart by military forces and scientists of the countries involved – under the most rigid and ruthless security restrictions'.

One of those disks crashed in the Sahara desert but was too much destroyed to be of some use. Three others crashed in the United States, two of them in very good condition. The fifth crashed somewhere in the British Isles, and the last one came down in one of the Scandinavian countries: these two were almost undamaged too . . . In all of them were found bodies of members of their crews. They were 'little men' and ranged in height from about 32 to 46 inches. They were dead in all cases . . .[1]

Regarding the Air Force officer's reference to Homestead AFB, the well-known comedian and musician, Jackie Gleason, who was a UFO enthusiast, claimed to have been shown alien bodies at Homestead, as I described in *Alien Liaison*. According to Gleason's second wife, Beverly McKittrick, her husband came home one night in 1973, visibly shaken, explaining that he had just returned from Homestead where, thanks to his friend, President Richard Nixon, he had been taken to a top-secret repository where alien bodies were stored.[2]

According to the Air Force officer the alien creatures had 'insect-like eyes, like an inverted tear-drop'. Supposedly, two creatures who had survived a crash, or crashes, were killed by an Air Force policeman outside Kirtland AFB, in Albuquerque, New Mexico. This provoked a phenomenal response by the deceased creatures' colleagues, who demonstrated the ease with which they could control local weather. Communications were established. The aliens insisted on the return of the two corpses and contact with the US military, represented by an Air Force major, allegedly was initiated in the late 1940s, in the south-west desert.

PERCEPTION MANAGEMENT

I first heard stories similar to these in the early 1980s, most of which originated with the Air Force Office of Special Investigations (OSI). Thus it was of interest to learn that, according to the officer, by the late 1980s, at least a hundred OSI personnel had knowledge – in varying degrees – about the alien presence.

Currently headquartered at Andrews AFB, Maryland, the OSI was founded in 1948 and patterned after the FBI. In 1998, its personnel included 430 officers, of which 385 are special agents; 1047 enlisted, including 714 special agents; 422 civilians, including 224 special agents; and 439 Reserve individual mobilization augmentees, 397 of whom are special agents.[3] OSI's main duties are counter intelligence and criminal investigations and operations, sometimes including deception, referred to euphemistically as 'special plans'. The OSI has a long history of involvement in UFO investigations. In 1998 I was invited to discuss the UFO subject at the Defense Airborne Reconnaissance Office (DARO) in the Pentagon. Major General Kenneth Israel, then director of DARO, told me that, if any organization was currently involved in UFO investigations, it most likely would be the OSI.[4]

In spite of the likelihood of disinformation, or 'perception management', which invariably includes *some* factual information, much of what the Air Force source disclosed is new and, to say the least, interesting.

UNITED STATES BASES

John's source claimed that bases within the continental

United States were sited in Alaska, New Mexico and West Virginia. George Adamski, the first person to claim publicly to have met extraterrestrial beings and the first to state that aliens had established bases on Earth, remarked in a private letter that he had learned from a marine engineer in Alaska that spacecraft landed on a regular basis in a certain area in that state. The unnamed engineer claimed to have seen humanoid beings there, varying from three to six and a half feet in height.[5] As I have shown in *Alien Base*, many of Adamski's claims cannot be dismissed.

Regarding the alleged alien base in New Mexico, the officer stated categorically that this was sited in the vicinity of the Manzano Weapons Storage Area, in the Manzano Mountains, close to Kirtland AFB. In previous books I have alluded to incidents involving intrusions by unknown aerial craft at Manzano, in areas where nuclear weapons are kept and inspected. Reports of some of these incidents have been released under provisions of the Freedom of Information Act.[6,7]

The base in West Virginia was said by the officer to be located in the mountainous, heavily forested Monongahela National Forest in the farthest northern part of Pocahontas County, some 225 miles south-west of Washington, DC. The approximate centre of the base was given as about eight statute miles north-north-east of Durbin, WV. In 1987 John drove around the area, which appeared exactly as his source described it to him. He found no evidence of anything unusual. Neither did another investigator, who explored the area in 1998 on my behalf, interviewing several local residents, including a police officer, none of whom could recall any unusual activity, including UFO sightings, in the area. According to John's source, the base was 'vacated' in 1988, yet the constable, a man in his forties, had lived in the immediate area all his life and often hunted wild game with his dog, sometimes camping overnight inside the forest area said to contain the alien base. He had never experienced any phenomena suggesting UFOs or an alien presence, neither had anyone else he knew in the community.

Of incidental interest, taking into account rumours

associated with the Arecibo Observatory in Puerto Rico, 15 miles to the south of the alleged base is the National Radio Astronomy Observatory at Green Bank, where Project Ozma, the first SETI initiative, began in 1960. Green Bank is located slightly south-west of the centre of the only federally legislated National Radio Quiet Zone in the US, a 13,000-square-mile area established to protect the observatory – and a classified Navy facility about 30 miles to the east of it – from signals that interfere with radio telescopes and other sensitive electronic equipment.[8]

EXCAVATION, VACATION AND REACTIVATION

The bases were said to be constructed by the aliens using their craft as 'boring' machines, allegedly with some assistance from the military. 'My source said the aliens were capable of excavating to astounding depths,' John told me. Interestingly, Rubens Villela, the Brazilian scientist, informed me that in 1978 the aliens he communicated with required a base in Ibituruna Mountain, Minas Gerais State, supposedly for some of their craft and for obtaining certain minerals. With Villela acting as an intermediary, authorization from the owner of the land was granted to use a 35-metre-square area where the aliens intended to excavate to depths of 160 to 260 kilometres! 'I protested that the depth was unbelievable, that we on Earth had only dug to 10 kilometres,' said Villela.

'But you yourself recognize that your technology is somewhat behind ours,' came the response.[9]

Earth's crust (the lithosphere) is only about seven kilometres thick beneath the oceans and up to eighty kilometres thick in the continents, below which lies the upper mantle (the asthenosphere). Presumably, alien technology can deal with the high temperatures and molten rock found at such depths.

The US Army was charged with guarding a number of the bases. 'The aliens are there doing their own thing,' claimed the Air Force officer. 'We're there to keep them secure.' All the bases, worldwide, are allegedly 'vacated' at periodic intervals, usually after no more than six months, then later returned to and 'reactivated'. Although the officer did not give a location for the Caribbean base, in my opinion it is Puerto Rico.

PACIFIC OCEAN BASES

I asked John if the Air Force officer had revealed any clue as to the location of the two Pacific bases, said to be the largest on our planet. 'I think he said one was about half-way between California and Hawaii,' he replied, 'but he seemed to waver on that point. I had the impression that the other was in the South Pacific.' Interestingly, another military reporter I know claims to have knowledge relating to an alien base in the Hawaii area. I also learned from a further source about the alleged existence of a base in the Marshall Islands. Although these islands, like the Hawaiian Islands, are located in the North Pacific, rather than in the South Pacific Ocean, the following story may be relevant, particularly since disinformation about the actual location of bases seems to be the name of the game.

Harold (Hal) Starr was a pioneering UFO researcher and Arizona State Director of the Mutual UFO Network (MUFON), who wrote and spoke on over 500 daily syndicated radio programmes on the subject, heard in seven English-speaking countries. On 13 January 1990, Hal told me, he was on the air with his amateur radio equipment when he heard a call from a very familiar place, Kwajalein, in the Republic of the Marshall Islands. As a US Army radio officer in the Second World War, Hal's first post overseas had been to Kwajalein, so he immediately responded. Because of the supposedly sensitive nature of what was revealed by this operator and another radio 'ham', real names will not be given. Both hold doctorates and work for a major aerospace firm and a well-known think-tank. For purposes of identification, the first radio operator is referred to as 'Bill' and the second as 'Allen'. I have proof of the true identity of both these individuals, if not of their background.

After establishing a rapport, Hal asked Bill what he was doing in such a remote place. Bill responded that he had a doctorate in a specialized field of physics and worked there on some advanced equipment in his capacity as a research and development scientist. He claimed his work was so bizarre and complicated that it would not be believed; that it defied basic laws of physics, and went on to say that there were several large American companies employed at Kwajalein and operating under top-secret conditions. (Almost certainly, Raytheon was the company that employed him.) He explained that he was not at liberty to be too specific, having taken a security oath. Aware that work on a project known as the Strategic Defense Initiative (SDI, or 'Star Wars') was under way somewhere in the Pacific Ocean at that time, Hal asked Bill if that was his line of work. He replied that this was only part of the activity at the base.[10]

Between 1946 and 1958 the US conducted some 66 nuclear bomb tests in the Marshall Islands. In 1959 the Kwajalein Missile Range was established. 'All of our high-tech strategic systems have some relationship to the Kwajalein facility,' said a Pentagon spokesman in 1985. 'If we didn't have Kwajalein we wouldn't be able to test such long-range stuff over open, largely uninhabited areas of the earth's surface.'[11] Currently, Kwajalein is the only US range capable of testing all classes of ballistic missiles and has tracked launches from sites such as Vandenberg Air Force Base in California, 4300 miles distant, and the Pacific Missile Facility in Hawaii, 2400 miles away. Raytheon Range Systems Engineering is responsible for Integrated Range Engineering and Kwajalein Logistics Support, employing a total of more than 2300 Raytheon people. Located on Roi-Namur in the Kwajalein Atoll are probably the world's most sophisticated radar systems, spanning nearly the entire frequency range. 'These systems essentially track, identify and describe the activities of missiles and other objects in space,' reports Dick Sherman of Raytheon.[12]

Bill went on to tell Hal that his field of specialized work had been moved to Kwajalein from Nevada. Hal assumed that 'Nevada' referred to the Nellis Air Force Base Test Range (including Groom Lake, or 'Area 51'), where it is rumoured that captured alien spacecraft have been 'reverse engineered' and test-flown (see *Alien Liaison*). Hal himself had learned

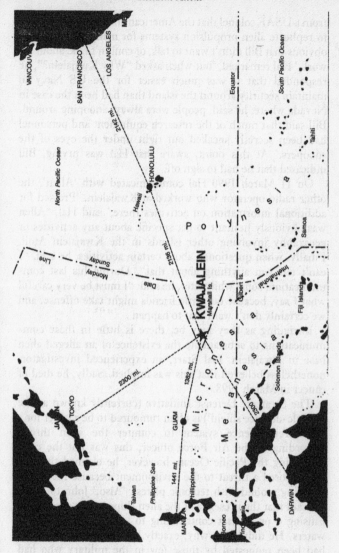

Figure 28. A map of the Pacific Ocean showing Kwajalein in the Republic of the Marshall Islands.

from a USAF colonel that the Americans had been attempting to replicate alien propulsion systems for many years. 'It was obvious that Bill didn't want to talk, or couldn't talk, about his work,' Hal remarked, 'but when asked "Why Kwajalein?", he responded that it was much easier for the US Navy to maintain security around the island than had been the case in Nevada where, he said, people were always snooping around. Bill said that much of the research equipment and personnel had been secretly sneaked out right under the eyes of the snoopers.' At this point, aware that Hal was prying, Bill indicated that he had to sign off.

On 11 March 1990 Hal communicated with 'Allen', the other radio operator who worked at Kwajalein. 'Pressed for additional information on activities there,' said Hal, 'Allen was obviously hesitant to get specific about any activities or geography involving other islands in the Kwajalein Atoll. Finally, when questioned about certain activities, he said, "I can't tell you anything about that". During his last communication, some while later, he said: "I must be very careful what I say, because our little friends might take offense, and we certainly don't want that to happen . . ." '[13]

Intriguing as they may be, there is little in these communications to substantiate the existence of an alleged alien base in Kwajalein. Hal Starr, an experienced investigator, nonetheless believed that this was implied. Sadly, he died of cancer in March 1998.

The Strategic Defense Initiative (currently known as the 'missile-defence shield') is often rumoured to be a cover for a top-secret defence system to counter the alien threat. According to the Air Force officer, this was not the case. Regarding the Pacific Ocean, however, he claimed that the aliens posed a threat to the environment because they were 'messing around with tectonic plates'. 'Also,' John told me, 'he said that the presence of the alien ships in our oceans was causing – or at least contributing to – the warming of the waters. He didn't say why, exactly.' Supposedly, the aliens had been requested by those few in the military who had access to them to vacate their undersea bases. The request was ignored.j327

AUSTRALIA BASE

John's source disclosed that an alien base was located at, or near, Pine Gap, 15 miles from Alice Springs, in Australia's Northern Territory. America's most secret facility in Australia, Pine Gap is a Joint Defense Space Research Facility sponsored by both the American and the Australian defence departments. Established by the Central Intelligence Agency in 1966 and run jointly by the National Reconnaissance Office and National Security Agency (NSA), it serves principally as a downlink site for reconnaissance and surveillance satellites. In *Alien Liaison* I cite the 1989 report by three hunters who claim to have witnessed a 'camouflaged door open up in the grounds of the base and a metallic circular disk ascend vertically and soundlessly into the air before disappearing at great speed'. I also alluded to the claim by one of my most reliable sources that an alien base existed at an unspecified location in Australia.[14] This information was first published in 1991, several years after the officer mentioned Pine Gap to John.

On one occasion, the Air Force officer himself claims to have seen craft and met two of the beings, at or near Pine Gap. I have not been given any details. In this connection, I am reminded of the information given to George Adamski, as long ago as 1949, by a government scientist and former commanding officer in the Chilean Air Force, who claimed that a large 'space laboratory', 1400 miles from Sydney, had been in operation since 1948, and that 'space ships could be landing there [and that] a communication system could be going on through this laboratory between earthmen and spacemen'.[15] Pine Gap is about 1250 miles from Sydney. As revealed in *Alien Base*, Adamski held a US Government Ordnance Department identification card which gave him access to military bases, and he had regular meetings with military contacts who passed him sensitive information.

It is also of incidental interest to note some circumstantial evidence provided by the late Patrick Price, an exceptionally gifted psychic employed by a CIA contractor in the 1970s.

According to Captain Frederick H. Atwater, a retired US Army officer also involved at the time in highly classified 'remote viewing' experiments for the CIA and the Defense Intelligence Agency, as well as for the Army's Intelligence and Security Command, Price had remotely viewed four alien bases on Earth, one of which was located under Mount Ziel, Northern Territory. Mount Ziel lies some 80 miles west-northwest of Pine Gap. Price believed the base contained a mixture of 'personnel' from the other bases, one purpose being to 'transport new recruits, with an overall monitoring function'. The other bases were said to be under Mount Perdido in the Pyrenees, Mount Inyangani in Zimbabwe, and, coincidentally, in Alaska, under Mount Hayes. Price described the occupants as 'looking like *homo sapiens*, except for the lungs, heart, blood and eyes'.[16,17]

TECHNOLOGY TRANSFER
According to the Air Force officer, the alien craft used a form of electromagnetic propulsion, taking advantage of the Earth's magnetic field.[18] They were capable of faster-than-light speeds (presumably for interplanetary travel). It is pertinent to compare the officer's comments about alien propulsion with the information provided by Brazilian Navy intelligence officers, in 1958, to Dr Olavo Fontes:

> Examination of instruments and devices found aboard these disks showed that they are propelled by an extremely powerful electromagnetic field. Evidence shows it is a rotating and oscillating high-voltage electromagnetic field. Such a kind of field obviously produces some type of gravity effect not yet understood . . . Unfortunately, the more important problem was not solved: how these fields were produced and what was the source of the tremendous amount of electric energy released through these fields. No clues were found in any of the disks examined. Apparently they got their power from nowhere. There is, on the other hand, evidence that the large UFOs use some type of atomic engine, as [the] power-source suggests that they are able to transmit electric power through radio beams as we now send it through wires. Some of the devices found inside of the small disks could well serve to receive and to concentrate the electric power

[in] this way.[19]

George Adamski, who claimed to have travelled on board both small and large alien craft, learned that electromagnetic and electrostatic forces were employed in the propulsion system of these particular smaller craft. Within Earth's atmosphere, he was told, the discs 'travel along the planet's geo-magnetic lines of force',[20] as partially corroborated by the officer. The smaller discs that Adamski flew in were incapable of generating their own power to any great extent and were dependent on the larger craft for on-board 'recharging'.[21] Another American contactee, Sid Padrick, taken on board a 75-foot-diameter disc in 1965, learned that the power source of that particular craft was transferred to it from a much larger, cigar-shaped spacecraft.[22]

The Air Force officer disclosed that the aliens were sharing some of their technology with us. Just why they were doing so was not made clear. I speculate that it might be in exchange for the use of our planet as a base of operations. In any event, much of what they were doing, the officer explained, was an extension of what we ourselves were doing. 'We'll have to rewrite our physics textbooks in due course,' he said. We were already advancing in areas of research that touched on their technological expertise, such as the use of the torus (used to contain plasma in nuclear fusion reactors). 'Plasma physics is the key,' declared the officer. The aliens are highly advanced in the physics of light, well beyond our laser technology. Apparently, 'we make good pupils' and have adapted well to this new technology.

The aliens are capable of dealing 'mentally' with any local intruders on their territory, John learned. It seems paradoxical, even ludicrous, that elements of the US Army would be needed to provide additional security, yet, according to the officer, the aliens are not omnipotent and become vulnerable once isolated from the protection of their craft or from their hand weapons (used largely for defensive purposes). In fact, they are rather afraid of us.

Jorge Martín has obtained some information (or disinformation?) which corroborates an alleged US Army–alien liaison. In April–May 1992 military exercises conducted by forces of American and some Latin-American countries, given the name 'Operation Curtain' ('Operación Cortina'), were conducted at Fort Chaffee, Arkansas. According to a US Army officer belonging to a Special Forces unit attached to the Puerto Rico National Guard contingent, one of these exercises involved trying to prevent the 'enemy' from blowing up a mock bridge. No group had been successful: the enemy succeeded in infiltrating every time. Although it was forbidden to use infrared (IR) night-vision goggles to observe the enemy's tactics (because of exercise testing limitations), on one occasion, as the enemy approached, the Puerto Rican troops resorted to IR. Through these goggles, they observed small figures – invisible to the naked eye – crawling along the ground. Supposedly, the figures were about four feet tall, with slim, white bodies, long arms with four fingers on the hands, and large black eyes.

Subsequently, the Puerto Rican contingent was ordered not to discuss the incident. 'Although it seems incredible,' said Martín's source, 'it seems that the US armed forces are in contact with non-humans, and in that exercise these non-humans showed our troops just what their own technological and psychical capacities are.'[23]

According to John's US Air Force source, access to information about the alien situation is denied to all but a few in the US intelligence community. For those 'in the loop', there is occasional liaison with the aliens at their bases, presumably limited to the technology transfer. Some military personnel who had been 'introduced' to the aliens were unable to cope psychologically, John told me. One person became so 'unhinged' by the experience that he had to be taken to the Army's Walter Reed Hospital in Washington, DC.

'What would happen', 'John' once asked his source, 'if I came out with all this, naming you?'

'We'd just make you look very foolish,' replied the officer.

TAKE-OVER
The officer emphasized that he did not have all the answers. '*I* don't know,' he would say to John, 'but someone else may

know.' He disclosed that more than one alien species was here. Further compounding the issue, there appeared to be a conflict of interests, as Rubens Villela also learned. 'There has been hostility between some of them,' said the officer. 'We don't want to get into the middle of *that*!'

'He did not know where they originated, except that it was in our galaxy,' John told me. 'He said they are physical beings, not demons coming from multi-dimensional realities. He was clear about that.'

> I asked him about abductions. He said he had little knowledge of that, except that they happened – he didn't dispute it. He was particularly concerned that children had been taken, and speculated that the abductions might have something to do with genetics. They don't give a damn about our souls.
>
> He told me that the aliens could reproduce the limbs of human amputees because they, unlike human scientists at that point, knew how to regenerate nerve cells.

The aliens – at least, those the officer knew of – are neither concerned with our politics nor national boundaries and seemed very detached about our problems in general. It was no longer a question of Earth being simply a 'way station' – they are here on a permanent basis. 'They're after this planet,' claimed the officer.

ELEMENTS OF TRUTH

How much truth is contained in the Air Force officer's disclosures? 'I've always been intrigued by what I was told, but I never had enough faith in it to vouch for it,' 'John' concedes. 'I've been checking it out in bits and pieces, here and there, through the years and too much of it now rings false, including the base in West Virginia . . . and the purported eyewitness account of aliens and humans working together in Australia.'

Knowing that the officer had approved of my book, *Above Top Secret*, I requested John to re-establish contact and ask if he would be prepared to meet me. He did so, by telephone, in September 1998.

I reminded him that he had told me about actually seeing an alien ship and aliens on the ground in Australia, and asked him, bluntly, 'Did that actually happen?' He finessed the question, replying, 'Lots of things happened.' He remained unresponsive, continuing to talk around the question. I let it go, and took another tack, asking whether he would be willing to meet with you, in the assurance that you would protect him, and tell you what he had told me. He said he would need some time to think about it, and would get back to me. He did not, so I called him. He said he had decided not to speak to you [but] did not elaborate.

'We may not have seen the end of this,' said John. 'Maybe something is going on that I can't perceive or imagine. I'm not through poking around . . .'

In my estimation, although laced with disinformation and lacking in crucial details, the information provided by the senior Air Force officer is essentially true. This would explain the uniquely high degree of security classification applied to the subject since the 1940s, as confirmed in a once Top Secret memorandum by Wilbert Smith, a Canadian government scientist: 'The matter is the most highly classified subject in the United States Government, rating higher even than the H-bomb,' he wrote in 1950.[24] Many others in a position to know have confirmed as much. Andrew Lownie, my agent, learned from a former CIA deputy director of operations that the subject is 'the most sensitive in the intelligence community'. 'It is still classified above Top Secret,' wrote Senator Barry Goldwater, former Chairman of the Senate Intelligence Committee, in 1975. 'I have, however, heard that there is a plan under way to release some, if not all, of this material in the near future.'[25] The officer's disclosures, in my view, are part of that plan.

If some aliens are here on a permanent basis, those few who are aware of the fact understandably remain reluctant to admit as much. As Jorge Martín was informed by a US Navy officer in referring to the presence of an alien base in Puerto Rico, military authorities had been well aware of the situation for many years but did not know how to explain it to the public. 'One of the principal fears of the government,' explained the officer, 'is that the sudden knowledge of the truth might cause a panic and, above all, a paralysis of worldwide economic activity . . .'[26]

A gradual release of the facts may be the only way forward. As I mentioned in the Introduction, towards the end of an important speech before the 42nd General Assembly of the United Nations in September 1987, President Ronald Reagan made an extraordinary statement. 'I occasionally think how quickly our differences worldwide would vanish if we were facing an alien threat from outside this world,' he said. 'And yet, I ask, is not an alien force already among us . . . ?'[27] Reagan had two sightings of UFOs, one of which occurred during a flight in 1974 when, as Governor of California, he ordered his pilot to chase it.[28] He also discussed the alien threat with President Mikhail Gorbachev during the Geneva Summit in 1985. 'The US President said that if the Earth faced an invasion by extraterrestrials,' confirmed Gorbachev during a Kremlin speech, 'the United States and the Soviet Union would join forces to repel such an invasion . . .'[29] And during a private showing of *ET* at the White House in 1982, Reagan leaned over to Steven Spielberg and murmured: 'If only people knew how true all this was.'[30]

RESIDENT ALIENS

In Chapter 1, I refer in part to the story of Inocencia Cataquet, who claims to have encountered undersea alien craft in Puerto Rico in 1988. Cataquet told Jorge Martín that he subseqently communicated with human-type aliens who, as in the case of Iván Rivera Morales (Chapter 17), seemed to 'materialize' out of balls of light. They explained to Cataquet that they were capable of travelling among dimensions. Impending 'geological changes' will endanger all life on Earth, they declared, necessitating their taking and preserving the genetics of all species – including humankind – with which to repopulate Earth in the event of global catastrophe. Other alien beings, they said, were conducting similar work, although their intentions toward us were not good.[31]

Although claims by abductees and contactees – *and* aliens – should be regarded critically, it is prudent not to dismiss them all. With their advanced technology, it is probable that aliens know a great deal more about Earth's geological structure than do we. The theory of global plate tectonics, for example, was born only in 1967. As David Sington, co-author of *Earth Story*, puts it succinctly, the theory explains 'how the outer shell of the Earth is divided into a small number of vast pieces, called plates, which are in constant motion relative to one another ... water plays a crucial role in lubricating the motion of the plates – without it there would be no plate tectonics.'[32] If the US Air Force officer's remark about the aliens 'messing around with tectonic plates' in the Pacific is based on fact, one can only wonder if this was done to control or limit seismic activity. Perhaps this is for our benefit but, if they are resident aliens, it is just as likely to be for their own. No wonder, then, that they are so concerned about impending geological and ecological disturbances.

Given that several species, possibly with conflicting interests, seem to be based here, temporarily or permanently, what might be their agenda? Some may well have our best interests in mind, as Rubens Villela learned. 'These cosmic visitors proclaim a genetic origin linked to our own species on Earth, though they inhabit a dying planet, where we would have to manipulate time and space dimensions to reach,' he wrote to Michael Collins, the Apollo 11 astronaut, in 1979. 'They desire an alliance without fear [and] offer us protection against impending cosmic dangers . . .'[33] But it is not that simple. Again, as Villela also learned, certain other alien species are inimical to humans.

Astronomers and exobiologists regularly remind us that not only is Earth unique in the solar system, it may also be unique for light years around. If this is the case, a corollary is that our planet has attracted those from elsewhere who stand to benefit from its exploitation. 'Your world is marvellous,' Julio Fernández, the Spanish abductee, was told. 'Its biological richness is unbelievable, [with] many of the things that we need, and that we do not have . . .'

Even if some alien beings remain well–disposed towards us, there is no doubt that others pose a threat. People have been abducted and, in a few cases, they have not returned. People have been traumatized and sometimes they have died as a result of their encounters. Animals have been killed. What the purpose of all this is I do not yet know, but clearly there is a requirement. Hybridization might be part of the agenda. Most abductees have been told that this is for our benefit, but I believe it just as likely to be for their own. Are these aliens creating a hybridized species adapted to living on Earth? If so, to what end?

Whatever the threat posed by certain alien species, I believe we have much more to fear from our own kind. I, for one, would welcome an official disclosure to the effect that we share this planet with denizens of other planets.

It might be just the sort of shock we need.

NOTES

1 Letter from Dr Olavo T. Fontes to Coral Lorenzen, 27 February 1958.

2 Good, Timothy, *Alien Liaison*, p. 93.

3 *Air Force Times*, 7 December 1998, p. 34.

4 Interview, the Pentagon, 6 May 1998.

5 Good, Timothy, *Alien Base*, p. 252.

6 Ibid., pp. 340–1.

7 Good, Timothy, *Beyond Top Secret*, pp. 378, 381–4.

8 *Popular Science*, January 2000.

9 Letter to the author, 5 November 1999.

10 Monograph by Hal Starr, provided for the author, 11 July 1997.

11 *Washington Times*, 26 June 1985, quoted in Dibblin, Jane, *Day of Two Suns: US Nuclear Testing and the Pacific Islanders*, Virago, London, 1988, p. 6.

12 Sherman, Dick, *Raytheon News*, 20 May 1996.

13 Monograph, 11 July 1997.

14 Good, *Alien Liaison*, pp. 98-9.

15 Good, *Alien Base*, p. 252.

16 Miley, Michael, 'Former US Military Intelligence Officer Suggests Four "Alien" Bases on Earth', *UFO Magazine* (US), vol. 13, no. 3, 1998, p. 7.

17 Miley, Michael, 'Room With An Alien View: Part Two', *UFO Magazine* (US), vol. 13, no. 5, 1998, pp. 37–8.

18 Regarding UFO propulsion technology, much has been written. I particularly recommend *Unconventional Flying Objects: A Scientific Analysis*, by Paul Hill, the late NASA scientist, Hampton Roads Publishing Co., 134 Burgess Lane, Charlottesville, Virginia 22902, 1995.

19 Letter to Coral Lorenzen from Dr Olavo T. Fontes, 27 February 1958.

20 Adamski, George, *Flying Saucers Farewell*, Abelard-Schuman, London, 1961, p. 39, cited in *Alien Base*, p. 119.

21 Adamski, George, *Inside the Space Ships*, Arco Spearman, London, 1956, p. 53, cited in *Alien Base*, p. 122.

22 Good, *Beyond Top Secret*, p. 368.

23 Martín, Jorge, 'Operation Curtain: Joint Military Exercises with Aliens?', *Flying Saucer Review*, vol. 43, no. 1, Spring 1998, pp. 3-6, translated by Gordon Creighton from *Evidencia OVNI*, no. 14, 1997.

24 Memorandum to the Controller of Telecommunications from W.B. Smith, Senior Radio Engineer, Department of Transport, Ottawa, 21 November 1950.

25 Letter to Shlomo Arnon from Senator Barry Goldwater, United States Senate, Washington, DC, 28 March 1975, reproduced in *Beyond Top Secret*, p. 505.
26 Martín, Jorge, 'Strange UFO events in Lajas', *Evidencia OVNI*, no. 11, 1996, p. 46, translated by Gordon Creighton.
27 United Nations verbatim transcript, 21 September 1987.
28 Good, *Alien Liaison*, pp. 64–5.
29 Speech by President Mikhail Gorbachev at the Grand Kremlin Palace, Moscow, 16 February 1987, published in *Soviet Life*, May 1987, p. 7A.
30 As confirmed by Steven Spielberg's press office.
31 Martín, Jorge, 'Blond aliens on El Yunque', *Evidencia OVNI*, no. 16, 1997, p. 6, translated by Margaret Barling.
32 Lamb, Simon and Sington, David, *Earth Story: The Shaping of our World*, BBC Books, 1998, pp. 8, 9.
33 Letter to Michael Collins from Rubens Junqueira Villela B.Sc., 21 January 1979.

Appendix

Some recommended UFO journals

Evidencia OVNI
CEDICOP Inc., PO Box 29516, San Juan,
Puerto Rico 00929-0516, USA
(NB Spanish language)
evidencia@rforest.net
www.rforest.net/evidencia

Flying Saucer Review
FSR Publications Ltd, PO Box 162,
High Wycombe, Bucks, HP13 5DZ, UK
fsreview@hotmail.com
www.fsreview.net

International UFO Reporter
J. Allen Hynek Center for UFO Studies,
2457 West Peterson Avenue, Chicago, Illinois 60659, USA
infocenter@cufos.org
www.cufos.org

Journal of UFO Studies
J. Allen Hynek Center for UFO Studies
2457 West Peterson Avenue, Chicago, Illinois 60659, US
(NB An annual journal publishing mostly scientific papers)

Lumières Dans La Nuit
BP 3, 86800 Saint Julien-L'Ars, France

MUFON UFO Journal
Mutual UFO Network, PO Box 369,
Morrison, Colorado 80465-0369, USA
mufonhq@aol.com
www.mufon.com

Skeptics UFO Newsletter
404 'N' Street SW
Washington, DC 20024, USA

UFO: Rivista di Informazione Ufologica
Centro Italiano Studi Ufologici
CP 82, 10100 Torino, Italy
cisu@ufo.it
www.ufo.it

UFO*BC Quarterly
11151 Kendale Way, Delta,
British Columbia, V4C 3P7, Canada
www.ufobc.org

UFO Magazine
Lloyds Bank Chambers, West Street, Ilkley,
West Yorkshire, LS29 9DW, UK
QPIL@ufomag.co.uk
www.ufomag.co.uk

UFO Magazine
PO Box 15325, North Hollywood, California 91615, USA
www.ufomagazine.com

UFO Newsclipping Service
#2 Caney Valley Drive, Plumerville, Arkansas 72127–8725,
USA

Books and other material relating to UFOs
Those requiring books, videos, etc., on the UFO subject, which are not available in shops or are out of print, should contact: Arcturus Books Inc., 1443 SE Port St Lucie Blvd., Port St Lucie, Florida 34952, USA
Phone (+1) 561-398-0796; Fax (+1) 561-337-1701
rgirard321@aol.com

Index